Dreams and Visions in African Pentecostal Spirituality

Global Pentecostal and Charismatic Studies

Edited by

William K. Kay (*Glyndŵr University*)
Mark J. Cartledge (*London School of Theology*)

VOLUME 45

The titles published in this series are listed at *brill.com/gpcs*

Dreams and Visions
in African Pentecostal Spirituality

*The Sub-Saharan Horizon
of the Pneumatological Imagination*

By

Anna M. Droll

BRILL

LEIDEN | BOSTON

Cover illustration: Lost in a Day Dream. © Erin Ashley. Used with kind permission by the artist.

Library of Congress Cataloging-in-Publication Data

Names: Droll, Anna M., author.
Title: Dreams and visions in African Pentecostal spirituality : the Sub-Saharan horizon of the pneumatological imagination / by Anna M. Droll.
Description: Leiden ; Boston : Brill, [2024] | Series: Global Pentecostal and charismatic studies, 1876-2247 ; volume 45 | Includes bibliographical references and index. | Summary: "Euro-Western descriptions of knowledge and its sources fall short of accommodating the spiritual, experiential terrain of the imagination. What of the embodied, affective knowing that characterizes Pentecostal epistemology, that is, the distinctive Pentecostal-Charismatic knowing derived from dreams and visions (D/Vs)? In this stunning ethnographic work, the author merges African scholarship with an investigation of what visioners say about the significance of their D/Vs for Christian life and spirituality. Revealing data showcases case studies for their biblical and theological articulations of the value of D/V experiences and affirms them as sources of Pentecostal love, ministerial agency, and the missionary impulse"– Provided by publisher.
Identifiers: LCCN 2023029528 (print) | LCCN 2023029529 (ebook) | ISBN 9789004541214 (paperback) | ISBN 9789004541221 (ebook)
Subjects: LCSH: Pentecostalism–Africa. | Reformed epistemology. | Africa–Church history. | Dreams–Religious aspects–Christianity. | Visions–Religious aspects–Christianity.
Classification: LCC BR1644.5.A35 D76 2023 (print) | LCC BR1644.5.A35 (ebook) | DDC 269/.4096–dc23/eng/20230823
LC record available at https://lccn.loc.gov/2023029528
LC ebook record available at https://lccn.loc.gov/2023029529

Typeface for the Latin, Greek, and Cyrillic scripts: "Brill". See and download: brill.com/brill-typeface.

ISSN 1876-2247
ISBN 978-90-04-54121-4 (paperback)
ISBN 978-90-04-54122-1 (e-book)
DOI 10.1163/9789004541221

Copyright 2024 by Anna M. Droll. Published by Koninklijke Brill NV, Leiden, The Netherlands.
Koninklijke Brill NV incorporates the imprints Brill, Brill Nijhoff, Brill Schöningh, Brill Fink, Brill mentis, Brill Wageningen Academic, Vandenhoeck & Ruprecht, Böhlau and V&R unipress.
Koninklijke Brill NV reserves the right to protect this publication against unauthorized use. Requests for re-use and/or translations must be addressed to Koninklijke Brill NV via brill.com or copyright.com.

This book is printed on acid-free paper and produced in a sustainable manner.

*For my grandmother Transita Minero
who taught me to love Jesus Christ*

Contents

Acknowledgements XI
List of Figures and Tables XIII
Abbreviations XIV

1 **Dreams and Visions in African Pentecostal Spirituality** 1
   1 Dreams, Visions, and Pentecostal Epistemology 2
      1.1 *Dreams and Visions in Africa: Piercing the Veil for Pentecostal Knowing* 4
      1.2 *A Dream in Dar es Salaam* 5
   2 Methodology: Mark J. Cartledge: Practical Theology for Charismatic Practitioners 6
      2.1 *Renewal Methodologies* 8
      2.2 *Renewalist Hermeneutics* 11
      2.3 *Experience and Affectivity* 12
   3 Concepts for Exploring Dream and Vision Narratives 13
      3.1 *The Big Dream and the Spontaneous Dream or Vision Narrative* 14
      3.2 *Root Metaphor and Piercing the Veil* 15
      3.3 *Populations, Codes, Frequencies, and Associations for Narrative Analyses* 17
   4 Author's Location, Thesis, and Map of This Book 19

2 **Dreams, Visions, and Near East Religions** 24
   1 Dreams and Visions and Hebraic Theology 26
      1.1 *Dreams, Visions, and Patriarchs* 27
      1.2 *Dreams, Visions, Kings, and Prophets* 29
      1.3 *Dreams and Visions in the Apocrypha and Jewish Thought* 33
   2 Dreams and Visions in Christianity 34
      2.1 *Dreams and Visions in the New Testament and Early Church* 35
      2.2 *Dreams and Visions in Late Patristic Thought* 38
      2.3 *Aquinas, Kant, and Swedenborg on Dreams and Visions* 40
   3 Dreams and Visions in Islam 47
      3.1 *Dreams and Visions in the Qurʾān and Hadith* 48
      3.2 *Dream Manuals and Their Transmission in Islam* 51
      3.3 *Dreams and Visions as Legitimizing Elements in Islam* 53
   4 Conclusion 57

3 **Dreams and Visions in African Contexts** 59
  1 Dreams in Traditional African Religions 60
    1.1 *Dreaming and the Akan* 61
    1.2 *Dreams and the Diola of Senegambia* 64
    1.3 *Islam and Dreaming among the Tukolor Weavers* 66
  2 Dreams and Visions in the AICs and among Zambian Baptists 67
    2.1 *Dreams and Visions in New Movements of West Africa* 68
    2.2 *Dreams and Visions and the Bantu Prophets* 70
    2.3 *Dreams and Visions among Zambian Baptists* 73
  3 Opoku Onyinah on Pentecostal Dreams, Prophecy, and Angels 75
    3.1 *The Role of Dreams and Visions in Abisa* 76
    3.2 *The Sleeping State and the Diagnosis of Witchdemonology* 79
    3.3 *The Sleeping State and Angelology* 81
  4 Conclusion 83

4 **Epistemology: African Perspectives** 84
  1 Knowledge, Ontology, and the Holy Spirit 85
    1.1 *Voices from African Studies* 86
    1.2 *Voices from African Christianity* 92
    1.3 *The Holy Spirit and Knowing* 96
  2 Nigerian Perspectives for Dreams and Visions Analyses 100
    2.1 *Pentecostal Principle and Emergence for Dreams and Visions Analyses* 101
    2.2 *Piercing the Veil for Dreams and Visions Analyses* 104
    2.3 *Spiritual Warfare and Dreams and Visions* 110
  3 Conclusion 113

5 **The Big Dreams of African Pentecostals**
  Visionary Impact and the Christian Life 115
  1 Continuity and Discontinuity: Dreams and Visions and the Spirit in Africa 117
    1.1 *Spirit Hermeneutics and Universal Dreams* 117
    1.2 *The Spirit and Ancestor Dreams* 121
    1.3 *The Agency of the Spirit and Pentecostal Visioners* 127
  2 Dreams and Visions and the Christian Life 135
    2.1 *Visioners and Spirit–Word–Community* 136
    2.2 *Dreams, Visions and Practical Spirituality* 138
    2.3 *Attitudes in the Church toward Dreams and Visions* 142
  3 Conclusion 147

6 Dreams and Visions and the Pentecostal Warrior
Prayer, Identity, and Agency 148
  1. Dreams and Visions and the Pentecostal Pray-er 150
     1.1 *Dreams and Visions and the Pentecostal Warrior* 153
     1.2 *The DAME Dream or Vision and Pentecostal Agency* 161
  2. Dreams and Visions and Pentecostal Agency 163
     2.1 *The Agency of Visionary Women* 164
     2.2 *Visionary Love and Ministerial Agency* 169
     2.3 *The Visionary Church and Missionary Agency* 173
  3. Conclusion 177

7 African Dreams and Visions for Pentecostal Epistemologies 178
  1. African Dreams for African Pentecostal Theology 179
  2. African Dreams for Western Pentecostal Epistemologies 182
     2.1 *Religious Language and Hearing God's Voice* 183
     2.2 *Relational Knowing and Orthopathy* 187
     2.3 *Embodied Knowing* 192
     2.4 *Knowing in the Trialectic of Spirit–Word–Community* 194
  3. Conclusion 197

8 Conclusion
Dreams, Visions, and the Missiological Spirit 200

Appendix 1   Written Survey and Interview Guide 207
Appendix 2   Coding for Surveys and Personal Interviews 210
Glossary 212
Bibliography 213
Index 224

Acknowledgements

This project would not have been conceived without the gracious invitation to come to Ghana in 2011, therefore I want to appreciate Rev. Ebenezer Asamoah of Kumasi and Rev. Paul Manso, former General Superintendent of the Assemblies of God, Ghana. The research was made possible with the help of various assistants and translators: thank you to Fatimatu (Dorcas) Mensah of Ghana, Raymond Ajagbe, David Omih and Chidinma Agu-Price of Nigeria, Rev. Amos Tchenawou and Akowoe Folly-Koué of Togo, and Elias Francis Mkata of Tanzania. Many thanks also to several others I am unable to name here who made me feel at home and like a true family member. Special thanks to the family of Rev. Dr. Prince Onyemaechi for the worshipful devotions full of song in their home in Enugu, Nigeria. Those early mornings were so nourishing.

I also want to appreciate the faculty of Fuller Theological Seminary, as well as the Center for Missiological Research, which provided the financial support for my research. In addition, my colleagues at Fuller Theological Seminary who ran and continue to run this academic course with me deserve mention. Your fellowship has been so important and added so much meaning to my presence on campus. My time at Fuller was deeply formative for me and your friendship added to it.

My sincere gratitude to my advisor Amos Yong will reverberate through the years ahead. I hope to employ all he has so patiently imparted to me. The timely meeting with him was nothing short of miraculous. I, having scheduled an appointment in the CMR department to discuss the possibility of pursuing the PhD in the School of Intercultural Studies, was informed by David Scott that Dr. Yong had begun his post as Director of the Center for Missiological Research on that very day. Thus began a mentorship which has required Dr. Yong's tireless attention, a season I will treasure forever.

Other scholars were crucial to my learning experience as overseers of my tutorials, so much thanks must go to Kelly Bulkeley, John J. Travis (both having served as committee members), and Elias Bongmba. Also, for their role as committee members, I want to appreciate Clifton Clarke (especially for pointing me to important texts), and colleagues Uchenna Anyanwu and Irene Amon for their comments and encouragement. Dave H. Scott and Nimi Wariboko also gave important input. Lastly, my appreciation goes out to Toyin Falola for giving his time to serve me as the outside reader of the dissertation which has become this book.

It is necessary to acknowledge the men and women of the Assemblies of God who nurtured my understanding of Pentecostalism, but especially for how they valued and still value education as spiritual formation. They provided classrooms where I could take the journey that is Pentecostal theology and which developed into the turn toward research. To Rev. Connie Pack, founder of Global Bible Institute, and other educators—Richard and Janie Cook, Ken Moren, and Charles Adams, thank you for nurturing both mind and spirit.

To my husband, Raymond, and daughters Regina, Anjulí, and Rose, thank you for cheering me on to completion of my project. To my grandson Joshua, thank you for lightening my heart with your precious ways. And finally, praise be to God, *Otito diri Chineke!*

Figures and Tables

Figures

1 Dialectics in the Spirit   10
2 Dreams and visions of pneumatological imagination   110
3 Dreams and visions value and experience percentages   124
4 West Africa possible D/V sources percentages   128
5 Dreams, visions and Spirit–Word–Community   196

Tables

1 Seminarians and universal dreams   118
2 Dream and vision themes of seminarians   139
3 Nourishing/spiritually edifying dreams and visions   141

Abbreviations

AICS   African Initiated Churches
DAME   The D/V experience that is directive, affirming, motivational, or encouraging
D/V   Dream or vision experience
SS D/V   The D/V experience which is marked by spiritual significance

CHAPTER 1

Dreams and Visions in African Pentecostal Spirituality

> Pentecostals live in a world where God can be relied on to communicate, even when it messes up a good night's sleep.
> PAUL ALEXANDER, *Signs and Wonders*[1]

∴

> In the vision I saw a piece of white paper floating down.
> I went to pick it up and read what was written on it, "Jesus for addicts."
> Magesté Merope, Lomé, Togo[2]

∴

The way people know—that is, their epistemology—is a philosophic question that has been a topic for discussion in the West for some time, yet often in circles unconcerned with non-Western contexts and equally disinterested with pentecostal knowing. Sources of knowledge, the means by which one can know, and the purpose of knowledge are all topics pertaining to epistemology, and many who live south or east of Euro-Western regions understand the issue of knowing differently than those who seem to dominate the conversation in the West and beyond. The idea of a spiritual knowing as enabled by the Spirit of Christ adds another dimension of complexity. What of the "God sightings," spiritual experiences, uncanny foresight, senses of intuition, knowledge ascertained during prayer, dreams and visions and the like which are attributed by

---

1 Paul Alexander, *Signs and Wonders: Why Pentecostalism is the World's Fastest Growing Faith* (San Francisco, CA: Jossey-Bass, 2009), 130.
2 This is from a conversation with Magesté Merope at a conference in Accra, Ghana in 2015.

Pentecostal-Charismatics to the agency of the Spirit?[3] Are these to be "written off" as enigmata, cognitive anomalies of the type reserved for psychological analysis only? It seems that Western philosophy has no room for them as *legitimate* elements of knowing.

Non-Western epistemics may not, necessarily, reflect the antithesis of Western constructs. Yet it is unclear to what degree the influence of Western ideas has had an impact. During research, the proposal to conduct interviews among seminarians of one African seminary was rejected. The discussion with the academics in charge yielded their assumption, "[d]reams and visions are not important to our students' Christianity." The resistance was unexpected since a few years prior a resident professor had shared that dreams and visions which guide the students toward biblical education are often shared by students in their applications. To add to the complexity, the senior academic was non-African.[4]

1 Dreams, Visions, and Pentecostal Epistemology

This book argues that the experiences of visioners, themselves, can inform regarding the significance of dreams and visions for knowledge and for spirituality.[5] This book asks: how might dreams and visions (D/Vs) experienced and interpreted by some Pentecostals point to a distinct expression of pentecostal epistemology?[6] In other words, how does a Christian orientation emphasizing

---

3 See James K. A. Smith, *Thinking in Tongues: Pentecostal Contributions to Christian Philosophy* (Grand Rapids, MI: William B. Eerdmans Publishing Company, 2010), 48. He refers to "God sightings" as the term offered by Pastor Swartwood of Cornerstone Vineyard Fellowship for "where they saw the Spirit living and active" in their everyday lives.

4 See also chapter 5, fn. 58.

5 The term "visioner" was used by Nigerian scholar Umar Danlfulani in an interview in Jos, Nigeria (see chapter 4). He spoke extensively on the value of dreams and visions among his ancestors of the Mupun. "Visioner" was used by other interviewees in West and East Africa, as well, and functions as the term "visionary" does in the American context when used as a noun. While the visioner may have experienced an isolated event, there are visioners (also sometimes referred to as prophets) who are known within the Christian faith community for this ability to "see." Research escorts in Togo, Nigeria, and Tanzania led me to such visioners. General Superintendent of the Assemblies of God (President) Rev. Mitré of Togo pointed out the propensity of missionaries and evangelists to have D/V experiences and suggested *L'Ecole Internationale d'Evangelisation et de Relation d'Aide* as a research site. Research revealed that visioners may interpret the experiences alone, but most often interpretation of the experiences involved others.

6 When coming across the capitalizing of the word "Pentecostal" it should not be read as we read it in the Euro-West and especially the US. It does not refer only to Classic Pentecostals but

a Spirit-ed knowing—a pneumatological epistemology—demonstrate itself in how Pentecostals experience and interpret their dreams and visions? Do their experiences indicate that D/Vs inform for living, just as information received by "conventional" means of transmission? And if so, to what extent do they inform? This quest for understanding pentecostal (or Pentecostal) epistemology is also the quest for the pneumatological imagination, that is, the Spirit (in)formed mind.

What this book offers is the first focused examination of Pentecostal-Charismatic dreams of its type. While it is of a similar genre as the work of one scholar who analyzed the dreams of Zambian Baptists, Nelson O. Hayashida (see Chapter 3), and though it interfaces in some ways with other projects,[7] this analysis of Pentecostal-Charismatic dreams and visions offers an inductive exploration of 357 dream and vision narratives and an appraisal of their significance for African pentecostal spirituality. Therefore, it stands on the shoulders of prior work while also standing apart by engaging with a larger population of narratives, by employing multivariate statistical testing, by interacting more extensively with African scholarship, and by using Spirit hermeneutics for tracing what visioners say about Spirit agency. That emphasis has enabled deeper engagement with the theological assumptions of visioners.

---

is intended as a much more inclusive term signifying Spirit-emphasis across many denominations and church movements and is interchangeable with "Pentecostal-Charismatic." The word "pentecostal" will be used sometimes as it is here, in a way that refers more specifically to Spirit-attributes of the spirituality.

7 Hayashida was intrigued with comparing the Baptist experience of dreams and visions with that of congregants of the AICs (African Initiated Churches). He gathered 189 dream narratives from among three Baptist populations. Therefore he offers observations between dreaming in the various populations using available resources describing the AIC valuation of dreams, such as M. L. Daneel's research among AIC churches. It required that Hayashida pull together information from his own literature review of sources and he admits, "[i]t would be appropriate to state at the outset that I have not seen a systematic (typological) study of AIC dreams and visions." See Nelson O. Hayashida, *Dreams in the African Church: the Significance of Dreams and Visions Among Zambian Baptists* (Atlanta, GA: Rodopi, 1999), 75–120 and 282–288, citation 282. I also see some correlation between my work and that of Jean-Daniel Plüss who included vision narratives from case studies in Europe in his *Therapeutic and Prophetic Narratives in Worship* (1988) and to whom I return to comment on further in my concluding chapter. There is also some similarity with the work of Claudia Währisch-Oblau which featured dreams and visions in her case studies of immigrant missions from Africa to Southern Europe. See *The Missionary Self-Perception of Pentecostal/Charismatic Church Leaders from the Global South in Europe: Bringing Back the Gospel* (Leiden: Brill, 2012).

1.1 Dreams and Visions in Africa: Piercing the Veil for Pentecostal Knowing

The purpose of the project was to assess the experience of D/Vs and to find out what visioners make of them for Pentecostal-Charismatic spirituality. What was discovered was that there is a high value of dreams and visions as important sources of knowledge among the participants. The West African seminarians, along with other West Africans and also East Africans, the majority from Tanzania, offered a host of narratives for the study.

According to these men and women, the true state of things can be revealed to the visioner through a dream or vision. In line with Nigerian scholar Nimi Wariboko who writes about the Pentecostal capacity for "piercing the veil," visioners understand D/V experiences as events by which knowledge from the noumenal realm is accessed. This belief generates the high value of D/Vs as assets for living life by the Spirit. It also inspires the caution and care given to interpreting the experiences—along with the messages they carry—with discernment, as visioners seek to make spiritual and personal application to their lives. What is evident is that piercing the veil is a coveted experience, so that those who have many D/Vs are considered blessed while those who have no such experiences are pitied. The Dreams and Visions Project brings the voices of these visioners, and therefore the theology and practices pertaining to D/Vs, to the forefront that they might speak for themselves.

The answer to the question regarding pentecostal knowing in African contexts has an application that is more than expository. It opens the conversation up to consider how ill-fitting Euro-Western concepts of epistemology are when it comes to understanding pneumatological imagination and Pentecostal-Charismatic spirituality. This is because knowing has been understood within Western philosophy primarily as a cerebral exercise for the production of abstract conceptualizations. Therefore, Euro-Western descriptions of knowledge and its sources fall short of accommodating the spiritual, experiential terrain of the imagination and of embodied, affective knowing.

Scholars in and outside of the Pentecostal-Charismatic movement have encountered evidence of the elasticity of pentecostal knowing. They note that the criteria for a knowing of the Euro-Western brand are incongruent with the knowing of pentecostal intuitions.[8] Yet, there has not been a pentecostal

---

8   Mark J. Cartledge asserts that epistemology needs to be redefined in terms of "recent philosophy and the nature of knowledge within Pentecostal and charismatic faith communities." See *Practical Theology: Charismatic and Empirical Perspectives* (Eugene, OR: Wipf and Stock, 2012), 4. Steven J. Land writes, "[t]herefore, to do theology is not to make experience the norm but it is to recognize the epistemological priority of the Holy Spirit in prayerful receptivity."

inquiry that engages seriously with D/Vs as samples of generative knowledge *with an aim to highlight distinctive characteristics of pentecostal epistemology.* For example, the way D/V experiences can produce impetus for social engagement marks this way of knowing as essentially practical. It points to pentecostal epistemology as being open to a way of knowing that is as efficacious as it is elastic, by normative Western terms. An encounter with a woman in Dar es Salaam drove that point home. Meeting her was a key event that served to indicate that samples of this distinctive epistemology might be gleaned from Tanzanian visioners.

1.2 A Dream in Dar es Salaam

We sped along the streets of Dar es Salaam, catching glimpses through the car's backseat windows of local storefronts, passing vehicles, and the colorful clothing of the men and women on foot. Our driver occasionally talked over his shoulder to us in the smooth rhythms of Swahili—the purer version of the dialect, other East Africans have said—while I took in the fresh sensations of my surroundings and filed them away with the memories of my first visit to Dar es Salaam in 2015. We were being taken to experience the work of a woman who had become highly respected in the church for her impact among what we would call in the US the "at-risk" youth population. Elias Francis was my host, a lawyer by vocation and also the national secretary of the board of directors that would guide the planting of the Teen Challenge ministry, a faith-based effort first started in the US. Its goal is to reach substance abusers and other forgotten members of society with a recovery program. The Teen Challenge program offers a biblically based method for overcoming life-controlling issues. Today Francis played the role of chaperone and host for this lone representative of Global Teen Challenge on my mission to promote GTC awareness among Assemblies of God (AG) leadership. I was scheduled to meet several

---

See *Pentecostal Spirituality: A Passion for the Kingdom* (New York, NY: Sheffield Academic Press, 1993), 38. Also, anthropologist André Droogers and sociologists Donald E. Miller and Tetsunao Yamamori have stood outside Pentecostalism suggesting that serious scholarship be applied to the relevance of the Holy Spirit to Pentecostal studies. Droogers writes: "In any case, both currently and in the past, whatever the theoretical framework used, most attention is given to factors that are external to Pentecostalism itself," and "[a] good starting-point may be the central place given to the presence of the Holy Spirit." See André Droogers, "Globalisation and Pentecostal Success" in André Corten and Ruth Marshall-Fratani, *Between Babel and Pentecost: Transnational Pentecostalism in Africa and Latin America* (Bloomington, IN: Indiana University Press, 2001), 41, 45. See also Donald Miller and Tetsunao Yamamori, *Global Pentecostalism: the New Face of Christian Social Engagement* (Berkeley, CA: University of California Press, 2007), 219–221.

ministers reaching the marginalized outside the walls of the church in those three weeks.

"So tell me about your doctoral work," Francis asked above the din of radio and vehicles. I shared about my curiosity regarding the role of dreams and visions in Pentecostal spirituality, about my own experiences and those I had heard of from West Africans I knew, and about my special interest in how individuals incorporate the experiences into their daily life. I had a hunch that dreams and visions might inspire Christian spirituality to be expressed in public ministry and wondered particularly how women might be impacted by them. When we arrived, we were ushered from the car to an open area of a few tables and several plastic chairs under an awning in front of a luncheonette. There, a group of about twenty youth were gathered, and on the ground was a collection of items that represented the crafts and skills they had learned in the program. After the customary introductions, we watched as the woman stood to explain her ministry. Francis and I were immediately caught off guard. Her initial remarks left us amazed and we exchanged a glance that registered our surprise. In English she shared, "I had a dream. In the dream, I saw the map of Tanzania and, when I woke up, I felt God was telling me that I must reach all of the youth of our nation. So I have begun here." On that day I knew that my transcultural investigation on dreams and visions was to extend from West to East Africa to include the Tanzanian context. Within eight months I would return to interview her and twenty-four others in Dar es Salaam about their dream and vision experiences.

The remainder of this introductory chapter accomplishes three things. First, it presents the approach of Mark J. Cartledge as a methodology for this work. Then, it explains how narrative analysis was conducted using concepts from dream researcher Kelly Bulkeley, and using frequency tables and multivariate analyses to locate significant associations. Lastly, the chapter closes with a map of how the rest of this book will unfold.

2 Methodology: Mark J. Cartledge: Practical Theology for Charismatic Practitioners

The methodology presented here is a blend of empirical and theological approaches—a meeting of social sciences with theology. It rises out of the controversy about the possibility of such a marriage, with concerns for the integrity of both disciplines. For some, religious sociology seems to take undue advantage of empirical methods while for others, sociology of religion holds the determinants within analysis to constrictive standards, those in accord with epistemic assumptions. The blending of the approaches for the examination of faith and practice from a pentecostal perspective is the achievement of the interlocutor presented in this section. Mark J. Cartledge represents constructive pentecostal theology attentive to the importance of the pragmatic in a spirituality conscious of the agency of the Spirit.[9]

Mark J. Cartledge is the British scholar who holds a unique place in Pentecostal-Charismatic academics for his role in shaping practical theology from a charismatic (pneumatological) perspective. He is an ordained minister with the Church of England and the Principal at the London School of Theology in the UK. His charismatic theory of research resonates with how this project germinated in a Spirit-ed orientation.

Cartledge rode the pneumatological winds that were impacting the UK about the same time that other key scholars were sensing the need for Spirit emphasis from their own contexts. For example, at about the time that Cartledge was engaged in his seminal work on prophecy and glossolalia in the church (in the 1980s early 1990s), Allan H. Anderson of South Africa was lamenting the lack of scholarship on the Holy Spirit in African contexts, and Steven J. Land in the US was articulating his benchmark treatise on Pentecostal spirituality.[10] Awareness of the need to emphasize the person and work of the Spirit in academic scholarship was blooming, as was also evident in the founding of the Society of Pentecostal Studies in the USA as early as 1970, and the launching of its *Journal of the Society of Pentecostal Studies* (now *Pneuma*) in 1979. Cartledge locates himself in the fourth movement of Pentecostal-Charismatic scholarship, the first being that of Pentecostal historians, then biblical scholars, systematic theologians, and finally practical theologians. In this milieu, Cartledge went on to publish *Practical Theology: Charismatic and Empirical Perspectives* (2003, 2012) among many articles, and more recently published *The Mediation of the Spirit: Interventions in Practical Theology* (2015).[11]

---

9   Cartledge, *Practical Theology*, 12–14.
10 See Allan Anderson, *Moya: The Holy Spirit in an African Context* (Pretoria, South Africa: University of South Africa, 1991) and Steven J. Land, *Pentecostal Spirituality: A Passion for the Kingdom* (New York, NY: Sheffield Academic Press, 1993). It should be noted that also at this time a volume endorsed by Philip D. Cliff of Westhill College, Birmingham, was published: Mary Chinkwita's theologically funded treatise on dreams in Malawi, *The Usefulness of Dreams: An African Perspective* (London: Janus Publishing Co., 1993).
11 Mark J. Cartledge has also written *Testimony in the Spirit: Rescripting Ordinary Pentecostal Theology* (UK: Ashgate, 2010), *Narratives and Numbers: Empirical Studies of Pentecostal and Charismatic Studies* (Leiden: Brill, 2017), and edited and contributed to *Megachurches and Social Engagement: Public Theology in Practice* along with Sarah L.B. Dunlop, Heather Buckingham, and Sophie Bremner (Leiden: Brill, 2019), among other more recent works.

Cartledge began to research prophetic activity in 1986 and developed a combination of approaches for the task. He asserts that research methodology can be understood as having three aspects. There is the "overall approach in terms of epistemology" pertaining to the nature of knowledge and its relationship to reality, that is, its "*a priori* understanding of what constitutes knowledge in relationship to the reality beyond language or what we might call ontology."[12] Methodology can also be understood in the sense of its "procedure of process of investigation," but also in the sense of describing the tools specific to the approach. Tools may be many and used in combination.[13] Therefore, this section turns now to Cartledges's Renewal methodologies for an overview of epistemic assumptions, a look at his "dialectics in the Spirit," and an examination of the appropriate tools for research.[14]

2.1   Renewal Methodologies

In *Practical Theology*, Cartledge describes how he used Renewal methodologies in his exploration of the New Church movement in the UK during the Charismatic Movement. As a participant observer, he collected observations and narratives (through interviews) at Aigburth Community Church and analyzed them for how they reflected prophetic activity. He assessed the nature of charismatic worship, the practice of glossolalia, and the characteristics of women's involvement in the prophetic, among other topics. Later, in *The Mediation of the Spirit*, he discusses the significance of investigating theological narratives of religious experiences because of their relevance to spirituality. In particular, "to frame pneumatology and experience within the discourse of spirituality" is to remedy the neglect of tracing the role of the Spirit in the community of faith.[15] In fact, the neglect is notable in how Scripture can be read making no provision for pneumatology, reflected as well in the tendency to approach practical theology without reference to the mediation of the Spirit. His conclusion is that not only has religious experience been devalued, but "the role of pneumatology in practical theology is virtually nonexistent."[16] On the other hand, Cartledge explains, those concerned with a pneumatological assessment look for the mediation of the Spirit, not only in the analysis of

---

12   Cartledge, "Can Theology be 'Practical'? Part II: A Reflection on Renewal Methodology and the Practice of Research," *Journal of Contemporary Ministry* 3 (2017) 20–21.
13   Ibid., 21, 29.
14   Cartledge offers a diagram "Dialectics in the Spirit" in *Practical Theology*, 28, see Figure 1.
15   Cartledge, *The Mediation of the Spirit: Interventions in Practical Theology* (Grand Rapids, MI: William B. Eerdmans Publishing Co., 2015), 51.
16   Ibid., 58.

biblical texts, but in order to define and characterize spiritual praxis for ecclesiology and soteriology. Cartledge's attention to pneumatology continues until today heart deep in research using Renewal methodologies. For example, he co-edited *Megachurches and Social Engagement: Public Theology in Practice* (2019) involves "an inter-disciplinary, team-based approach that includes case studies of five megachurches in London."[17]

As mentioned, Cartledge charted out an epistemological approach, a methodology of dialectics, and a selection of appropriate tools for his work. What Cartledge refers to as the "standpoint" of the researcher is what pertains to the overall approach guided by the epistemic assumptions of the researcher. According to Cartledge, it is funded by the personal experience and practice of the researcher—demonstrating that the researcher cannot be "compartmentalized" or aspects of being sufficiently "bracketed out"—and will influence even the choice of how one develops and uses tools for investigation. "This standpoint or way of being and thinking is part of who we are as people … It provides a set of motivations to research certain kinds of things."[18]

In effect, Cartledge was critiquing long entrenched assumptions regarding the idealism of Enlightenment "objectivity" and the possibility of a type of "pure" approach to what can be known. Rather, the knower is a participant in the empirical process by bringing his or her standpoint to the work, a fact that is not necessarily an epistemic hindrance to finding the meaning in that which is known, especially when a standpoint (à la Cartledge) is acknowledged.[19] Therefore, Cartledge has set the table for an unapologetic pentecostal

---

17   Cartledge, "Can Theology be 'Practical'?", 28.
18   Ibid., 30. See also *Practical Theology*, 24 and *The Mediation of the Spirit*, 45.
19   Comments by Henning Wrogemann are helpful here. He represents a turn toward self-awareness as a German theologian recognizing the call for a new intercultural hermeneutic for a global context. In regard to those in contexts beyond our familiarity, "[w]hich paradigms of perception do these people believe to be "significant," and which aspects of reality serve to carry meaning for them? … Which paradigms do other people believe to be encoded in their social world?" He also asserts that the hermeneutical lens should be tempered by sensitivity to one's own location and the liabilities that particularity may bring to cross cultural understanding. Comprehension is not easily achieved without the release of bias and the awareness of expectations and ideologies that act like lenses that obstruct truly knowing the other. See Henning Wrogemann, *Intercultural Theology: Intercultural Hermeneutics*, vol. 1, English edition (Downers Grove, IL: IVP Academic, 2016), 38, 57–86.

   Also, Craig Keener notes that faith is an epistemic commitment "which is consistent with the mind of the Spirit." He writes, "Epistemically, Christians need be no more reticent about their starting convictions than are others." Craig Keener, *Spirit Hermeneutics: Reading Scripture in Light of Pentecost* (Grand Rapids, MI: William B. Eerdmans Publishing Co., 2016), 163.

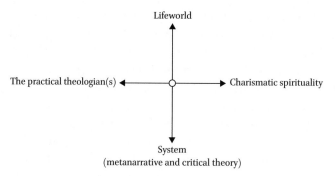

FIGURE 1   Dialectics in the Spirit

appraisal of the facts of pentecostal theory and praxis. Also, when epistemological assumptions are recognized and acknowledged there can be a clearing of the air regarding assumptions that may impede research, or positively, those that may enhance it. Cartledge's dialectics in the Spirit describe the method of investigative procedure for research and is depicted by the metaphor of engagement along two perpendicular poles (see figure 1).

The pole running west-east involves the theologian as the starting point as he or she lives dynamically situated in dialogue with epistemic commitments to charismatic spirituality (the Bible read with attention to Spirit agency). From that vantage point questions emerge to ask of the lifeworld of the subject.[20] At the same time, another pole runs north-south across this one in the model. It depicts the dynamic of investigative discovery as the subject in his or her lifeworld is brought into encounter (in the mind of the researcher) with scholarship (the theologian's literature reviews) and the elements of the theologian's epistemic system (metanarrative), which for the charismatic practitioner is a particular en-Spirited Christian theology. The intersection of these dialectics is therefore dynamic, and according to Cartledge, self-perpetuating toward more questions and more discoveries and perhaps toward suggestions for transformation of the church.[21]

The tools Cartledge chose for guiding the multiple encounters involved in the dialectics in the Spirit are both qualitative and quantitative. The analyses of data gathered through observations and interviews are the focus since

---

20   Cartledge describes lifeworld in the following comments, "I shall use the word 'lifeworld' to denote the particular concrete setting of a circumstance under study. This is the one pole of the dialogue with which I believe practical theology is engaged." See *Practical Theology*, 17.
21   Ibid., 28–30.

narratives and testimonies are the key to understanding the values and intuitions leading to prophetic activity in charismatic spirituality. Also, Cartledge's intra-disciplinary approach invites a variety of voices to speak into his topics of interest. For Cartledge, "[k]nowledge is to be gained both by participation and by reflection, by engagement and detachment."[22] His comment and methodological approaches demonstrate that charismatic epistemology embraces an assessment of knowledge on more than just the level of intellect. This epistemology also holds to expectancy of divine agency in regard to the source of knowledge and interpretation of it in relation to the Spirit. Renewal methodology demonstrates a practical theology that anticipates encountering "the person and work of the Spirit in a dramatic or ordinary manner."[23]

2.2   Renewalist Hermeneutics

In Cartledge's dialectics in the Spirit model, he employs Renewalist hermeneutics that requires that biblical engagement be brought out from the margins and into a more prominent role in practical theology. It allows for open engagement with dimensions of Scripture reading relevant to the researcher who incorporates biblical reflections for application in academics. Cartledge describes the initiative he took in developing this empirical-theological method. He adopted a method used by Johannes van der Ven, but also *adapted it* in accord with his own theological intuitions. Van der Ven had used the communicative action theory of German sociologist Jürgen Habermas, an element Cartledge felt unsuitable for his own approach.

Within the framework, Cartledge incorporated Renewalist hermeneutics based on the Paraclete sayings in John's gospel as a methodological lens.[24] The adaptation was a bold move on Cartledge's part and he supported it by asserting, "[s]cripture does provide points of departure for theological thinking and action, even if it is intertwined in experience or religious practice."[25] Referring to the academy of practical theology as "under the spell of social science," Cartledge suggests an awakening from the neglect of biblical engagement and offers five points to consider for a practical-theological reading of Scripture that can inform research.

Cartledge describes the first dimension important to engaging with Scripture as a practical theologian as *"hermeneutically reflexive."* This involves being open at the outset regarding "starting points and commitments," both

---

22   Cartledge, *Practical Theology*, 82.
23   Cartledge, "Can Theology Be 'Practical'?", 30.
24   Cartledge, "Can Theology Be 'Practical'?", 31.
25   Cartledge, *The Mediation of the Spirit*, 43.

theological and theoretical, that inform the researcher's approach to biblical texts. The practical theologian also reads Scripture to find the *"explicit or implicit praxis of communities and individuals"* and weighs the inferences that can be gleaned. Thirdly, assessing the human-divine relationship in terms of *"agency and the relationship between the different agents* in biblical texts" is important for understanding such relationships in the church and the world today.[26] The fourth dimension to this reading is *"holistic"* and involves reading texts in relationship to broader contexts and across genres. This leads to learning from all voices on a topic and allows one to "acknowledge and explore plurality, but also identify harmony and unity."[27] Lastly, bringing *"contemporary questions and issues emerging from lived reality* to the text" is part of the dialectic between the texts and the sociocultural context in view. It ensures relevant interaction between both and the continuation of the "hermeneutical circle" for "renewed praxis."[28] This turn toward the Scriptures is also a turn toward the priority of the Spirit and is important for the analysis of D/Vs in this study, as well.

2.3   *Experience and Affectivity*

The connection between experience and affectivity lies at the core of Cartledge's practical theology. The epiphany regarding the significance for theology of the idea that affectivity generates impetus for beliefs and practices was a pivotal moment for Cartledge. It inspired him to come to the conviction that theologians need to reverse the trend of neglecting experience and giving it only "cursory attention."[29] It had become clear that from experiences and their reports are hulled the real elements that point to theory and practice in spirituality.

Cartledge was impacted specifically by how American theologian Steven J. Land highlights the role of affectivity in his articulation of Pentecostal spirituality.[30] He realized that Land's assessment of experience and affectivity as indicators of collaboration with Spirit agency in communities and individuals is key to research. The link between the affections and praxis has prepared a milieu in which practical theology can be a means of locating notions of the

---

26   On this topic, Ghanaian Esther Acolatse offers "biblical realism" as a hermeneutic that offers the right "epistemological fit" for understanding the ontological realities set forth in Scripture. See chapter 4.
27   Cartledge, *The Mediation of the Spirit*, 46.
28   Ibid., 45–46, all italics belong to Cartledge.
29   Ibid., 53.
30   Ibid., 24–25. See also Land, *Pentecostal Spirituality*, 43–44.

mediation of the Spirit. The discovery of that correlation explains Cartledge's fascination with the pentecostal practice of testimony, which is embedded in Pentecostal narratives. While the Holy Spirit is an elusive object for research, the empirical assessment of that which *subjects claim about the Spirit's agency* is not.

The link between affectivity, that is, emotions, feelings and deep affections, and the experiences that promote it is a vital thread that will be picked up again in the presentation of data hulled from the D/V narratives. It will be demonstrated that people were moved by dreams and visions toward transformation of identities and toward various decisions and courses of action. Their visionary experiences were vital sources of impetus toward caring for others with a caring they first experienced through the D/Vs in which they report that God was speaking. Affectivity is, therefore, a key element in Pentecostal epistemology and spirituality in respect to how the experiences are transposed into religious meaning and spiritual practice.

3   Concepts for Exploring Dream and Vision Narratives

The Dreams and Visions Project consisted of collecting and analyzing dozens of dream narratives from Pentecostal-Charismatic visioners primarily of Ghana, Togo, Nigeria, and Tanzania. The narratives, some collected in surveys and some through recorded interviews later transcribed and treated as texts, were noted for their differing qualities, and specifically in terms of what visioners said about them. Herein is found their religious meaning and significance. The work of American dream researcher Kelly Bulkeley is brought out in this section to provide a starting point for approaching this work of narrative analysis in the Dreams and Visions Project. Bulkeley is a psychologist of religion and researcher of dreams who has studied the link between dreams and religious beliefs and practices for about three decades.[31]

Bulkeley's work has built on the original work of Freud, Jung, and William James in the area of dreams, yet he asserts "The nocturnal imagination remains largely unexplored territory for this still-young field."[32] Bulkeley has taken the

---

31 Bulkeley is also director of the Sleep and Dream Database, and editor of the multidisciplinary journal *Dreaming*, which is published by the American Psychological Association. He is also a Visiting Scholar at the Graduate Theological Union in Berkeley, California, and former President of the International Association for the Study of Dreams. I am indebted to him for his attention through directed studies throughout most of 2017.
32 Kelly Bulkeley, *Big Dreams: The Science of Dreaming and the Origins of Religion* (New York, NY: Oxford University Press, 2016), e-book, 6.

study of dreams intentionally along the vein of religious studies and writes, "[d]reams are a primal wellspring of religious experience."[33] His recognition of the value of D/V experiences to spirituality has qualified him to make unique contributions to this project.

3.1 The Big Dream and the Spontaneous Dream or Vision Narrative

One of the important concepts Bulkeley articulates for dream research is the significance of analyzing the "big dream." The term big dream was first used by Carl Jung in his assessment of the significance of this type of experience vis á vis the more common "little dream." Jung concluded that little dreams were less weighty since they were reflections of the day to day affairs and general psychic conditions of the dreamer, while the big dream marked unique psychic experiences. Jung wrote, "[s]ignificant dreams … are often remembered for a lifetime, and not infrequently prove to be the richest jewel in the treasure house of psychic experience."[34] For Bulkeley, these memorable and impactful big dreams are especially significant for how they are linked to the origins of religious beliefs and practices.

Bulkeley explicates using a metaphor he attributes to the Scottish philosopher David Hume to communicate the value of the big dream. Hume and some who followed after him referred to the "Black Swan" as a highly significant phenomenon amongst the more common "white swan" phenomena. It was part of the logic which eschewed inductive reasoning in favor of a suspicion of generalizations, promoting deductive reasoning and the value of larger sample sizes for empirical studies. Bulkeley writes, "The Black Swan is a metaphor for the fragility of conventional knowledge and the surprising importance of rare events."[35] Of significance to Bulkeley is that the Black Swans among oneiric experiences can explain much about the cognitive beginnings of religious concepts and origins.

Bulkeley points out that the idea that religiosity and spirituality have primordial roots in D/Vs and their interpretations is not new but has, rather, been recognized throughout pre-modern and modern times. This study brings that fact to light in Chapter 2 where D/Vs are examined in light of Near East religions. Recognizing that the thesis of connection between dreams and spirituality is not new, Bulkeley has devoted his energies to affirming and substantiating it. Therefore, he writes, "I want to put this classic thesis to the scientific

---

33   Bulkeley, *Big Dreams*, 8.
34   Bulkeley, *Big Dreams*, chapter 1, fn. 3, referencing C.G. Jung, "On the Nature of Dreams," in *Dreams*, translated by R.F.C. Hull (Princeton, NJ: Princeton University Press, 1974, 76).
35   Bulkeley, *Big Dreams*, 2.

test by clarifying and improving it with better data, sharper analysis, and a broader evolutionary framework."[36]

It is notable that in the case of this project three of the field sites chosen for research were, in fact, selected due to the unsolicited sharing of a dream or vision (during ministry engagements) that had all of the hallmarks of the big dream. Ghana became a return destination due to the big dream account offered in 2014 by the Muslim man who converted to Christianity and was told in the vision to go back to his village. Togo became a return destination due to the vision report given by Magesté Merope when we met in West Africa in 2015, and a return to Tanzania became imperative after hearing the big dream of a female evangelist. These big D/Vs were all reported some time after the visionaries had experienced them, and yet they were narrated with a passion, clarity, and a sense of wonder that had withstood time. But beyond those characteristics, these D/Vs experiences were also charged with a special quality which infused the visionary with a burst of impetus for social engagement, as will be shown in Chapter 6.

The written survey posed crucial questions which were meant to draw out the big dream or vision and its impact. They read, "[c]an you share about a dream or vision that was significant to you? Did the dream or vision impact you? If yes, how?" (See Appendix 1). When examining the surveys, as well as the transcribed interviews, this contribution to the project was looked at carefully. That is because they represented spontaneous and not prompted content (prompted by a specific question), and according to Bulkeley, the memorable, impactful dream is most likely the big dream. Therefore, these "spontaneous" contributions would be likely to yield indications of spiritual significance and religious meaning.

3.2 *Root Metaphor and Piercing the Veil*

Bulkeley's explanation of the concept of the root metaphor and how it relates to dreams brings the awareness of how D/V experiences can reflect overarching concepts. This prepares the way for appropriating "piercing the veil" as a metaphor for this project. Such a metaphor provides a construct or "banner" under which we can figuratively place the D/Vs and their interpretations while examining how they are transposed into spiritual meaning by visioners. Bulkeley builds upon a "theory of religious metaphor" and draws from key philosophers and theologians who each highlight certain aspects about how metaphors or metaphorical thinking functions in the human experience. He

---

36   Bulkeley, *Big Dreams*, 3.

borrows from their concepts to give life to the idea of the root metaphor for dream research. It is helpful to touch briefly on each aspect.

Bulkeley refers to the work of George Lakoff and Mark Johnson for its clarity in describing the way people not only use metaphors but *think metaphorically*. Lakoff and Johnson drive home that "metaphorical thinking is basic to *all* human conceptual thinking."[37] They contend that people not only employ metaphors for describing the intangible concretely, but that the processing of human experience is naturally guided by the tendency to understand one experience by means of another. So the senses and perceptions process new experiences by means of reference to others, that is, metaphorically.

To be more explicit, as Bulkeley renders their ideas, "[t]he metaphors we use ... always have some basis in our experiences ... our metaphors reflect our *interactions* with our bodies, our physical world, and our culture."[38] But metaphorical thinking not only draws from experience, it in turn *shapes* experiences by effecting behaviors, goals, attitudes and perceptions. Therefore, metaphorical thinking is vitally connected to cultures and their social realities, though metaphors render only partial reflections of the whole psychic milieu, or necessarily a bias for one metaphor (aspect of the lifeworld) over another. A last relevant point Lakoff and Johnson offer is that "metaphorical thinking ... enables us to see how reason and imagination are united ... [it is] a product of *both* rationality and imagination."[39]

Bulkeley also notes theologian Don Browning's expansion of Lakoff and Johnson's concept of metaphorical thinking. Browning looks at how metaphorical thinking can encompass "metaphors of ultimacy," as well. He posits that psychologies, for example, put forth "comprehensive understandings of life" much in the same way as the religions, so that adherents are guided through "deep metaphors" toward a certain worldview which answers ultimate concerns.[40] Theologian Sallie McFague concurs with Browning's observation on the importance of metaphorical thinking. She points out that it is "the way language and, more basically, thought works." She asserts that it is "what we do when we interpret: we see "this" as "that," we find the thread of similarity with

---

37 George Lakoff and Mark Johnson, *Metaphors We Live By* (Chicago, IL: University of Chicago Press, 1980), 56–60. See Kelly Bulkeley, *The Wilderness of Dreams: Exploring the Religious Meanings of Dreams in Modern Western Culture* (Albany, NY: State University of New York, 1994), 135.

38 Bulkeley, *Wilderness of Dreams*, 135.

39 Lakoff and Johnson, *Metaphors We Live By*, 193. See also Bulkeley, *Wilderness of Dreams*, 136–137.

40 Don Browning, *Religious Ethics and Pastoral Care* (Philadelphia, PA: Fortress Press, 1983), 58. See Bulkeley, *The Wilderness of Dreams*, 136–137.

the familiar in the unfamiliar situation and move beyond where we were before as we work through the process of "is and is not" toward new understanding."[41]

McFague also brings an intriguing contribution to metaphorical thinking by exploring the way religious metaphors—or "root metaphors" (borrowed from Paul Ricoeur who is mentioned ahead)—can revitalize religious thought for fresh relevance in contemporary contexts. She points out that religion may seem irrelevant today, but that overlooked religious metaphors have power to speak in fresh ways, for example, in the way the metaphor of God as mother can speak with relevance to women. Therefore, McFague is optimistic that fresh root metaphors can shape minds for a revitalization of Christian faith.

Lastly, Bulkeley refers to French philosopher Paul Ricoeur, who he notes inspired both Browning and McFague. Bulkeley highlights Ricoeur's explicit acknowledgment of dreams in connection with religious meaning. Ricoeur suggests a "second naivete," that is, a "postcritical" assessment of what a root metaphor expresses about those who find meaning in it.[42] Paul Ricoeur's assertion that root metaphors speak so as to inform regarding the importance of symbols and their meanings for reflection on human life makes for an apropos springboard into these D/V analyses. Kelly Bulkeley and the other interlocutors have explained how the root metaphor speaks about the deeper meanings embedded in metaphorical thinking revealed in dreams or visions, or in the reflections about them.

A religious metaphor did surface while assessing the dreams and visions in this project. As already mentioned, the idea of gaining access to the true state of things or "piercing the veil" of the phenomenal (what can be experienced with the senses) communicates the value of D/V experiences for pentecostal knowing. That metaphor will be discussed in more detail in Chapter 4.

3.3 Populations, Codes, Frequencies, and Associations for Narrative Analyses

The Dreams and Visions Project was approved by the Center for Missiological Research at Fuller Theological Seminary in California. Data collection took place from July through September in 2017 in Ghana, Togo, Nigeria, and Tanzania,[43] and an extension for follow-ups through emails or by phone was

---

41 Sallie McFague, *Metaphorical Theology: Models of God in Religious Language* (Philadelphia, PA: Fortress Press, 1982), 37, 57–59. See Bulkeley, *Wilderness of Dreams*, 140–141.
42 Paul Ricoeur, *Freud and Philosophy: An Essay on Interpretation* (New Haven, CT: Yale University, 1970), 496. See also Bulkeley, *The Wilderness of Dreams*, 145.
43 I have spent about 9 months cumulatively in African contexts since 2011, primarily in the locations of the research.

permitted through August of 2018. There were 212 original participants. Some completed a written survey and were interviewed, as well. Some submitted only a survey, and others were only interviewed. 137 surveys were examined. A total of 77 interviews were conducted. Unfortunately, 17 of the interview recordings were lost; 60 were retained for use as data. In light of the loss of some interviews, the measurable data represents the participation of 197 individuals: 31 women (21 audio interviews, 10 survey submissions) and 166 men (39 audio interviews, 127 surveys). Also, several participants contributed with more than one D/V narrative. For example, four participants each contributed with nine narratives.[44]

Participants were contacted and interviewed at Pentecost Theological Seminary of Ghana (PTS), Trinity Theological Seminary of Legon (TTS), Ghana, Evangel Theological Seminary of Jos, Nigeria (ETS), and *L'Ecole Internationale d'Evangelisation et de Relation d'Aide* in Lomé, Togo (The International School of Evangelism and Counseling).[45] A handful of seminarians who participated were from the neighboring nations of Burkina Faso, Congo, Liberia, and Sierra Leone. Other West African participants were contacted in Brong-ahafo, Ghana, and the cities of Ibadan, Jos, and Enugu in Nigeria. Participants who were not contacted at the seminaries were invited by research escorts because of the participant's proclivity toward D/V experiences or simply because of their availability.[46] Among non-seminarians, a few Ugandans and a Kenyan participated along with Tanzanians in Dar es Salaam. Data collection required 6 research escorts and translations from French, Igbo, Ewe, and Swahili to English and vice versa.

There were two groups of data, the first drawn from the written surveys, and the second set drawn from the transcriptions of the personal interviews (221 pp.).[47] Examination of the texts involved coding the narratives by looking at the D/V text, but also (in the case of the personal interviews) by looking

---

44   As already mentioned, 357 narratives were examined.
45   Written surveys were not used in Togo but only interaction through personal interviews. I made that decision because of the success I felt I had with personal interviews in Ghana.
46   All of the research escorts were associates I already knew through my work with the Global Teen Challenge Africa ministry. I served GTCA from 2014–2017 as Communications Coordinator.
47   The data is contained within three main documents that are in my possession: the "Dreams and Visions Transcription" (221 pages of the personal interviews transcriptions), the "Dream Narratives from the Audio Recordings of the Dreams and Visions Project" (32 pages of excerpts of major dream and vision contributions found in the Transcription), and "Spontaneous Dream and Vision Reports from Surveys" (23 pages extracted from the surveys).

at the content surrounding it. Narratives were coded demographically and with other signifiers such as CL for clergy and other codes for denomination, if one was revealed, but also with other pertinent references. Some of the codes include coding of references to the Holy Spirit in the written surveys (hs, HS, or HSS depending on how often Holy Spirit was mentioned), the use of Scripture noted in oral or written data (SCR), the report of an audition in oral or written data (A = an audible voice during the experience), and the reference or descriptive of spiritual warfare in oral or written data (SW) for example (see Appendix 2).

The frequency of types of information was also gauged, first in simple percentages of occurrence and then using multivariate computations. An example of a simple frequency is the count of how many foreknowledge/warning D/Vs were mentioned from among 17 dream reports offered by seminarians of Trinity Theological Seminary in Ghana. Those foreknowledge/warning D/Vs appeared 47% of the time, or 8 out of 17 times. The frequencies were put into tables and are shown in Chapter 5. The statistics which reveal *associations of variables*, indicated through multivariate testing (of several variables) also gave information about the nature of the D/V experience.

4   Author's Location, Thesis, and Map of This Book

In keeping with Cartledge's attention to self-disclosure regarding epistemic assumptions, I offer here a brief preamble before sharing the overview of this book. At the close of 1999, I experienced a personal Pentecost with tongue-speaking while alone in prayer and meditation on Acts Chapter 2. The new millennium dawned soon after, and came with an enhanced vigor and Spirit-dynamic for life with the strong impression that prayers sung for "More Love, More Power" were actually fulfilled and being fulfilled. This research project finds its orientation in that Spirit emphasis. The project was conceived and approached with a heightened appreciation for Holy Spirit agency in myself, the Church, and the world. It was with this sense of the accessibility of the transcendence and immediacy of the Spirit's intervention in daily life that the vision for the project developed over time.

My presence in Africa was actually the result of a prophetic word delivered in London by a British (non-African) prophet of a charismatic church. He approached me to deliver the message that people from many nations of Africa were waiting for me. I found it astounding since I had no connection at that time with any persons from Africa, but the next Sunday while visiting another church in London the invitation came from a Ghanaian minister.

It explains the arrival, along with my husband, of this fair-skinned woman of Scotch-Irish and Mexican descent in West Africa in 2011. In the midst of missional activity through intermittent visits spanning 2011 and 2016, the curiosity about the possibility that dreams and visions were epistemological founts impacting the lives of men and women had solidified into the focus of this book. Assumptions regarding the capacity of the Spirit to lead one to agency are, therefore, embedded in the genesis of this project.

The people of Africa, their lives and their customs, have been historically a focus of study in the West as a result of diverse motivations, both honorable and dishonorable.[48] In the course of this project, I found myself engaging with the works of sociologists, anthropologists, and scholars of religious studies, each one having traveled a pathway to this field of study. The circumstance of "being led by the Spirit" may be considered by some as an unusual mode of arrival, but that is precisely the point of this project. If dreams and visions (and their pursuant "prophetic words") understood as the messages of the Spirit do matter to Pentecostal-Charismatics, then the pneumatological imagination is an epistemological reality worth exploring. And so are its associated manifestations and effects, since they demonstrate that this way of knowing is "alive in our midst."

I have learned that the past portrayals and interpretations of the realities of things "African" have been plagued by distortions. These renderings of African culture have often been funded heavily by Western epistemic constraints and the assumptions associated with white values and white privilege.[49] I cannot claim immunity from the mindsets which have so deeply infected American worldview. My hope is that I have engaged as a learner in spite of (and in some sense because of) the nature of the particularity I bring. I also hope that the epistemic tools I have brought have been used to enhance knowledge about the actualities of epistemology in African contexts, rather than obscure them. The matter is of crucial importance to Pentecostal studies at large. This is especially true in light of the trend toward global theological tables where dialogue on theology and praxis can be exchanged. With true understanding of African

---

48 Missions entwined with the scandal of the slave trade exemplify the latter. I think of the exploratory mission of Thomas Bowdich on behalf of the British Empire in 1817. Its purpose was "to conduct a mission to Ashantee, for the purpose of establishing the trade with that kingdom." See Thomas E. Bowdich, *Mission from Cape Coast Castle to Ashantee: With a Descriptive Account of that Kingdom* (London: Griffith and Farran, 2015), vi.

49 Kwame Anthony Appiah addresses the "invention of Africa" along these lines. See *In My Father's House: Africa in the Philosophy of Culture* (New York: Oxford University Press, 1992).

contributions, it may be possible to arrive at a convergence of the horizons of self-understanding and pentecostal affinity in matters epistemological, reflecting Pentecostalism as a truly distinctive and transcultural phenomenon.

Since the study was birthed from within the standpoint of Western Pentecostalism and from one who also makes claims to experiences of spiritual dreams and visions, there are also theological assumptions to wade through. Yet, the goal was to remain aware of dissonance in sensibilities, when it arose, while allowing the narratives to have their full impact as the central focus. In respect to the conclusions drawn from data, fallibility besets every interpreter. As the study hopes to show, the journey through the data was made with the aim of portraying the Pentecostal-Charismatic epistemology of the participants on its own terms.

This book details a quest to find out how the dreams and visions of African Pentecostals in certain contexts express a distinctive epistemology—that is, a unique way of knowing—that characterizes pentecostal spirituality. This pentecostal epistemology is grounded in "piercing the veil" to the unseen or noumenal, through the experience of dreams and visions. This knowing is marked by visioners' serious engagement with D/Vs in their contexts with the Holy Spirit at the core of epistemic assumptions. How exactly do dreams and visions experienced and interpreted by some Pentecostals in African contexts point to a distinct expression of pentecostal epistemology? And why does it matter? Does the topic inform in ways that are constructive to theology within African contexts? How about beyond those contexts? The argument for the significance of D/Vs unfolds in the following chapters and requires an explanation, first, of how dreams and visions are defined in this project.

The distinction between dreams and visions is not a sharp one, since the understanding for many visioners is that dreams *contain* visions. The two terms are actually linked together in two significant Scriptures referenced by the participants, Numbers 12:6 and Joel 2:28. Numbers 12:6 reads: "Hear now My words: if there is a prophet among you, I, the Lord, make Myself known to him in a vision; I speak to him in a dream." Additionally, Joel 2:28 reads, "And it shall come to pass afterward that I will pour out My Spirit on all flesh; Your sons and daughters shall prophesy, Your old men shall dream dreams, Your young men shall see visions." Accordingly, this project notes a very fine line drawn, at times, between dreams and visions and uses the terms together generally (D/V). The separate terms "dream" or "vision" are used according to how the visioner identified his or her experience(s).

Episcopal scholar of Christian dreams and visions, Morton Kelsey (see Chapter 2), also accentuates the blurred lines inferred by the Greek terms for the visionary experience. In his important volume *God, Dreams and Revelation*

(1991), Kelsey offers twelve terms found in biblical accounts, "each of them a different way of saying that one had come into contact with some reality other than that perceived with the physical senses."[50] The term used eleven times in the book of Acts is perhaps the best reflection of how "D/V" is used in this project. Kelsey writes that ὅραμα (*horama*) "is used to translate the Hebrew words for both dream and vision, and since it can refer to the state in which one receives a vision, it may also refer to the dreaming state."[51] Ghanaian Joseph Quayesi-Amakye explains, regarding visions, that a "closed vision" is what may be experienced while almost dozing or in a trance-like state. An "open vision" is what may be experienced while awake with eyes open.[52]

In order to situate the project within the broader conversation of dreams and visions in the religions, C explores D/Vs as spiritual phenomena within religions of the Near East. In Chapter 3 the discussion turns to D/Vs in spiritualities in African contexts, including Christianity. Chapters 2 and 3 demonstrate the continuity of the valuation of D/Vs with long established oneiric traditions. Chapter 4 narrows the focus to the epistemological soundings of African scholars as the discussion prepares to segue into the analyses of the data collections. The chapter discusses what is being said by African scholars about indigenous knowledge, epistemology in respect to ontological issues, and the agency of the Holy Spirit. Chapter 4 also discusses certain important concepts (such as "piercing the veil") offered by Nigerian Nimi Wariboko that will be referred to in the analyses of the data. Chapter 5 presents the data from the dream narratives and discusses the most obvious and pertinent

---

50   Morton T. Kelsey, *God, Dreams, and Revelation* (Minneapolis, MN: Augsburg Fortress, 1991), 82–87. On pp. 82–86, Kelsey points out other Greek words which refer to dreams or visions or are associated with the visionary experience such as *onar* (dream; Matt. 1:20; 2:12; 2:13, 19, 22; 27:19), *enypnion* ("a thing or vision seen in sleep;" Acts 2:17; Jude 8), *horasis* (vision; Acts 2:17; Rev. 9:17), *optasia* (a supernatural vision in the sense of the self-revealing of the divine; Luke 1:22; 24:23; Acts 26:19; 2 Cor. 12:1), *ekstasis* ("it can denote a state in which a person's ordinary consciousness has been suspended by God's action"; Mark 5:42; Luke 5:26; Mark 16:8; Acts 3:10; 10:10; 11:5; 22:17), *ginomai en pneumatic* ("'to become in the spirit' signified a state in which one could see visions and be informed or spoken to directly by the spirit"; Matt. 4:1; Mark 1:12; Luke 4:1; 1:41), *ephistēmi, paristēmi* (some reality such as the Lord or an angel stands by in the day or night, Acts 10:30; 23:11; 27:23, *angelos* or *angel* (messenger or "divine being sent by God, *daimonion* or *diabolos* (demons or devil), the verbs *blepō, horaō* and *eidō* ("the vision is referred to as the action of seeing"; Mark 9:9; Luke 9:36; Rev. 1:2, 11), *apokalypsis* ("any disclosure in the realm of spirit that was formerly hidden"; Rom. 16:25; 1 Cor. 14:6, 26; 2 Cor. 12:1, 7; Galatians 2:2.
51   Ibid., 83.
52   Joseph Quayesi-Amakye, *Prophetism in Ghana Today, Prophetism in Ghana Today: a Study in Trends in Ghanaian Prophetism*, (Scotts Valley, CA: CreateSpace Publishing, 2013), 12–13.

observations: this pentecostal epistemology recontextualizes certain traditional concepts to reframe them for Pentecostal knowing and also demonstrates a practicality for meeting real needs. Then, Chapter 6 continues in the analysis of data by exploring how findings contribute to understanding the links between prayer and D/V experiences, the impact of the experiences for identity-shaping, and how D/V experiences release impetus for missions.

The quest for the pneumatological imagination comes to a close in Chapter 7 where the discussion turns to the way D/V valuation and this pentecostal epistemology draw from traditional African sensibilities. The chapter also explores how they complement and enhance Pentecostal studies in the West. Chapter 8 closes the discussion with a look at what D/Vs and their interpretations might also indicate about the missiological Spirit.

CHAPTER 2

Dreams, Visions, and Near East Religions

Now, by the power of the Holy Trinity, who is without beginning or division,
I begin my interpretations.
Syrbacham, dream interpreter of the king of India,
ca. 800–1075 AD.[1]
On the day before his death … the prophet Muḥammad announced … "when I am gone there shall remain naught of the glad tidings of prophecy, except true dreams."
JOHN C. LAMOREAUX[2]

∴

I sleep, but my heart is awake; it is the voice of my beloved!
Song of Solomon 5:2

∴

Scholarship drawn from the study of oneiric traditions, that is, the study of societies that value dreams and dreaming, points to the fact that dreams were important to people of ancient cultures. Dream lore was valued in ancient India, Egypt, and Mesopotamia and manuals of dream interpretations have survived from these ancient peoples. One of the earliest of these was found in Egypt and dates back to the 18th century BC. Another book of ancient

---

1 *Achmetis Oneirocriticon* 1.3–14, ca. 800–1075 AD, found in John C. Lamoreaux, *The Early Muslim Tradition of Dream Interpretation* (Albany, NY: State University of New York Press, 2002), 142. Apparently Syrbacham was explicitly Christian. See also Elizabeth Sirriyeh, *Dreams and Visions in the World of Islam: A History of Muslim Dreaming and Foreknowing* (London, UK: I.B. Tauris and Co Ltd, 2015), e-book, loc. 2032. She reports from the same source a quote from Syrbacham, "[v]ery great wisdom is the gift of divination and the interpretation and decipherment of dreams that God has proclaimed to all." Here also Syrbacham substantiates dream interpretation with Jesus' words: "To the one who loves Me, My Father and I will come and tarry with him."
2 John C. Lamoreaux, *The Early Muslim Tradition of Dream Interpretation*, 4.

dream lore is the Indian *Atharva-Veda* which dates back to the 5th century BC. It contains a portion titled "Treatise of Dreams," which draws from even earlier material and discusses predictive dreams. There is also a Babylonian dream manual among the findings of the library of Assurbanipal of Nineveh in Assyria, dated 669–626 BC.[3] A perhaps more popular extant work pointing to the value of dreams is the ancient Gilgamesh Epic produced by the Sumerian and Babylonian culture which dates as far back as 2000 BC. In it, gods and goddesses appear in the dreams of the protagonist, and dreams also guide him in his victories over the enemy.[4]

Dreams were regarded as vehicles of otherworldly knowledge, visionary experiences gained by "piercing the veil" for bringing their benefits from the unseen realm into the everyday experience of the waking life. This value of dreams and other oneiric beliefs and practices of the Near East represent the cultural attitudes that were imparted to the religions historically linked to Abram of Ur: Judaism, Christianity, and Islam. This chapter is a survey of the attitudes toward D/Vs in these religions, beginning first with a look into the Old Testament writings, the Apocrypha, and the annals of Jewish thought. Then, an overview of D/Vs as portrayed in the New Testament, the works of the Church Fathers, and the theological outlooks of Thomas Aquinas, Immanuel Kant, and Emmanuel Swedenborg will be presented.

It will become apparent that conflicting ideas regarding D/Vs had already set solidly into Christian discourse by the 18th century. Closing this chapter, a view into the rich oneiric tradition of Islam will include D/Vs reflected in the Qur'an and the *hadith*, the transmission of dream manuals, and the use of D/Vs for legitimizing religious and political figures in Islamic societies. This chapter situates D/Vs in African Pentecostalism as part of a broader, universal appraisal of spiritual experiences, yet one which reflects a distinctive use of a Spirit hermeneutic that engages biblical narratives for pentecostal epistemology.[5]

---

3   Roger Caillois, "Logical and Philosophical Problems of the Dream," in G.E. von Grunebaum and Roger Caillois, editors, *The Dream in Human Societies* (Berkeley, CA: University of California Press, 1966), 23–24.
4   Kelsey, *God, Dreams, and Revelation*, 54.
5   While this chapter appeals to historical accounts, the universal appraisal of D/Vs is by no means a thing of the past. Dream researcher Kelly Bulkeley writes, "[m]any modern Westerners are dissatisfied with the existential meanings provided by their culture. The rationalism, commercialism, and individualism promoted so vigorously in the modern West do not always lead to a fulfilling, meaningful life ... So modern Westerners interested in dreams are simply exploring a realm of religious meaning that humans have been exploring for the same reason throughout history." See Kelly Bulkeley, *The Wilderness of Dreams: Exploring the Religious Meanings of Dreams in Modern Western Culture* (Albany, NY: State University of New York Press, 1994), 213.

1 Dreams and Visions and Hebraic Theology

Foundational to the Hebraic understanding of dreams and visions in spirituality is the belief that Yahweh initiates communication through dreams, visions, and auditory experiences. The experiences are often portrayed in the Old Testament as being linked to the act of prophesying, that is, declaring the messages of God. For that reason, Old Testament scholar David C. Hymes currently at Northwest University suggests that Hebrew semantics indicate a blending of concepts so that dreams, visions, and prophecy should be understood as triadic and often intersecting.[6] Morton Kelsey, former mentee of Carl Jung as well as professor at the University of Notre Dame in Indiana, expresses the relationship of the dream and vision by describing the dream as the vehicle for the experience of the vision. Therefore, experiences are not easily categorized as either dream or vision, and rather, resist the Western penchant for precise descriptors.[7]

Both Hymes and Kelsey will contribute to the subsequent discussion on D/Vs in the Old Testament. Their material will inform for understanding the role of D/Vs in the lives of the patriarchs of Judeo-Christian faith, the way that D/Vs figure prominently in the story of Israel's kings and prophets, and the attitudes toward D/Vs as reflected in the Apocrypha and later Jewish sources. What will become clear is that, more important than technicalities regarding the distinctions, if any, between dream and vision, is the bigger picture portraying Old Testament D/V accounts as the stories of divine encounters. Hymes asserts, "[d]reams have been the means for some Israelites to experience a theophany that would transform their lives, with grave import to the covenantal community."[8] It was so for Abraham, Jacob, Joseph, and many prophets and foreign kings in the story of the birth and history of the nation Israel.

---

[6] David C. Hymes, "Toward an Old Testament Theology of Dreams: A Pentecostal-Charismatic Perspective," *Australasian Pentecostal Studies* 14 (2012) 75.

[7] Kelsey, *God, Dreams, and Revelation*, 33. He points out that, while Num. 12:6 and Job 20:8 describe dreams and visions in parallel fashion, attempts at firm distinctions should be avoided. That is because some Scripture references only refer to "a vision of the night," (1 Samuel 3:15; Job 20:8; Isaiah 29:7; Daniel 2:19 and 7:2) or relay "In the night I saw" as in Zech. 1:8. The broad semantic base in the biblical languages is also substantiated by Bart J. Koet. See "Divine Dream Dilemmas: Biblical Visions and Dreams" in *Dreaming in Christianity and Islam: Culture, Conflict, and Creativity,* Kelly Bulkeley, Kate Adams, and Patricia M. Davis, eds. (New Brunswick, NJ: Rutgers University Press, 2009), 18.

[8] Hymes, "Toward an Old Testament Theology of Dreams," 61.

1.1   Dreams, Visions, and Patriarchs

The role that Morton Kelsey has played in bringing the dreams and visions of Judeo-Christian tradition into scholarly purview should not be overlooked. His volume *Dreams: The Dark Speech of the Spirit* (1968), which was later published in its revised and expanded form as *God, Dreams and Revelation: Christian Interpretation of Dreams* (1991), predates other important research.[9] For example, Nelson O. Hayashida, who studied dreaming among Zambian Baptists (see Chapter 4) and Kelly Bulkeley, whose work was featured in Chapter 1, both refer to Kelsey in their work. Kelsey, also an Episcopal priest, explained how his exposure to the value of dreams in Jungian therapy led him to the discovery of their importance in Christian tradition. He writes, "I began to reread the New Testament with a greater open-mindedness, and I was surprised by what I found."[10]

As reported by Kelsey in *God, Dreams and Revelation*, the first mention of a dream experience in Scripture also immediately follows the experience of a vision. It is the incident in which confirmation of Abram's call to relationship with Yahweh is given (Gen. 15:1), as well as revelations about the future (Gen. 15:4, 13–16). The significance of this D/V experience cannot be overstated since it was the initiation of God's covenant with Abram through the ritual of sacrifice. Kelsey writes, "In a numinous and mysterious experience that touched a person to the depth, God turned his promise to Abram into the Covenant, the effective contract between God and human beings."[11]

When encounters with angels are included as visionary experiences, as they are in Kelsey's material, it is apparent that visions were not only selectively granted to Israel's patriarch, Abram. The poignant scene of the angel comforting Hagar, who was to bear Abram's child Ishmael, is followed by several other angelic visits, first to Abraham and Sarah (whose names had been changed), to Lot in Sodom, and to Abraham's grandson Jacob who wrestled with God, otherwise referred to as an angel in Hosea 12:4.[12]

---

9   The work of Patricia Cox Miller is an example of a subsequent, deeper dive into the oneiric tradition of Greco-Roman, Jewish and Christian traditions. See *Dreams in Late Antiquity: Studies in the Imagination of a Culture*, 1994.
10 Kelsey, *God, Dreams, and Revelation*, 27.
11 Ibid., 36.
12 Ibid., 82, 84–85. Kelsey lists visions of angels among the twelve expressions of visionary experiences and notes that they represent reality in terms other than the materiality we are accustomed to. It is worth bringing up here that it seems that the reference to angelic visits as visionary should be qualified. Would it be better to think of angelic experiences in terms of Hyme's model of intersecting sets, where angelic visits may or may not be visionary, per se? If the angel appears in ontological materiality for all to see, as in the

Dreams become particularly significant in the narratives of the lives of Jacob and his son Joseph. The dream that Jacob had while sleeping outdoors on his journey to Padan Aram was a pivotal spiritual experience for him. In the dream, angels were ascending and descending a ladder into heaven. It so moved Jacob that he concluded that the location was the "gate of heaven." The conviction of God's immanence led him to mark the place by pouring oil on the rock he had slept on (Gen. 28:18). Jacob responded to the dream by vowing his tithe to Yahweh: "Of all that You give me I will surely give a tenth to You" (v. 22). The religiosity of the event has carried forward until today in the Judeo-Christian practice of the tithing of one's resources to give to God's purposes.

The life of Joseph demonstrates D/V experiences as pivotal to the major events marking his enslavement and subsequent rise to power in Egypt. The dreams that Joseph shared with his brothers, of their sheaves in the field that bowed down to him, and of the eleven stars, sun, and moon that also bowed to him fueled the hatred already simmering. After being sold by them into slavery and then being cast into prison due to the allegations of Potiphar's wife, more dreams figured prominently. His skill at interpretation brought him before Pharaoh to interpret the divine messages in the dreams of the seven gaunt cows and the seven thin stalks of grain. Joseph's interpretation and wise counsel catapulted him to the role of overseer of Pharaoh's operations, and specifically of the feeding program that would sustain Egypt and surrounding nations during the seven years of famine.

Hymes takes note of the scholarship that has yielded observations about the D/Vs of the Old Testament. He recognizes that Assyriologist A. Leo Oppenheim offered a landmark Western typology of dreams, locating two distinctive types of Near Eastern dreams, the "message dream" and the "symbolic dream."[13] Oppenheim added that the dream was viewed by visioners as conveying knowledge from the gods and its existence as a phenomenon was reflected in its frequent use as a literary device. The experience was also often marked with the hearing of an audible voice and is better assessed, according to Oppenheim, as a "theological" event.[14] Also, a certain type of message dream of the theological type, such as that which results from the ritual of incubation, was understood as plain and not requiring interpretation.

---

case of the angels who visited Lot in Sodom (Gen. 19:5), might there be a need for a more nuanced understanding of angelic interventions?

13   Hymes, "Toward an Old Testament Theology of Dreams," 64. See Leo Oppenheim, "Mantic Dreams in the Ancient Near East" in von Grunebaum and Caillois, *The Dream in Human Societies* (Berkeley, CA: University of California Press, 1966), 341–350.

14   Oppenheim, "Mantic Dreams in the Ancient Near East," 347–348.

Hymes reports that Frances Flannery-Dailey and other dream researchers have built upon Oppenheim's work. For example, Flannery-Dailey uses Oppenheim's form-critical method for delineating twenty-eight dream accounts in the Old Testament.[15] But in Hymes' perspective, Oppenheim has not allowed for D/V experiences that do not fit neatly into either the "message" or "symbolic" typology. Hymes concludes that it is more helpful to learn through language study and the nuances that study offers wherever terms are used. It means that studying the "broader semantic field of dreams and visions without dividing the two" is imperative when examining the dreams in Hebraic writings, thus expanding the pool of pertinent material.[16]

In any case, message dreams are a distinct category of dream and the characteristic dream experience of the Hebrew patriarchs, whether directly or symbolically relayed. Additionally, message dreams carry an effect that extends far beyond the visioner him or herself to include impact on descendants or the nation Israel.[17] It should also be noted that the divine messages appear to have an even farther reaching purview, even for impacting other nations and their kings, as was the case in Joseph's life, which is discussed in the next section.

1.2 *Dreams, Visions, Kings, and Prophets*

Accounts of D/V experiences pepper the narratives of the kings and prophets of Israel. They are embedded in the story of the role of the prophet in Israel, which in essence was bound to the ability to "see" and to the function of the "seer" who delivers God's message. The mention of prophets and dreams and visions in Numbers 12:4–6 is taken up by Kelsey and Hymes in their discussions about the validation of D/V experiences in the lives of prophets in Israel. Hymes notes the passage as a key reference to understanding Hebraic D/Vs. This particular pericope has Moses' reputation as the central focus since the narrative describes how God came to Moses' defense at a time of tension with the people. It also describes D/Vs as normative communication for prophets of God.

Hymes also shows that by looking back at the preceding texts in Numbers 11 the value of prophets and prophecy in Israel is apparent. The chapter is also an important part of the context for establishing Moses' affirmation from God in chapter 12. The fact that prophets are necessary is indicated through

---

15 Frances Flannery-Dailey, "Lessons on Early Jewish Apocalypticism and Mysticism from Dream Literature," in *Paradise Now: Essays on Early Jewish and Christian Mysticism*, ed. April DeConick (Atlanta, GA: Society of Biblical Literature, 2006), 233.
16 Hymes, "Toward an Old Testament Theology of Dreams," 65.
17 Ibid., 78–79.

Moses' comment, "Oh, that all the Lord's people were prophets and that the Lord would put His Spirit upon them!" (11:29). Hymes notes, "Moses is able to graciously wish that all Yahweh's people would become prophets and be given the spirit."[18] The subsequent verses spoken by Yahweh himself clarify that God does, in fact, speak to prophets, doing so through dreams and visions: "If there is a prophet among you, I, the Lord, make Myself known to him in a vision; I speak to him in a dream. Not so with My servant Moses; He is faithful in all My house. I speak with him face to face" (Num. 12:6–8a).

Hymes writes, "Num. 11–12 therefore gives both purpose and means to normative prophecy that could be experienced by all with divine communication as its center."[19] It might be added that the texts offered a fitting affirmation of the D/V experiences of Abraham and the patriarchs while also positioning Israel for the centuries of prophetic ministry to follow after settling in the land of Canaan.

The introduction of a long line of kings for Israel, and later for the kingdom of Judah, is tied to the prophetic role of a small boy, Samuel. His ability to know and "see" on Israel's behalf was to guide them in the selection of a king and through difficult times in the years to come. As Kelsey observes about Samuel's initial experience reported in 1 Samuel Chapter 3, "[t]his vision-dream of Samuel's opened up a new era, and in several places Samuel is described as the seer, the one who sees beyond ordinary things."[20] Kelsey also refers to statements attributed to Israel's first king, Saul, that give an indication of the value of dreams in those days. In a time of desperation for spiritual guidance Saul disobeyed Mosaic law and consulted a medium in order to contact the spirit of Samuel. Saul's complaint to Samuel reads, "I am deeply distressed ... God has departed from me and does not answer me anymore, neither by prophets nor by dreams" (1 Sam. 28:15).

In the case of King David, the prophet Nathan received a message for David by means of a vision at night that gave instructions regarding the building of a house for the Lord. Nathan was informed that it would be a project that David would prepare for, but which would be implemented by his son (2 Sam. 7). Solomon was the fulfillment of that promise and had his own encounter with Yahweh through a dream he experienced after sacrificing a thousand burnt offerings. In that dream, God responded to Solomon's request for "an understanding heart to judge Your people" (1 Kings 3:9) by stating, "see, I have given

---

18 Hymes, "Toward an Old Testament Theology of Dreams," 86.
19 Ibid., 87.
20 Kelsey, *God, Dreams, and Revelation*, 39.

you a wise and understanding heart, so that there has not been anyone like you before you, nor shall any like you arise after you" (1 Kings 3:12).[21]

Biblical scholars note the resemblance of the account of Solomon's dream with the practice of dream incubation that was customary in the Near East. Hymes refers to the work of E. L. Ehrlich on this point (*Der Traum im Alten Testament*, 1953). Old Testament scholar James L. Crenshaw also makes mention of Solomon's experience at Gibeon as reflecting the practice of incubation "by which a devotee of a particular deity slept at a sanctuary hoping to receive a visit."[22] The practice will be commented on in the discussion ahead regarding D/Vs in Islam. It is sufficient here to be reminded that attitudes related to dream lore in Israel's history developed within the milieu of the general appreciation of, and practices related to D/Vs in the surrounding cultures of the Near East.

Kelsey observes that the farther the kings wandered from Yahweh, the less frequent were dreams and visions. He writes, "[b]ut as the kings of Israel got into more and more trouble, the record of their own dreams ceased. Instead, we are told that the word of the Lord came to Elijah and Elisha."[23] There were a series of miraculous events associated with Elijah's prophetic role in Israel, including receiving the ministration of an angel in the wilderness and revelation that came audibly in the "still small voice" (1 Kings 19). Another event was the vision his servant Elisha saw of the chariots of fire whisking Elijah away. A vision also came to Elisha's servant as Elisha prayed for him, as is reported in the dramatic account of the servant's "open vision" of the "mountain full of horses and chariots of fire all around Elisha" in 2 Kings 6.[24] These episodes are followed by other examples among the Hebrew prophets who also proved to be prolific visioners.

Kelsey approaches the problem of D/Vs through the prophets that were to follow in Israel's history: Isaiah, Jeremiah, and Ezekiel. All three were visionaries, and Kelsey notes that in their writings the scrutiny of prophetic utterances was not overlooked. Therefore, the issue was not with the dream or vision as

---

21   James Crenshaw renders the translation of Solomon's request as asking for "a *hearing heart* to judge" the people of God. See James L. Crenshaw, *Old Testament Wisdom: An Introduction* (Louisville, KY: Westminster John Knox Press, 2010), 44.
22   Ibid., 44. Also, for a vivid rendering of the practice of incubation in the Grecian cult of the god Asclepius see Patricia Cox Miller, *Dreams in Late Antiquity*, 109–117.
23   Kelsey, *God, Dreams, and Revelation*, 40.
24   An open vision is what may be experienced while awake with eyes open. See Quayesi-Amakye, *Prophetism in Ghana Today*, 13.

vehicle for the messages from Yahweh. The concern was with the truthfulness and authenticity of both messenger and message. Isaiah is forthright in his rebuke, alleging that the rulers of Jerusalem had "made a covenant with death" (Is. 28:15), but as Kelsey notes, "[t]hen he shifted the burden back upon the people who demanded deceitful things and would not listen to the prophet who told them what he really saw."[25]

The prophet Jeremiah admits that time will test the veracity of prophetic D/Vs (Jer. 28:9), but the comparison of dreams with chaff found in Jeremiah's message from God earlier in the chapter present a more disparaging view (Jer. 23:28–29). Echoing Kelsey, Hymes brings clarity by arguing that it is not the valid dream that is being portrayed as offensive, but the use of dreams to draw people away from Yahweh. Borrowing from the work of Thomas Overholt, scholar of Religious Studies, Hymes comments, "[i]n this way, Jer. 23 follows the lead of Deut. 13:2–6 which condemns the inappropriate use of a valid methodology."[26] Likewise, the prophet Ezekiel, the seer with perhaps the most unusual visions which include otherworldly creatures, also warns the "foolish prophets who follow their own spirit and have seen nothing" (Ez. 13:3).

Amos, Hosea, Obadiah, Micah, Nahum, Habakkuk and Zechariah are all noted by Kelsey as among the minor prophets who experienced visions. The visions of Zechariah were particularly extensive and began with what Zechariah "saw in the night" (Zech. 1:8). Kelsey notes that the book of Daniel stands apart from the books of other prophets and is classified as more similar to the books of Job and Esther, together commonly known as the "writings." The content of the book is remarkable for how it offers "a field day" for one interested in D/Vs, reinforcing their value and showing that the ability to interpret them was a mark of wisdom.[27] Like Joseph, Daniel rose to notoriety because of his ability, in this case during the Babylonian exile. He interpreted the dreams of King Nebudchadnezzar but experienced many visions of his own. Kelsey, remarks, "The Book of Daniel is so much concerned with these experiences that it might well be subtitled A Romance of the Dream."[28]

---

25 Kelsey, *God, Dreams, and Revelation*, 44.
26 Hymes, "Toward an Old Testament Theology of Dreams," 82. Bart J. Koet concurs that inauthentic dreams were the concern in Jeremiah. See "Divine Dream Dilemmas: Biblical Visions and Dreams" in Bulkeley, Adams, and Davis, eds. *Dreaming in Christianity and Islam* (NJ: Rutgers University Press, 2009), 23.
27 Kelsey, *God, Dreams, and Revelation*, 49.
28 Ibid., 49.

1.3 Dreams and Visions in the Apocrypha and Jewish Thought

Kelsey introduces his material on D/Vs and the Old Testament Apocrypha by emphasizing that readers today do not generally recognize how authoritative the works were in Judaism. They are, in fact, part and parcel of the Greek translation of Hebraic works, the Septuagint. They were so widely esteemed that clear articulation between the Hebrew and Christian Bible only came later, a delineation noted in the writings of St. Jerome in the 5th century. Kelsey argues that the Apocrypha complements the works of the Old Testament by offering similar indications of the attitudes regarding D/Vs in Judaism in the time of Jesus. He reports that, in particular, six books of the Apocrypha deal with dreams and visions: 2 Esdras, the book of Tobit, the Greek version of Esther, the Wisdom of Solomon, Ecclesiasticus (the wisdom of Sirach), and 2 Maccabees.[29]

In the Greek version of Esther, it is a dream experienced by Mordecai that is threaded throughout the account and which Mordecai considers revelation of God's purposes fulfilled. In 2 Maccabees, Kelsey reports on an account of a dramatic vision experienced by Heliodorus, one similar to that of Saul of Tarsus. In Ecclesiasticus, the mention of dreams is ambivalent, that is, both doubtful of dreams and yet showing recognition of certain dreams as being granted by God. Kelsey concludes, "[t]he authors of the Old Testament and the Apocrypha had a belief about dreams and visions that they considered important … This was one way in which God, the Most High, or Yahweh, spoke what needed to be said to men and women."[30] As found in the Old Testament writings, the possibility of encountering lies and inauthentic accounts is taken into consideration in the Apocrypha, yet, without discounting the value of dreams.

Kelsey explains that the Babylonian Talmud is considered second only to the Old Testament in theological importance for Judaism. The material was written between the third and sixth centuries AD and represent the works of esteemed rabbis. Reflective of the fact that there are four chapters on dreams in the first section of the Talmud, Kelsey writes, "Rabbi Hisda said that an uninterpreted dream was like an unread letter."[31] In regard to "bad" dreams, Kelsey observes from Talmudic writings, "[t]he bad ones often were more valuable since they led to repentance and had a more transforming effect."[32] Another indication of the value of dreams in Judaism is that the intellectual leaders

---

29   Kelsey, *God, Dreams, and Revelation*, 49–51.
30   Ibid., 51.
31   Ibid., 52.
32   Ibid., 52.

believed in their value to the point that dream interpreters were even paid for their services.[33]

Kelsey refers to other notable indications of receptivity of D/Vs in Jewish history. The historian Eusebius mentions the works of the Jewish philosopher Philo, the Alexandrian scholar who apparently wrote five volumes on dreams. Two of those works are mentioned in Philo's extant works. The theologian Maimonides, who wrote in the medieval era, referred specifically to the human capacity for prophetic dreams in his work *The Guide for the Perplexed*.

Dreams were also valued in the Kabbalist movement, as is reported in the book *Rosenbaums of Zell* which features dreams as vehicles for "illumination." This volume also records the dream experiences of Reb Hile Wechsler who lived about 1880. He dreamt repeatedly of "the extinction of the Jewish community in Germany" and thought deeply upon the dreams, voicing publically his conclusion that Jews should return to Palestine.[34] Dreams were relevant as well in the Hasidic tradition. For example, the Rabbi Eisik of Cracow "followed his dreams and was led in the end to a great treasure."[35] Another example of the enduring value of dreams in Jewish tradition is the fact that the 16th century book on dream interpretation by Jacob Almoli, titled *Pitron Halomot*, was republished in 1902 in New York City.[36]

2   Dreams and Visions in Christianity

Transmission of literature—or lack of it—can reflect censorship indicative of an underlying value system. Kelsey argues that this is no less true in the case of Christian works. What survived over the centuries points to transmission due to the estimation of which works were *deemed* important for academic or ecclesiastic consumption. Kelsey argues that lack of transmission of material regarding dreams and visions in Christian spirituality is notable. He writes, "[t]here are thirty-eight thick volumes of ante-Nicene, Nicene, and post-Nicene fathers that seem to have been rather carelessly indexed in relation to dreams

---

33   James Crenshaw sheds insight on the struggle that some intellectuals did have with accepting D/Vs as valid means of knowledge. He offers that that the account of Solomon experiencing the dream on mount Gibeon no doubt impacted the second century sage Ben Sira, but Ben Sira nevertheless opposed "the practice of predicting the future by means of dreams" and was ambivalent, at best, regarding dreams and spirituality. See Crenshaw, *Old Testament Wisdom*, 29, 44.
34   Kelsey, *God, Dreams, and Revelation*, 53.
35   Ibid., 53.
36   Ibid., 54.

and similar subjects."[37] Kelsey notes that the omissions reflect the biases or preferences of the editors and can therefore be poor reflections of the material that was actually available. He also observes that "[t]here has been no serious study of the thinking of the church fathers on the subject of dreams for at least two centuries."[38]

This section continues to rely heavily on the work of Morton Kelsey since he provides a careful examination of the way that biblical passages about D/Vs have been interpreted by the early Church and through subsequent centuries. In other words, it examines the reception history in the church of the biblical passages that speak of D/Vs experienced by prophets and other persons of Old and New Testaments. The material enlightens in regard to the high valuation of D/Vs and the biblical support for a positive theological assessment in early Christianity. Kelsey also examines the attitudes of those guiding the Church early on. The section includes his comments on the Apostolic Fathers and D/Vs, the attitudes of other early thinkers of the Eastern and Western Church, and the pertinent ideas of medieval theologians. It is, therefore, to the trajectory from appreciation to ambivalence in the story of D/Vs and Christianity that the conversation now turns.

2.1 Dreams and Visions in the New Testament and Early Church

Kelsey points out that the gospels are replete with D/V experiences, especially in the accounts of Jesus' birth. Beginning with the vision of the angel Gabriel that Zacharias experienced while serving in the temple, and the annunciations to Mary by Gabriel and to Joseph in a dream, the narrative gives a prominent place to D/V experiences. The shepherds saw angels announce Jesus' birth in Bethlehem, and the magi and Joseph received dreams of warning and guidance that kept them from Herod's wrath. It was Joseph's third divine dream experience while in exile in Egypt that guided him away from a return to Judea so that he chose rather to go to Nazareth.[39]

Kelsey argues that the authors of the gospels and book of Acts held to the traditional high value of D/V experiences. Therefore the accounts are sprinkled with such experiences from the lives of Jesus and his disciples. The most significant examples are the auditory and visionary experiences connected

---

37 Kelsey, *God, Dreams, and Revelation*, 99.
38 Ibid., 100. Kelsey's line of research required that several works be translated from Latin into English, including some of the pertinent works of Augustine and Gregory the Great along with a 16th century volume written by Benedict Pererius. That volume produced by Pererious investigates the value of dreams to Christian spirituality.
39 Kelsey, ibid., 87.

with Jesus' baptism when the Holy Spirit came upon Jesus like a dove and the voice of the Father affirmed his Son. Kelsey posits that the temptations of Jesus incited by the devil were also visionary experiences. Also, a striking vision was experienced by Peter and the disciples who saw Jesus transfigured and Moses and Elijah appear to them.

The last dream account of the gospel of Matthew records the dream of Pontius Pilate's wife who warned her husband to "have nothing to do with this righteous Man" because she "had suffered greatly in a dream because of Him" (Matt. 27:19). The most memorable of D/V accounts in the book of Acts include the visions of Peter and Cornelius, the life transforming vision of Saul on the road to Damascus—along with the vision of Ananias—and the dreams and other visions experienced by Paul.

Paul was directed to Macedonia through a dream, and later, was moved by a vision of an angel to encourage his desperate shipmates during the shipwreck on route to Rome. Paul's remarkable vision of being taken up to Paradise, as recorded in his second extant letter to the Corinthian churches, is another extraordinary account. The apocalyptic visions of the apostle John recorded in the book of Revelation are the most illustrious examples of the visionary experiences of those who followed Jesus.[40]

The climate reflective of the attitude toward D/Vs in the days of the Apostolic Fathers is portrayed in several volumes treasured among early Christians. Two of these are the *Shepherd of Hermas* and the *Martyrdom of Polycarp* and both of them feature dreams and visions. It is reported that Polycarp, the bishop of Smyrna, dreamt prior to his martyrdom of his pillow catching fire. He felt that the symbolism signified his impending death.[41] Of New Testament apocryphal writings, Kelsey lists the *Acts of the Holy Apostle Thomas* as containing anecdotes regarding dreams and visions. Kelsey shares that rather than communicating caution in regards to visionary experiences, the Fathers continued in the spirit of the New Testament. He writes, "I found that when these men spoke of dreams, it was almost always to express a positive view."[42]

Irenaeus, the bishop of Lyons in the 2nd century, and several others followed in the understanding of D/Vs held by Justin Martyr. That understanding maintained the value of these experiences for Christian spirituality. Martyr believed that the dream life supported the argument "that souls do not cease after death … because they give hint of human participation in a more-than-physical

---

40   Kelsey, *God, Dreams, and Revelation*, 88–96.
41   Ibid., 101.
42   Ibid., 103.

world."[43] Martyr also maintained that dreams could be sent by evil spirits or by God, implying the need for discernment.[44] In *Against Heresies*, Irenaeus makes at least three references to biblical D/Vs: the dreams of Joseph in Matthew's gospel, the vision of Peter in Acts 10, and the dream of Paul in Acts ch.16. These instances were held up as evidence of intimacy with God and authentication of those who received them as followers of the true God.

Origen of Alexandria followed in the interpretation of the Bible of his spiritual mentor Clement. Both of them understood D/Vs as significant for Christian life. Origen makes reference to the experiences of Jacob, Daniel, the dreams and visions surrounding Jesus' birth, and the paradigm shifting vision received by Peter in the New Testament. He refers to them as revelatory works of God. Tertullian of Carthage discussed sleep and dreams in eight chapters of his *De Anima (A Treatise on the Soul)*. In the introduction to his volume the *Martyrdom of Saints Perpetua and Felicitas*, he links the experience of dreams and visions to Joel's prophecy and to God's concern for the Church.[45]

The bishop of Carthage in 250 AD, Thascius Cyprian, made reference to Job and to the Patriarch Joseph when defending visionary experiences. Hyppolytus of Rome referred to the prophet Daniel when explaining the value of dreams. In the days of the emperor Constantine, the tutor of Constantine's son, Lactantius, produced the volume *Epitome* in which he showed that Jesus Christ was the fulfillment of the Spirit-inspired visions of the Old Testament prophets.[46]

---

43   Kelsey, *God, Dreams, and Revelation*, 104.
44   Discernment is a pivotal issue to the visioners from the Dreams and Visions Project. Patricia M. Davis also notes three criteria for discerning divine dreams in Christianity: approval of the religious community, conformity with the sacred scripture, and good fruits demonstrating a perceived beneficial effect. See Patricia M. Davis, "Discerning the Voice of God: Case Studies in Christian History" in Kelly Bulkeley, et. al., *Dreaming in Christianity and Islam*, 45.
45   Kelly Bulkeley cites Christian martyr Perpetua as a significant case study for understanding the phenomenon of the "big dream." He writes, "[b]ig dreams are often quite coherent, highly structured, and easily remembered." See Kelly Bulkeley, *Big Dreams: The Science of Dreaming and the Origins of Religion* (NY: Oxford University Press, 1016), e-book, loc. 3925–4170. Citation found at loc. 1497. Also, Patricia Cox Miller offers a female rendering of Perpetua's dreams as reflecting liberationist or perhaps Montanist influence. Miller reads Perpetua's diary of dreams "as both *reflective* of *and* resistant to the sexual politics of her community." See Miller, *Dreams in Late Antiquity*, 166.
46   Kelsey, *God, Dreams, and Revelation*, 99–114.

2.2 Dreams and Visions in Late Patristic Thought

The 4th century ushered in an era of deliberations among Christian leaders confronted with heretical influences such as Arianism and the sectarianism of the Donatists. It gave rise to a flock of theologians and apologists of both the Latin and Greek speaking Church who each contributed to the work of theological self-reflection. Understanding where the concerns of the Church lay in that era is helpful for comprehending the content of the writings produced at the time. Kelsey points out that, in spite of the dominant preoccupations, the works of Athanasius, bishop of Alexandria, also share regarding his attitude toward D/Vs for Christian spirituality.

In his work *History of the Arians,* Athanasius includes a reference to the visionary experience of Daniel regarding the Antichrist. Athanasius presents Daniel's experience in a positive light, even suggesting a link between the vision and the appearance of Constantius as emperor of Rome. But Kelsey sees the work of Athanasius in his later years, the writing of *Life of St. Antony*, as even more indicative of the approval of dreams and visions. There Athanasius cites St. Antony's references to the revelatory capacity of Elisha the prophet who exemplified for Antony a truly intimate relationship with God. Kelsey comments, "[h]is interest in Antony shows his own religious aspiration and his belief that the soul can be given direct communication with the nonphysical, the spiritual world, without the mediation of reason."[47]

In the Eastern Church, Gregory of Nyssa wrote a major work titled *On the Making of Man* in which he discusses sleep and dreams. There he references the D/Vs of Joseph and Daniel and holds the men up as "worthy of evident Divine communication."[48] In his sermon titled "In Praise of Forty Martyrs," Gregory shared his own personal dream of a visitation from the martyrs, a dream which impacted him to seriously undertake his own Christian life and witness.[49] Gregory's brother, known as Basil the Great for his courage displayed in confronting the Arian emperor Valens, and who was bishop of Caesarea of Cappadocia, echoed the opinion of Gregory. In his work *On the Spirit,* Basil discusses how the Spirit communicated through dreams with Joseph and Jacob. In *The Hexaemeron*, Basil refers to Numbers 12:6–8 where it is stated that God spoke to prophets through a dream or vision. Nevertheless, he did warn Christians regarding some dreams that deceive, and that in response to

---

[47] Kelsey, *God, Dreams, and Revelation*, 122.
[48] Ibid., 123.
[49] This type of dream is similar to the ancestor dream common among visioners of this project.

the dreams of a certain Eustathius who claimed to have had dreams of Basil which Eustathius interpreted with a negative slant.

John Chrysostom, known as John the Golden-mouth, was the ascetic of Antioch who became known for his passionate and direct preaching in his role as Archbishop of Constantinople. Kelsey notes that his word was authoritative for the Church, to the point that he maintained influence even from a distance when banished. Most important to this discussion is his definitive approval of D/Vs as biblically sanctioned and spiritually significant as sources of revelation.

Chrysostom referred to Pentecost and the book of Acts when referring to the "grace" of dreams or visions, dreams being phenomena given to "those whose wills are compliant to God" and visions reserved for those in need of more startling manifestations.[50] In his discourses he cited the examples of Joseph the father of Jesus, Peter, and Paul, as well as the dreams of the Old Testament, those experienced by Joseph, Daniel, and Abimelech. Also, Chrysostom's theology of dreams offered a sophisticated distinction among dreams. He understood some dreams to reflect the state of one's soul, either one's "bad conscience or bad character," but also as experiences meant to "reveal spiritual reality," bring comfort from God, or give needed divine guidance.[51]

The voices of the Church in the West that figure prominently as ecclesiastic commentaries on dreams and visions are those of Ambrose, Augustine, and Jerome. Ambrose was bishop of Milan in the latter portion of the 4th century. Ambrose's letter to Theodosius, in which he calls him to repent because of a dream Ambrose had, is indication of Ambrose's attitude toward dreams. Another of Ambrose's dreams was actually reported by Augustine, who was his junior and who had been impacted by the life of the bishop. In *The Confessions,* Augustine explains that the whereabouts of the bodies of the martyrs Gervasius and Protasius had been revealed to Ambrose in a dream. But the high valuation of D/Vs that Ambrose had is best manifested in his book on the duties of the clergy. In it he calls attention to the experiences and abilities of Solomon, Joseph, and Daniel as coming from the Holy Spirit.

Augustine of Hippo believed that dreams and visions are given by God. He is credited with a sophisticated theory of epistemology in which the "inner eye" is capable of perceiving other than the corporeal or physical. So, for Augustine, "spiritual realities ... can present themselves directly to the inner eye."[52] Therefore, D/Vs can be sources of knowledge. Echoing the intuitions

---

50   Kelsey, *God, Dreams, and Revelation,* 128.
51   Ibid., 128.
52   Ibid., 134.

of Justin Martyr, who lived two centuries prior, Augustine believed that the abilities of the human psyche for these mental/visionary experiences serve as evidence of human existence after the death of the body. While Augustine offers a number of dream anecdotes, including the dream of his own mother Monica which encouraged her in regard to her son eventually coming to faith in Christ, it is Augustine's contemporary, Jerome, who offers biblical support for their value for Christianity. Jerome discusses dreams in his commentary on Jeremiah 23:25–32. He reflects on the responsibility of the Church to interpret dreams since believers have the word of God.

As Kelsey reports about Jerome's thoughts, "[d]reams can become idolatrous … when they are sought and interpreted for their own sake by those who are serving their own self-interest instead of God."[53] Jerome also reflected on Paul's visionary experience recorded in Acts 16 (the call to Macedonia) when he wrote on Paul's epistle to the Galatians. Therefore, Jerome followed suit with the positive attitude toward D/Vs that had been sustained through roughly the first four hundred years of the church's history.

So far, it has been argued that the early Church read the passages on dreams and visions in the Bible in a positive way, putting credence in visionary experiences as valued elements of Judeo-Christian tradition. The discussion has also mentioned some of the dreams that were recorded as significant in the lives of the Fathers and theologians of Christianity's early history. Ahead, the contours of the eclipse of dreams and visions are traced by first examining the stance of the medieval scholar Thomas Aquinas. He grappled openly with the biblical passages and arrived at a positive appraisal of the D/V experience for Christian spirituality, albeit, laced with caution due to the activity of demons. That optimism was ultimately eclipsed by the ideology of Immanuel Kant.

2.3   Aquinas, Kant, and Swedenborg on Dreams and Visions

For gauging the tone for the reception of D/Vs in the early modern era, the discussion turns to Thomas Aquinas, the theologian who featured as a prominent influence, at least institutionally, in the medieval Roman Catholic Church. With the help of other scholars, this essay proceeds to an evaluation of the ideas of Immanuel Kant. It is argued that the rationalist Kant is significantly responsible for the eclipse of dreams and visions in Christian thought. His confrontation with Emanuel Swedenborg's visionary experiences brought tension to the religious discussion about what constitutes valid knowledge.

---

53   Kelsey, *God, Dreams, and Revelation*, 137.

To be fair, the turn away from D/VS in Christianity can be spotted long before Kant, as scholar of Religious Studies John C. Lamoreaux points out. Lamoreaux highlights the monastic Antiochus of the 7th century who wrote about the dangers of paying attention to dreams in his instructions to monks of the Mar Sabas monastery near Jerusalem. Antiochus used Jude's epistle and the book of Sirach to support his view.[54] Thomas Aquinas had considerably more influence on Christian thought than individuals such as Antiochus. It is not difficult to see how Thomas Aquinas' role as *doctor angelicus* of the Roman Catholic Church in the 12th century caused his word on dreams and visions to carry significant weight. The context of that reflection on dreams and visions is noted, for example, in his work *Summa Theologica* where he interacts with a host of issues in conversation with Aristotle's philosophy. That is because the tide of interest in the works of Aristotle had risen by then and it required that the Church wrestle with how Aristotle's works were being used to critique long held Augustinian views.

Aristotle's influence was alarming to many in the Church, as historian Kenneth S. Latourette points out. Aristotle resisted the Platonic understanding of the "real" standing beyond the perceived. Yet, Plato's worldview had been adopted by Augustine, that is, to the degree that there was interface with biblical revelation. Latourette writes, "[i]t is quite understandable that the authorities of the Catholic Church took alarm at the popularity of Aristotle as interpreted by Averroes. Here was a heresy that might lure the intellectuals."[55]

Thomas Aquinas was able to navigate these precarious theological waters by formulating Christian theology using Aristotelian logic. A contextual aspect to note is that Aquinas was also reading Aristotelian philosophy as interpreted by the Islamic philosopher Averroes. According to Rena D. Dossett, Western accounts do not register just how impactful Averroes himself was to the development of Western humanism in European scholasticism. Dossett also comments on Averroes' influence on Thomas Aquinas. "His influences can be strongly felt in writings of St. Thomas Aquinas and the scholastic movement as a whole."[56] Reflecting on the logic guiding Aquinas' approach, according to Morton Kelsey, "[t]he Islamic medicine and astronomy and philosophy in that era was beginning to flood Europe ... There seemed to be no choice but to translate Christianity and the Bible point by point into the language of Aristotle."[57]

---

54   Lamoreaux, *The Early Muslim Tradition of Dream Interpretation*, 136–137.
55   Kenneth Scott Latourette, *A History of Christianity: Beginnings to 1500*, vol. 1 (San Francisco, CA: HarperSanFrancisco, 1975) 508.
56   Rena Dosset, "The Historical Influence of Classical Islam on Western Humanistic Education," *International Journal of Social Science and Humanity* 4:2 (2014) 88.
57   Kelsey, *God, Dreams, and Revelation*, 154.

Before examining Aquinas' views on D/Vs, it is necessary to share more about Aristotle's influence and how it challenged the epistemology embedded in the neo-Platonic views of the Church. Plato had certain ideas that Augustine felt could be viewed as intuitions of the fuller revelation of Christ and a biblical worldview. One important aspect of Plato's philosophy was the existence of the world of Forms crafted by a nondescript intelligent agency. In regard to how Plato saw the relationship between that world and what can be perceived in this realm, Diogenes Allen and Eric Springsted explain, "[t]he gap between the world of Forms and sensible reality is bridged."[58] Aristotle, on the other hand, "emphasized a study of the sensible world."[59] Aristotle did not hold to the concept of Forms, at least not in the sense of existence outside the cosmos, but rather "Aristotle found the permanent and the sources of order *within* the cosmos."[60] Therefore, for Aristotle the principles to be concerned with do not belong to Forms of another realm but are rather principles inherent to the things themselves. Also, the assumption that God can be known through biblical revelation was challenged. Consequently, Thomas Aquinas' epistemology included the belief that knowledge of the "nature of the divine being" was not possible, but only inferences regarding his attributes as could be deduced by reason.[61] The concepts seem to challenge the other-worldly aspects of Christian tradition, along with revelation through dreams and visions, yet Aquinas maintained the possibility of divine influence upon D/Vs. While Kelsey argues that Aquinas was ambiguous about dreams and visions for Christian spirituality, it is suggested here that, to the contrary, Aquinas' comments address the phenomena adequately and not unfavorably.

Aquinas' writings on the subject are found in *Summa Theologica* in which he reasons with careful adherence to Aristotelian emphasis on the senses and causality. Aquinas discusses dreams according to biblical references, in particular from the book of Numbers, and admits that dreams may have a divine source. It is clear that Aquinas considers the visions of dreams as arenas for the activity of various spirits, as he writes, "[b]oth a good and a bad angel by their own natural power can move the human imagination ... sometimes with alienation from the bodily senses, sometimes without such alienation."[62] He

---

58   Diogenes Allen and Eric O. Springsted, *Philosophy for Understanding Theology*, second edition (Louisville, KY: Westminster John Knox Press, 2007), 10.
59   Ibid., 80.
60   Ibid., 88.
61   Allen and Springsted, *Philosophy for Understanding Theology*, 108.
62   Thomas Aquinas, *Summa Theologica*, Aquinas interacts with Aristotle and Augustine in this passage under the heading "Whether an angel can change man's imagination." 1.111.3.

repeats his concern about the activity of other spirits when he writes that spirits of divination "make use of dreams."[63] Yet, Aquinas also wrote, "[t]here is no unlawful divination in making use of dreams for the foreknowledge of the future, so long as those dreams are due to divine revelations or to some natural cause inward or outward, and so far as the efficacy of that cause extends."[64]

Kelsey suggests that Aquinas "gave no directions on how we can be sure that they are from God ... The general attitude is that dreams are dangerous and rarely give us an experience of the Divine."[65] In Kelsey's estimation, Aquinas offered no clear instruction and had little to no enthusiasm for dreams and visions. This author questions the reasonableness of that pessimism, though, since Kelsey does mention that there have been some who refer to visions that Aquinas had during his life, even mentioning one vision which impacted Aquinas significantly at the end of his life. Kelsey shares that before his death Aquinas referred to experiencing revelations and that he "did come into direct relationship with God and ceased to write and dictate."[66] This seems to be corroborated by an episode reported by Aquinas' hagiographer, Bernard Gui. He relayed that Aquinas had experienced a vision of a deceased man, someone named Romanus, while in prayer. As Alan P. Darley reports it, in the vision, Aquinas probed Romanus regarding his experience of God, asking, "[h]ave you any immediate sight of God, or only by means of some image?" But to his dismay Romanus vanished.[67]

In this part of the discussion, the idea that the 18th century German philosopher Immanuel Kant fostered the eclipse of dreams and visions in Christian thought is considered. Kant was one of the major contributors to developing Enlightenment thinking in his day. A product of the rationalist tradition, he was schooled in the theories of Christian Wolff and the understanding of the importance of sense experience to epistemology. He explored how perception and experience were linked to distinguishing knowledge as "a priori" or "a posteriori."[68] Along with many other deep thinkers, he had felt the impact of Sir Isaac Newton's *Principia* (1687), a volume which brought to light a universe operating by rational, mechanical principles. The influence of the "new

---

63   Aquinas, *Summa Theologica*, 2–2.95.3.
64   Ibid., 2–2.96.6.
65   Kelsey, *God, Dreams, and Revelation*, 153.
66   Ibid., 156.
67   Alan P. Darley, "The Epistemological Hope: Aquinas versus Other Receptions of Pseudo-Dionysius on the Beatific Vision." *HeyJ* LIX (2018) 663–688. It is significant that Aquinas' vision came through prayer. In Chapter 6, the data of this project demonstrate significant association between visions and prayer.
68   Allen and Springsted, *Philosophy for Understanding Theology*, 155–157.

science of nature" brought optimism about a new age of intellectual development, while at the same time severe critiques of Christian ideology were being voiced.[69]

Kant was the contemporary of those bringing allegations against the Church. Pierre Bayle, Voltaire, and Edward Gibbons reported that Christianity stifles true rational understanding. Allen and Springsted write, "Bayle, although he claimed to be a believing Christian, never tired of claiming that the contents of Christian revelation were irrational."[70] Kant, on the other hand, sought to salvage Christian thought by means of incorporating new understanding and fresh articulation drawn from rationalist arguments. It can be argued that he did more harm than good in terms of imposing limits on Christian knowledge.

Kant's pursuit of a rational metaphysics led him to make conclusions about human perception, its limits, and how the human soul finds itself situated in the universe and in relation to God. David Hume of Scotland had made the assertion that there was a distinction between viewing events as "according to history" and viewing them "in the eyes of faith," placing biblical scholarship in its own category, presumably over against "scientific history."[71] Kant read this and other ideas of Hume and is credited with bringing Hume's thinking—for the sake of wrestling with its philosophical gaps—to the forefront. He pursued filling those gaps by articulating a metaphysics by which the processes of reason interacting with phenomena (appearances) could be rationally explained. Kant's reasoning led him to the conclusion that *noumenal* reality (the unseen aspect of reality) could not be verified since knowledge was limited to what could be perceived by the senses in contact with the material world. By the same token, the existence of God could not be deduced through pure reason nor through experience. For Kant, these were assumptions that necessarily showcased the distinction of faith.[72]

It was Kant's interaction with visionary Swedish Emanuel Swedenborg that some commentators register as the turning toward the devaluation of D/VS in Western Christianity. The exchange put the question of D/VS and Christian spirituality under theological scrutiny. It is true that Swedenborg's assertions of dreams and visions and contacts with spirits and otherworldly knowledge annoyed Kant. Geoff Nelson writes, "Kant's ridiculing of Swedenborg, particularly as it focused upon Swedenborg's use of his dreams as the motivation for this change, seemed to lead the way for Western culture in general to devalue

---

69   Allen and Springsted, *Philosophy for Understanding Theology*, 141.
70   Ibid., 141.
71   Ibid., 148.
72   Ibid., 161–167.

dreams."[73] To help examine Kant's critique of Swedenborg, the discussion here will engage Gottlieb Florschütz as an interlocutor. His commentary on the matter offers a closer look at Kant's objections to Swedenborg and Kant's own understanding of the limits of spiritual knowledge.

Florschütz engages with Kant's polemic titled, *Traüme eines Geistersehers— erläutert durch Träume der Metaphysik* (1766). In it, Kant describes Swedenborg's assumptions as "hopelessly ill-conceived and absurd testimony."[74] It should be noted, though, as Florschütz asserts, that Kant does not argue against the position of the human soul as a member of two spiritual worlds. Kant's strong stance on the immortality of the soul does not allow for truncating human existence from the other-worldly. Absent from the body after death, the soul returns to the "community it has always enjoyed with spiritual beings."[75]

In regard to the position of the human soul within two realms, the two theologians concur. It is the question of being able to perceive and interact with the other world while still resident in the body that Kant is concerned about. While Kant asserts that the human only experiences the present world, he does go as far as to articulate some experiential/ontological quality of this duality: "However, as a member of the spiritual world, it experiences and imparts the pure influx of non-material nature."[76] That influx marks the human soul as resident of the unseen world, and therefore Kant believes that death reopens "consciousness to clear perception."[77] So, matters of perception are the key to Kant's tension with Swedenborg. It therefore piqued him that Swedenborg admitted that humans live "in the company of spirits ... although ... quite unaware of it" and claimed that, in his own experience, God had opened his inner "reach" so that he could communicate with spirits.[78]

According to Florschütz, it was not that Kant had not considered the possibility of the experience of insights regarding, or sensations of, the "simultaneous spiritual and physical being."[79] He had been musing over the possibility within

---

73   Geoff Nelson, "Dreaming Through the Bible with Luther and Calvin" in Bulkeley, et. al., *Dreaming in Christianity and Islam,* 67. Nelson derives this stance from a conversation with Bart Koet of the Catholic Theological University of Utrecht, the Netherlands, see 70, n.13.
74   Immanuel Kant, *Traüme eines Geistersehers —erläutert durch Träume der Metaphysik* (1766) 96 in Gottlieb Florschütz, *Swedenborg and Kant: Emanuel Swedenborg's Mystical View of Humankind, and the Dual Nature of Humankind in Immanuel Kant* (West Chester, PA: Monographs of the Swedenborg Foundation, 1993), 158.
75   Florshütz, *Swedenborg and Kant,* 76.
76   Ibid., 36.
77   Ibid., 36.
78   Ibid., 76 and 95.
79   Ibid., 200.

his metaphysical framework prior to serious engagement with Swedenborg. But, as Florschütz points out, it is Kant's "critical theory of cognition" that weighed in heavily to temper his theology of the dual nature of humankind.[80] Kant could not agree on Swedenborg's terms with his "empirical dreams" and concluded that Swedenborg's claim that he was locating the thoughts of other beings in his spiritual interactions was in error. Kant was more comfortable with the "dreams of metaphysics" and the assumption that Swedenborg was being influenced by his own mind and intellect during his mystical episodes.[81] As an interesting twist, Kant made an unusual return to the topics after the publication of his polemic. Florschütz comments, "[t]he elderly Kant returned in a startling, radical way to Swedenborg as an individual and to his basic conviction that the sensible world was permeated by the other, spiritual world and affirmed this esoteric doctrine."[82]

What can be concluded about Immanuel Kant's influence on the eclipse of dreams and visions in Christian thought? It seems clear that Kant's theology did promote the eclipse. Perhaps, though, he did not see it as an entirely closed subject, since he returned to engage with Swedenborg's epistemologically permeable metaphysics. It can be concluded, though, that Kant's (at least, initial) understanding of the believer's cognitive limits does not allow for contact with the Holy Spirit, angels, or other spiritual entities through D/Vs. In light of his willingness to acknowledge the other-worldly realm as the home of spirits and the realm to which humankind returns after death, Kantian epistemology affirms the *noumenal* while keeping it classified as unverifiable. In other words, there *is* a veil and there *is* something behind it, but penetrating it is another matter. For Immanuel Kant (at least the younger Kant), Christians, or anyone else for that matter, cannot "go there" because all knowledge is subject to the constructs of Enlightenment rationalism.

In Chapter 4, the discussion will turn to Nigerian Nimi Wariboko's theology which articulates an epistemological elasticity for Pentecostalism similar to what Emanuel Swedenborg claimed. Wariboko asserts that Nigerian Pentecostals do, indeed, "go there" as they penetrate the veil of phenomenality by means of spiritual enabling through the Spirit. Experiencing the grace of "seeing eyes" and "hearing ears," and spiritual dreams and visions, the true state of things can be revealed and the noumenal laid bare. In a sense, Swedenborg's claims reflect a type of "last gasp" before charismatic rhetoric

---

80 Florshütz, *Swedenborg and Kant*, 297.
81 Ibid., 63.
82 Ibid., 63.

in that part of Europe retreated, at least from the theological table, for a long winter of Enlightenment.

3   Dreams and Visions in Islam

The turn away from the traditional, biblical appraisals of D/V experiences is even more obvious when a study of D/Vs in Islam is laid alongside Christian reception history. Kelsey notes, "[s]hortly after the death of [Pope] Gregory, the dream as a medium of revelation was given great emphasis in the new religion of Islam."[83] Consequently, despite sharing the same sacred writings which feature Abraham and his visionary descendants, especially Joseph, Christianity and Islam have produced contrasting trajectories in regard to D/Vs and spirituality. The volumes of dream manuals produced by Islam's scribes and theologians over the centuries attest to the fact that Islam's interaction with D/Vs was, and perhaps remains, a prominent feature of Islamic spirituality. In contrast to the course of events in Christianity, the genuine engagement with D/Vs among the religious elite clearly fostered the development of philosophical thought about the experiences.

Besides sharing the same cultural influences, the Near East religions of Judaism, Christianity, and Islam are mutually linked through the historical figures of the Bible. The characters that most impact the valuation of dreams in all three faiths are Abraham, Joseph, and Daniel. Beyond that mutuality, though, there are marked distinctions that characterize the reception of D/Vs in Islam that will be noted in these closing sections of the chapter. The work of John C. Lamoreaux, American scholar of Islamic studies, will serve to guide the discussion, especially due to his understanding of the nature of oneiric tradition in Islam.

References to D/Vs in the Qurʾān and in the commentaries of the scribes known as the *hadith* will be discussed, along with the phenomenon of dream manual transmission which is a prominent feature of Islamic tradition. The last topic to be explored is an aspect of the socio-political impact of D/Vs, that is, the legitimization of historical figures in Islam through D/V reports.[84]

---

83   Kelsey, *God, Dreams, and Revelation*, 143.
84   I want to appreciate John J. Travis here for his supervision of my tutorial on the topic of dreams and visions in Islam.

3.1 Dreams and Visions in the Qurʾān and Hadith

Since the death of the prophet Muhammad, his affirmation that "glad tidings" in the form of a dream can come to the righteous has sounded forth to devotees. As Lamoreaux records, "[o]n the day before his death ... the prophet Muḥammad announced ... 'when I am gone there shall remain naught of the glad tidings of prophecy, except true dreams.'"[85] Therefore, there is much in early Islamic writings about the value of a "true dream" and the verification of having had such a dream plays a major part of oneiric tradition. A reference to dreams as prophecy is also attributed to Muhammad: "A true dream represents one of forty-six branches of prophecy."[86] Those who recorded dream experiences also refer to another statement attributed to Muhammad, "There are three types of dreams: the good dream that is "a glad tiding from God" (Q 10:64), the dream in which our own souls speak, and the dream that Satan sends to make us sad."[87]

There is also the belief that the mediation of an angel named Sidīqūn, who is understood as one having access to the "Preserved Tablet," a reference to a "type of knowledge conveyed through the revelation of the Koran," is key to dream experiences.[88] There was, therefore, substantial validation of the D/V experience and theological support for an expectancy for revelation that can come through dreams and visions.

Islamic clerics appeal to biblical sources, but also to extra-biblical Islamic traditions about the biblical figures associated with dreaming, in their theological discourse supporting D/V experiences. For example, the prophet Daniel is noted as having delineated the four reasons that one forgets a dream.[89] Protocol for interpreting D/V experiences is found in the Qurʾān in portions discussing Jacob's warning to Joseph regarding divulging dreams to his brothers (Qurʾān 12:5).[90] More validation is found in the tradition about Abraham which reports that he received the command to sacrifice his son in a dream.[91] It is clear that attention to dreams is substantiated by these appeals to prophetic antecedence, but there is also reference to the experiences of the Prophet Muhammad.

---

[85] Lamoreaux, *The Early Muslim Tradition of Dream Interpretation*, 4.
[86] Muhammad M. al-Akili, *Ibn Seerin's Dictionary of Dreams According to Islamic Inner Traditions* (Philadelphia, PA: Pearl Publishing House, 1992), xv.
[87] Lamoreaux, *The Early Muslim Tradition of Dream Interpretation*, 20, 81.
[88] Ibid., 82.
[89] al-Akili, *Ibn Seerin's Dictionary of Dreams According to Islamic Inner Traditions*, xxii.
[90] Ibid., xxv.
[91] Ibid., xvi.

DREAMS, VISIONS, AND NEAR EAST RELIGIONS 49

The early revelations of the Prophet himself, as reported by his wife 'Aisha, were relayed through the experience of "true dreams."[92]

The *hadiths*—the writings which carry historical and religious authority for Muslims—contain a substantial amount of dream narratives, related anecdotes, and references pertaining to the Prophet's attitude toward dreams. Therefore, the Qur'ān and *hadith* both lay a foundational understanding of the value of dreams and their interpretations for Islamic spirituality.

The Sahih Bukhari is considered one of the authoritative *hadiths* available today. Its author, Abu Abdullah Muhammad bin Ismail bin Ibrahim bin Mughira al-Ja'fai, also known as al-Bukhari (194–256 AH), spent 16 years verifying the authenticity of the *hadith*, which totals 2,602 sayings. The collection contains nine volumes hosting books devoted to various themes. Among the myriad of religious topics considered of doctrinal and practical importance, material on dreams is included. For our purposes, the portion titled "Interpretation of Dreams" (vol. 9, book 87) is most relevant. It records the sayings having to do with Muhammad's personal dreams and their interpretations, and the dreams of others closest to him. These passages are significant for how they give support for Islamic attention to D/V experiences and their interpretations.

In the "Interpretation of Dreams," al-Bukhari's *hadith* reinforces the distinction between the good and bad dream. It reads, "[i]f anyone of you sees a bad dream, he should seek refuge with Allah from Satan and should spit on the left, for the bad dream will not harm him."[93] Another saying narrated by Abu Huraira and attributed to Muhammad is the instruction stating that whoever sees Muhammad in a dream will also see him in "wakefulness" and "Satan cannot imitate me in shape."[94]

It is clear, therefore, how dreams of Muhammad would be legitimizing social elements. In another saying, Muhammad reports that, while sleeping, "the keys of the treasures of the earth were brought to me til they were put in my hand."[95] Another dream with a militaristic connotation is mentioned, as well. Muhammad is believed to have said, "[s]ome of my followers were presented before me in my dream as fighters in Allah's Cause, sailing in the middle of the seas like kings on the thrones."[96] Also, a saying narrated by the prophet's wife 'Aisha records Muhammad's dream of betrothal, "Behold, a man

---

92   al-Akili, *Ibn Seerin's Dictionary of Dreams According to Islamic Inner Traditions*, xvi.
93   Muhammad b. Ismail al-Bukhari, *Sahih Al-Bukhari: In the English Language*, e-book, 9:87, 115.
94   Ibid., Number 122.
95   Ibid., Number 127.
96   Ibid., Number 130.

was carrying you in a silken piece of cloth and said to me, She is your wife, so uncover her, and behold, it was you."[97]

Al-Bukhari's material contains references to dreams scattered among other narratives, as well. In vol. 4, book 54, no. 490, a *hadith* narrated by the Prophet's wife 'Aisha records a dream in which the Prophet received insight after prayer to Allah. It came in the form of a dream that revealed that witchcraft had been used against him. Other excerpts in other volumes make references that show the value of dreams experienced by those close to Muhammad. For example, vol. 3, book 32, no. 232 describes how companions of the Prophet were shown in dreams that during the last week of Ramadan one can expect a special divine encounter on the night of *Qadr* (the night of power). Another example depicting dream lore is recorded in vol. 2, book 26, no. 638 in which is reported a dream experienced by Abu Jamra Nasr bin 'Imran Ad-Duba'i. The dream involves encouragement that he received to go on pilgrimage (*haj*). These excerpts provide religious validation for understanding dreams as a means by which special knowledge can be gained.

The *hadiths* of Islamic clerics also played a part in reiterating the value of dream incubation for Islamic societies. This is pointed out by Hidayet Aydar, Professor of Abrahamic Religions at Istanbul University. Aydar comments that though *Istikhara*, the practice of dream incubation, is not found in the Qurʾān, the prophets Abraham, Joseph, and Muhammad all received revelatory dreams, thereby sanctioning the seeking after divine knowledge. Also, many *hadiths* state that the prophet Muhammad taught forms of *Istikhara* to his followers.[98] Dream incubation has already been mentioned earlier in this chapter as a practice inherent to Near East cultures. The practice involves a posture of repentance and the prescription of certain actions done usually at night, such as the act of ablution (*ghusul*), certain prayers, repeatedly reciting the name "Allah," and laying on one's right side for sleep.[99] These actions are carried out by the devotee in order to bring on spiritual dreams for guidance.[100]

---

[97] al-Bukhari, *Sahih Al-Bukhari*, Number 139.
[98] Ibid., 126.
[99] Hidayet Aydar, "Istikhara and Dreams: Learning about the Future through Dreaming" in Kelly Bulkeley, et. al., *Dreaming in Christianity and Islam*, 128.
[100] See also Iain R. Edgar, *The Dream in Islam: From Qurʾanic Tradition to Jihadist Inspiration* (NY: Berghahn, 2011), e-book. In particular see Chapter 3: "Istikhara: Islamic Dream Incubation," loc. 1533–1782.

3.2 Dream Manuals and Their Transmission in Islam

Lamoreaux explains that dream lore was "transmitted in much the same fashion as other types of knowledge, whether Koranic commentary, traditions on the spiritual life, or information concerning the life of Muhammad and the formative period of Islamic history."[101] Dream manual transmissions developed from the original documentation of Muhammad's dream anecdotes to a formalized cultural form. *Muhaddiths* (early scribes who transmitted literature gathered from the *ahadith*) were the first to compile dreams, and then the *ulema* (the enlightened clerics) carried on the stewardship of the written tradition. Islamic tradition recognized dream interpretation within spirituality to the degree that many formalized manuals were written, unlike what we find to be present among Christian sources.

Lamoreaux asserts that the story of transmission of dream materials is part of "Islamicate discourse," that is, discourse that necessarily incorporates the voices of those who are not of Islamic faith.[102] The fact that Pst Achmet and Bahlūl, two Christians who both wrote at about the 4th century AH (10th century AD), most likely incorporated Muslim works into *their* dream manuals speaks to the blending of influences. The translation of the historically prized book of dream interpretation by Artemidorus from Greek to Arabic that same century was not insignificant. It proved highly impactful. As Lamoreaux points out, what actually got into the hands of Islamic clerics and scholars was the Nestorian Christian Ḥunayn b. Isḥāq's version of Artemidorus, which has its own coloring. For example, Lamoreaux notes that sometimes Ḥunayn changes "many gods" to "God" or to "angels," and in another passage the phrase "eating with Chronos" was changed to the innocuous "eating with a man."[103]

Therefore, Lamoreaux prefers to see Ḥunayn's version as an adaptation, since, "[o]n leaving Ḥunayn's hands, Artemidorus had not only been Arabicized. He had also been baptized, if not into the Christian faith, at least into the community of monotheists."[104] The translation came intact, though, with its Hellenistic rationalism exemplified by the calculated approach to dream interpretation. This is evident, for example, in the following approach to interpreting having seen a hernia in a dream: "A hernia is a symbol of injuries partly because the two words have the same numerical value and partly because everything that grows on the body without adding to its beauty or

---

101 Lamoreaux, *The Early Muslim Tradition of Dream Interpretation*, 40.
102 Ibid., 170.
103 Ibid., 48–49.
104 Ibid., 51.

strength ... symbolizes injuries and anxiety."[105] Therefore, for Islamic clerics to have absorbed Artemidorus' material signifies at least a tussle with its rationalism.

The intersection of Christian and Muslim influences is also seen in the fact that in the 11th century there was growing interest among the Byzantines in the advancements of Muslims in the Hellenic sciences. The medieval archbishop of Toledo, Spain (12th century) so esteemed Islamic scholarship that he authorized the translation of Arabic works into Latin. It was an era of authentic appreciation of Islamic learning, especially in Muslim engagement with the Hellenic sciences such as astronomy, astrology, medicine, and divination.[106] Literature on dreams and dream interpretation were part of the philosophic corpus of the works gaining attention and being circulated. Referencing especially the translated work of Artemidorus, Lamoreaux argues that in order to really understand dreams in Islamic tradition, one needs to "understand how non-Muslims were contributory participants to this discourse: how they mediated pre-Islamic philosophic traditions."[107]

It has already been noted that Muhammad's references to dreams carried much weight. Islamic oneirics also relies on figures of historical importance. One of these is Ibn Sīrīn who himself left no extant works but who is the subject of much content, for example, in the works of notable transmitters of tradition, Ibn Qutaybah and Abd Allāh al-Kirmānī.[108] Logs accompanying transmissions known as *riwāyahs* listed the history of dream manuals from generation to generation, not unlike the library cards used in the US to log readers of library texts. These recorded readers and authoritative transmitters of dream manuals which are used to authenticate the writings.[109] Researchers have gleaned from these documents to gain a better picture of Islamic dream traditions since they reveal the milieu of that day. For example, al-Husayn al-Khallāl's documentation of 7,500 persons known to be dream interpreters paints the picture of a society with profound receptivity to D/vs.[110] Additionally, the fact that the receptivity had saturated so as to become a prominent aspect of elite religious spirituality is evidenced in the works found in Andalusia, Spain. Lamoreaux

---

105 Robert White, *The Interpretation of Dreams: The Oneirocritica of Artemidorus*, translated by Robert White (Park Ridge, NJ: Noyes Press, 1975), 169.
106 Lamoreaux, *The Early Muslim Tradition of Dream Interpretation*, 153.
107 Ibid., 170.
108 Ibid., 42.
109 Ibid., 123.
110 Ibid., 17.

comments, "[i]n Andalusia, at least, dream interpretation was a shar'ī discipline, one avidly pursued by the ulema."[111]

As well as locating the prevalence and durability of dream lore in Islam, Lamoreaux points out that the indications of homogeneity of its content could possibly indicate a measure of censorship by clerics. That is because literature pulled from the broad spectrum of geographic and generational sources, and authors of "diverse cultural orientations within the early Muslim community," would be expected to be anything but uniform.[112] For example, Lamoreaux notes that symbols and their meanings did not change in the course of time but rather "Sufis, philosophers, and religious scholars all interpreted dreams in the same ways."[113]

That penchant for retaining traditional interpretations as passed down from previous transmitters characterizes the works as first and foremost the products of "conservators of an inherited tradition."[114] It is in the utilization of traditional works that creativity is seen, especially in the reliance on D/Vs for attaining social or political status. Examples of legitimizing techniques used in the Middle Ages as reported by scholars of Islam, Shahzad Bashir and Nozhat Ahmadi, and by Jörg Haustein, scholar of religions in Africa, are the substance of the next section.

3.3 Dreams and Visions as Legitimizing Elements in Islam

Lamoreaux serves again as a helpful interlocutor for a discussion on how D/Vs can serve to legitimize visioners. He explains that during the formative era of Islam, and on through development of Islamic dream lore, there were two avenues for legitimizing dreams and visions: through association with the dreamers of Hebraic history, and through association with Muhammad himself.[115] Lamoreaux writes, "[a]uthority in the formative period of the tradition was solely prophetic—whether that prophecy be pre-Islamic or Islamic."[116] Association with Muhammad is in actuality a broader concept than just a dream of the Prophet himself. It also included dreams in which his son-in-law 'Ali appeared, or others closely associated to the Prophet.

The legitimizing role of a religious person as an important aspect of dream theology is also evident throughout the development of Islamic history. These

---

111   Lamoreaux, *The Early Muslim Tradition of Dream Interpretation*, 129.
112   Ibid., 103.
113   Ibid., 80.
114   Ibid., 104.
115   Ibid., 42.
116   Ibid., 43.

dreams are not only verified among the "true dreams," but the visioners themselves are legitimized. Therefore, the endorsement of status through a whole array of elite figureheads associated with dream traditions in Islam has rendered D/Vs powerful elements of socio-religious politics in Islam.

Shahzad Bashir is Lysbeth Warren Anderson Professor of Islamic Studies at Stanford University. His scholarship is devoted to examining the Islamic sect initiated by Muhammad Nūrbakhsh in 15th century Iran. It offers a wealth of history on the transmission of Islamic beliefs regarding a returning messiah (*mahdī* or savior), an ideology that even included, for certain Sunnīs, the expectation of the return of Jesus.

In Bashir's volume *Messianic Hopes and Mystical Visions* (2003), he is especially concerned with explaining the socio-religious conditions under which Nūrbakhsh's messianic claims found success. Though Nūrbakhsh was definitely tagged as unorthodox to the majority, strains of the sect have survived until today in areas of Baltistan and Ladakh (located in Pakistan and Northern India). While the text is not featured as a treatise on dreams and visions in Islam, chapters 3 and 4, "Articulating the Messianic Message" and "Nūrbakhsh's Sufi Worldview," present an eruption of anecdotes on dreams and visions. These are described as key factors in the legitimizing campaign Nūrbakhsh generated.

Bashir makes frequent reference to a document written by Nūrbakhsh titled *Risālat al-hudā* which contains arguments for his status as *mahdī*. Bashir describes the writing as a rare self-portrait of a messianic personality and writes, "[i]n reading Nūrbakhsh's works, it is impossible not to notice the self-aggrandizement that permeates his whole discourse."[117] It is here that the dream and vision experiences of Nūrbakhsh and his contemporaries, along with appeals to numerology, genealogy, and even predictions of physical appearance in a *hadith*, are laid out for the reader. Regarding his own experiences, Nūrbakhsh reports a vision in which the prophet Muhammad's son-in-law 'Ali appeared to him to prophesy his ascendancy to leadership. Also in a dream, he saw himself revealed as the person who embodied mystical words "written in silver" which marked him as a blessed descendant of Muhammad.[118]

What is striking about the D/Vs reported in Nūrbakhsh's treatise is how many visions purported to have been experienced by those associated to him are used to ratify his own claims of being one deserving of the trust of the populace. The visions reported by others in the autobiography were crucial

---

117   Shahzad Bashir, *Messianic Hopes and Mystical Visions: The Nurbakhshiya Between Medieval and Modern Islam* (Columbia, South Carolina: University of South Carolina, 2003) 90.
118   Ibid., 97–98.

to his campaign. The list that promotes Nūrbakhsh as the *mahdī* includes reference to Shihāb ad-Dīn Jūrānī, who claimed seeing the angel Gabriel's sanction of Nūrbakhsh in a vision, and Khwāja Ishāq Khuttalāni, who saw the man illuminated with light. The power of these D/Vs that were carried into the public sphere where they supported Nūrbakhsh's claim to be the messianic figure depict an impact that is also noted by the UCLA scholar of Islamic Studies Nile Green.

Green mentions the significance of a dream that moves out of the private to the public sector in Islamic society, thereby demonstrating the special role played by public dreams over against the private dream. Green notes how such public dreams have had far reaching effects in societies politically and religiously. An example is in regard to the establishment of sacred spaces. The revelation through a dream pointing to the whereabouts of a shrine once dedicated to 'Ali the son-in-law of Muhammad, but which had been destroyed by Mongols, is one instance.[119] Dreams that publically elevated Sufi theologians through dream endorsements are another example.

Scholar of Iranian Studies Nozhat Ahmadi argues that dream interpretation rhetoric should be analyzed for its effects as a socio-political element in the Safavid Dynasty of Iran. That dynasty spanned from 1501–1722 AD. According to Ahmadi, dream interpretations were significant sources of knowledge in the society of that time, and especially the dreams of persons of power or status. Ahmadi shows that in the instance of the beginning of the Safavid reign in Iran, these weighed in heavily to effect or sway the attitudes of the populace. As he explains, the Safavids were Sunni (orthodox Muslims) assuming control among a people of the Shi'a sect. They were therefore motivated by a need to present themselves as God's appointed and to establish links with Shi'a beliefs.[120]

An example is found in the campaign of one Shaikh al Din. The hagiography of al-Din, who was an early leader of the sect of the Safavids, and which was written by Ibn Hazzas in 1391 AD, makes reference to several dreams. These were used to portray al-Din as one with prophetic gifts such as the ability to foretell the future. The dreams were also used to legitimize him as a religious and political leader by showing him as having been appointed for the calling of leadership since a child. Dreams also described al-Din as a man with a special

---

119   Nile Green, "A Brief World History of Muslim Dreams," *Islamic Studies* 54:3–4 (2015) 164.
120   Ahmadi notes that Safavid successors over the years did adopt Shi'ism. See Nozhat Ahmadi, "The Role of Dreams in the Political Affairs of the Safavid Dynasty," *Journal of Shi'a Islamic Studies* 6:2 (Spring 2013) 180.

connection to the prophet Muhammad and with links to Shi'ism.[121] One example of such a link to Shi'ism is manifested in a dream account in which "Imam 'Ali taught him to tie a special hat made of a red cloth (*parchih*) with twelve folds."[122]

This dream was experienced earlier by Shaikh Haydar in 1488 at a time when the Safavids' were in a clash with rulers and needed a reminder of their legitimacy to bolster morale. As Safavid rule extended and spread in Iran, other dreams of similar nature circulated on behalf of Safavid rulers. Ahmadi offers another example of legitimization with the dream in which Imam Muhammad Naqi (the ninth Shi'a imam) appeared to commission Khwajah 'Ali to lead the people of Dezful.[123] At this point, the discussion turns now to a relatively recent (early 1900s) incident of dream transmission in Islam that also reinforces the religious dream as a potent element of religious persuasion, this time in Africa.[124]

Scholar of religious studies in Africa, Jörg Haustein, presents fresh evidence to bear upon the events surrounding an Islamic dream account which circulated in East Africa in 1908. In that case, the motivation behind the "Mecca letter" (as it was referred to by the Germans) was feared by German colonial administrators of the day to be a political ruse. Perpetrators of its spread were even arrested. But Haustein argues for steering away from positing a political motivation targeting Tanzanian communities to understanding it as part of a "global chain letter" which had versions circulating in Cairo as early as 1877.[125]

---

121   The Shi'a is a sect that believes that the rightful succession of Islamic faith should have been passed to 'Ali, the cousin and son-in-law of Muhammad. They comprise about 10–13% of the Islamic population and reside mostly in Iran, Iraq, and Bahrain today. See Amber Pariona, "Differences Between Sunni and Shia Muslims" in *World Atlas*, 2018, accessed Oct. 17, 2018; https://www.worldatlas.com/articles/differences-between-sunni-and-shia-muslims.html.
122   Ahmadi, "The Role of Dreams in the Political Affairs of the Safavid Dynasty," 182.
123   Ibid., 184.
124   I also write of the legitimizing Pentecostal D/Vs shared between myself and the national director of Kairos Global Missions in Ghana. I note that the experiences demonstrate a similar en-Spirited worldview which also fosters trust in our working relationship. The D/V experiences override the customary "epistemological impasses" usually present in relations between people of the West and Africa. Found in Anna Droll "Pneumatological Epistemology and Missional Collaboration in Ghana," presented at the conference "Between Cosmology and Community: Religion and Sustainable Development" hosted by Humboldt University, Berlin, Germany, July 6, 2019.
125   Jörg Haustein, "Religion, politics and an apocryphal admonition: the German East African 'Mecca Letter' of 1908 in historical-critical analysis," *Bulletin of the School of Oriental and African Studies* 83:1 (2020) 99, 118.

Haustein brings several previously unexamined sources, copies of the letter in Arabic which had been relegated to a certain file kept by the Tanzanian National Archives, and offers them in a comparative study. The results offer exegetical indications regarding the actual breadth of the letter's transmission. Comparisons with versions outside of East Africa also add to the evidence that, rather than a device of political underpinnings, the letter reflected clerical concern for stirring up faithfulness to Islamic faith.

What is pertinent for application to this study is the way that the dream was legitimized, or made potent, by the claim to contain a message from the prophet Muḥammad. Šayḫ Aḥmad, the purported source of the letter, reported that Muḥammad had appeared to him in the dream in order to warn him that the people had lapsed into neglecting prayer, drinking alcohol, and gossiping. The letter admonished Muslims to repent before the impending final judgment. Haustein writes, "[t]he missive claimed to originate from the guardian of the Prophet's tomb in Medina and urged its recipients to a more faithful adherence to the tenets and practices of Islam."[126] Similar to the other examples cited of how the Prophet or others of his family figure as legitimizing elements in the religious dream, this dream carries with it the authoritative stamp of the "true dream."

4   Conclusion

This chapter has explained that while receptivity to dreams and visions in the Near East religions has been pervasive, it has not gone unchallenged by proponents of Enlightenment thinking. Additionally, the problems with D/Vs are not illegitimate concerns. Proponents of Judaism, Christianity, and Islam have voiced these explicitly, while most often retaining the value of the experiences for spirituality.

This book aims to show that the enduring viability of D/Vs as valid Christian and Muslim knowledge has been retained in the case of contemporary Pentecostal spirituality in African contexts. As in the Near East, visioners in African cultures have also contemplated their D/V experiences and sustained traditional attitudes regarding their usefulness or potential dangers. Pentecostals in this study also utilize a biblical lens, one they claim is oriented by the Spirit, with which they make their D/V assessments. Before an

---

[126]   Haustein, "Religion, politics and an apocryphal admonition", 95.

examination of the pneumatological imagination of those who participated in the Dreams and Visions Project, an overview of D/Vs in African traditional religions and in African Christianity is necessary. Therefore, it is to the topic of D/Vs in African contexts that the conversation turns in Chapter 3.

CHAPTER 3

Dreams and Visions in African Contexts

> Emitai was said to have revealed this to the woman in a dream.
> ROBERT M. BAUM[1]

∴

> When Lazarus was brought to the Zionist church, he at once recognized the white garments and the song from the dream he had had.
> BENGT G.M. SUNDKLER[2]

∴

> It was more than a dream.
> Michael Chisanga, Zambia[3]

∴

Ghanaian philosopher Kwame Anthony Appiah borrows the term "ethnophilosophy" from Father Placides Tempels, a Belgian missionary who reflected on the philosophical characteristics of Bantu thought.[4] While weighing the inherent shortfalls and naiveté accompanying Western anthropological assessments of philosophy in Africa, Appiah does register with the study of ethnophilosophy "as a useful beginning" for investigating African philosophy, if it is on African terms. For Appiah, it involves retrieving the concept of philosophy from the European colonial camp where intellectual reflection has somehow been

---

1 Robert M. Baum, *Shrines of the Slave Trade: Diola Religion and Society in Precolonial Senegambia* (Oxford: Oxford University Press, 1999), 101.
2 Bengt G.M Sundkler, *Bantu Prophets in South Africa*, 2nd ed. (Oxford: Oxford University Press, 1961), 269–270.
3 Nelson Osamu Hayashida, *Dreams in the African Church: The Significance of Dreams and Visons among Zambian Baptists* (Amsterdam: Rodopi, 1991), 221.
4 Kwame Anthony Appiah, *In My Father's House: Africa in the Philosophy of Culture* (Oxford: Oxford University Press, 1992), 94. Appiah refers to *La Philosophie Bantoue* published in 1945.

married to all things European or American. For example, Appiah challenges the dismissal of oral philosophies of African cultures, describing the assumption of irrelevance as being couched in typical Western bias. Appiah charges that Western bias regarding the criteria or nature of epistemology is something to be questioned, as he states quantum theory, itself, now points out.[5]

The discussion of African philosophy on African terms is relevant to an examination of how dream and vision experiences are situated as epistemological elements in the lives of the men and women who took part in the Dreams and Visions Project. The epistemic coordinates which have been normative for understanding D/V experiences help to inform regarding how the experiences are assessed today. The Dreams and Visions Project uncovered an epistemology rooted in philosophical approaches to dealing with personal forces (agencies) and existential concerns rather than a sequestered way of thinking fettered to the intellectual life of the abstract. Better put, the *intellectual life serves pragmatic purposes,* that of overcoming the factors working against human flourishing, and this can involve the assessment of D/V experiences for their use in everyday life. It is demonstrated in this chapter that the African experience of D/Vs offers an important contribution to authentic engagement with African epistemologies, and consequently, with African Pentecostalism.

This chapter is laid out in three sections. The first section explores the importance of D/Vs to the West African cultures of the Akan residing primarily in Ghana, the Diola of Senegambia, and the Tukolor of mainly Senegal and Mali. In the second section, the role of D/Vs in new Christian movements and among the Bantu prophets of South Africa will be examined. Included in this section is the research done by Nelson Hayashida on the dreams of Zambian Baptists. In the closing section of the chapter, Opoku Onyinah is consulted regarding Pentecostal dreams and prophecy in the experience of the Church of Pentecost. The chapter closes with Onyinah's experience with the agency of the angel Michael during sleep.

1   Dreams in Traditional African Religions

The embedded valuation of D/V experiences among people of African societies has not gone unnoticed by those within African contexts, nor by those without. For example, Kenyan theologian and philosopher John Mbiti argues that there was a strong awareness of the Supreme God as the giver of divine

---

5   Appiah, *In My Father's House*, 97.

dreams and visions among the religious of various African regions. He cites the value of D/Vs as experiences from God among the Gikuyu and Turkana of Kenya, the Nuba of Sudan, the Sonjo of Tanzania and the Lozi of Zambia.[6] In regard to the attitude toward the experiences among West Africans, anthropologists David Tait and Geoffrey Parrinder are among those who note the significance of dreams in West African cultures.[7] The section up ahead offers the observations of those who documented the value of D/Vs in West African societies in the past century. Mirroring the D/V appreciation reported by Mbiti in East Africa, the British anthropologist R. S. Rattray offers some of the first published work (1927) on the high value of dreams of the Ashanti people of the Akan situated in Kumasi of Ghana. Following a survey of Rattray's material, the contributions of Robert M. Baum in respect to the Diola people of Senegambia and those of Roy Dilley which shed light on dreaming among the Tukolor of Senegal and Mali will provide historical context for the more contemporary manifestations treated in this project.

1.1 *Dreaming and the Akan*

Captain Robert S. Rattray was appointed by the British authorities to explore the culture and beliefs of the Ashanti people of Ghana. He was head of the Anthropological Department set up by the colonial government and spent considerable time in the region most densely populated by the Ashanti, the city of Kumasi.[8] Rattray began to open a window into Ashanti epistemology as early as 1916 with a volume titled *Ashanti Proverbs*. He produced another volume titled *Ashanti* in 1923, and in his later work published in 1927, *Religion and Art in Ashanti*, Rattray engaged more extensively with Ashanti life. Rattray is considered a notable Africanist who offered the West firsthand exposure to Ashanti thought. He reports specifically regarding the dream lore of the people and wrote, "[a] survey of Ashanti religion would hardly be complete without some reference to dreams and dream interpretations."[9]

---

6 John S. Mbiti, *Concepts of God in Africa* (London: SPCK, 1970), 75, 151, 154, 200, 221, 224, and 245.
7 See David Tait, *The Konkomba of Northern Ghana*, 1961, Geoffrey Parrinder, *West African Religion: A Study of the Beliefs and Practices of Akan, Ewe, Yoruba, Ibo, and Kindred Peoples* (London: Epworth Press, 1949), and Robert Baum, *West African Women of God: Aliensitoué and the Diola Prophetic Tradition* (Bloomington: Indiana University Press, 2016).
8 The Anthropological Department was established in the Ashanti region (several hours north of the coast) and is not to be confused with the University of Ghana established some decades later in 1948.
9 R. S. Rattray, *Religion and Art in Ashanti* (Oxford: Clarendon Press, 1927), 192.

An observation Rattray makes that is pertinent to understanding dreams in Ashanti culture is the belief that the sleeping state is the condition by which the *sunsum* of a person may wonder about outside the body. The *sunsum* is one of the immaterial aspects of the human being, a topic to which the discussion will return. In fact, belief in soul or spirit travel is found across cultures, as anthropologists and dream researchers of dreaming in the Western Pacific have documented.[10] The sleeping state is therefore host to a broader range of experiences than the static dream containing metaphorical symbols. This is affirmed by the surveys and interviews that flowed from this project, warranting the use of "sleep experience" as, perhaps, the best term for referencing dreams and visions.

Rattray also notes the intimations of travel in the etymology of the term used to communicate "to dream" in the Ashanti dialect of Twi. He observes that the term *so dae* is closest to the phrase "to arrive at a place in sleep."[11] Also, the blurring of the delineations between dreams and visions that will be further discussed in Chapter 5 appear to be further nuanced with this introduction of the possibility of soul/spirit travel. Additionally, when the Apostle Paul explained to the Corinthians regarding his own "visions and revelations of the Lord," he was himself puzzled. "Whether in the body I do not know, or whether out of the body I do not know, God knows" (2 Cor. 12:2). It appears that it is left to the visioner to explain his or her own personal sense of the nature of the experience, and to the researcher to consider the fluidity of the metaphysical/ontological terrain.[12]

Rattray explains that the *sunsum* is not the only immaterial part of the human being, but that the *okra*, or *'kra* is sometimes used interchangeably with *sunsum*. Yet, the *'kra* is more often distinguished from the *sunsum*, and is rendered "soul" by Rattray, as he notes it is also rendered in the *Dictionary of the Asante and Fante Language*.[13] The work of Anthony Ephirim-Donkor (who

---

10   See Roger Ivar Lohmann, ed., *Dream Travelers: Sleep Experiences and Culture in the Western Pacific* (NY: Palgrave Macmillan, 2003) especially 2–3 where Lohmann writes, "[i]n Melanesia, Codrington (1891:208–209) reported shamans in what is now Vanuatu who used dreaming to travel in order to converse with the spirits in their own realms."
11   Rattray, *Religion and Art in Ashanti*, 193.
12   Lecturer Umar Danfulani of Jos, Nigeria affirmed the possibility of astral travel as a phenomenon during sleep in his interview on Aug. 22, 2017. Also, in a conversation with a young woman in Cameroon in Sept. of 2015, she divulged her travels during the sleeping state to the underwater world where she was engaged in the Mami Wata witchcraft cult. She was adamant that the place was real and that the experiences were not a dream.
13   Rattray, *Religion and Art in Ashanti*, 153–155.The dictionary Rattray referenced is one of the treasured legacies of philologist and German missionary Johann G. Christaller.

will be further consulted in Chapter 4) is important here for understanding the nature of *sunsum* as "spirit." Ephirim-Donkor explains *sunsum* as spirit by describing it as "a shadow, image, or double" as well as "anything intangible or unseen."[14] He adds, "[f]rom the realm of dreams, the Sunsum is thought to be an active agent capable of influencing objectivity having an independent existence."[15]

Therefore, Sunsum (*sunsum*), according to Ephirim-Donkor, is distinct from the physical. He continues, "[t]he Sunsum has an independent existence apart from its material object as Rattray has already noted ... [and] while it may appear that a Sunsum is an imprint of its host, the physical ... is instead an imprint of the Sunsum because the material is fleeting while the Sunsum is not."[16] This information helps to reinforce the broader possibilities of the dreaming state in Akan cultures. Also, if the *sunsum* is the part of the person that experiences outside the body, it is left ambiguous to what degree the *'kra* and *sunsum* might share the experience of the dream life together while stationary in the sleeping body.

One of the characteristics Rattray reports is the Ashanti tendency to dream of ancestors, with both pleasant and unpleasant effects. Taking into account Ephirim-Donkor's assertion that the self is literally an active agent in the dream, dreams of interactions with ancestors are not to be taken lightly.[17] Ephirim-Donkor writes, "[o]ne literally sees him/herself in dreams, and there is no reason to assume otherwise symbolically or figuratively."[18] He adds, "[t]he literal meanings of dreams are such that often relationships are strained because characters of relatives were villainously perceived in dreams."[19] Rattray gives an example of such a dream taken literally, "I have heard of a case of a sexual dream where the disclosure of the dream cost the owner his life."[20] Therefore, ancestors who appear as half animal and half human, or who try to lead you away (as to the spirit world) or who appear as cows to chase you must be dealt with through the proper prescriptions, either a sacrificial offering of food (for

---

14 Anthony Ephirim-Donkor, *African Personality and Spirituality: The Role of Abosom and Human Essence* (Lanham, MD: Lexington Books, 2016), 40.
15 Ibid., 40.
16 Ibid., 48.
17 Interviews in the Dreams and Visions Project showed how dreams of ancestors can cause distress for Pentecostal-Charismatics. Also, interpretations of those dreams can show ambivalence in the attitude toward having dream contact with one's ancestors.
18 Anthony Ephirim-Donkor, *African Spirituality: On Becoming Ancestors* (Trenton, NJ: Africa World Press, Inc., 1997), 57.
19 Ibid., 59.
20 Rattray, *Religion and Art in Ashanti,* 193.

those following traditional remedies), or as one Ghanaian Christian shared in an interview, through the power of consistent and effective prayers.[21]

1.2 Dreams and the Diola of Senegambia

Robert M. Baum is Associate Professor of Religion and African and African American Studies at Dartmouth University. He contributes significantly to West African studies through his research among the Diola communities of Senegambia. Baum was careful to narrow his analyses of religious change to specific instances within an area of five Esulalu townships, while providing a rich backdrop of cultural insights and historical events pertaining to the Diola people. His volume titled *Shrines of the Slave Trade: Diola Religion and Society in Precolonial Senegambia* (1999) is provocative for its combined use of written historical sources with first hand oral histories gathered over a period of almost four years of field study. His more recent publication, which reports on the tradition of prophetic female prophets among the Diola, is *West Africa's Women of God: Alinesitoué and the Diola Prophetic Tradition* (2016). It is drawn from twenty-five years of study on the phenomena of Diola encounters with Emitai, the supreme being. Both volumes are helpful for how they show the importance of D/Vs in Diola religious history, but also for how they describe an epistemology similar to that reflected in the Akan understanding of D/Vs and the sleeping state.

A major thematic thread in Baum's work is the validity of D/Vs as sources of knowledge and revelation for human flourishing, and as motivational for the establishing of new religious shrines. Baum reports that there are two ways in which Diola knowledge is acquired. It is transmitted from one generation to the next in the form of narrations, or it is revealed to the individual by means of dreams and visions, indicating "extraordinary mental powers" at work in the visioner.[22]

Spirit shrines were established to meet societal needs, as in the example of a shrine associated with powers for healing. In another instance: "Shrines of the forge had to be able to protect blacksmiths."[23] Individuals could be visited by the spirit shrine in dreams or visions, or "receive the spirit shrine" as Baum records, "[i]n the eighteenth century, Kooliny Djabune, of Kadjinol, received the spirit shrine, Cabai, during a time when his soul was said to have gone up to Emitai."[24] The Diola believe that it is the work of Emitai to endow one with

---

21 That interview took place in Brong-Ahafo, Ghana on July 22, 2017.
22 Baum, *Shrines of the Slave Trade*, 16.
23 Ibid., 47.
24 Ibid., 39.

the ability to "see" spirits. Baum writes, "Emitai's gift of special powers of "eye" and "head" enabled people to receive visions, to have important dreams, and to see the spirits."[25] Therefore, among the Diola there is a link between D/V experiences and the reception of knowledge and spiritual power for those who learn to benefit through engagement with spiritual agencies.

As indicated in Baum's mention of Kooliny "going up to" Emitai, one of the congruencies with Akan dream lore is Diola belief in the possibility of soul/spirit travel during the sleeping state. The correlation between sleeping and movement also encompasses the belief that spirits of others may come to the visioner (as noted above regarding shrine spirits) through a visitation while he/she is in the sleeping state. Baum reports that, for those chosen by Emitai, the immaterial self can leave the body and go to Emitai for personal instructions, and remain there for many days while the body is left sleeping. Therefore, not unlike the Akan, the Diola hold to the existence of a part of the self which is able "to leave the body and move about."[26] Baum adds, "[t]he soul could leave the body during dreams; a person's experiences in such dreams were considered real but lived within a different plane of existence."[27]

Baum observed an interesting characteristic of the Diola prophetic movement that took place in the thirty years prior to WWI. The rise of female prophets who claimed direct communication with Emitai occurred during that era concurrent with the encroaching presence of the Portuguese, French and British. The influence of the women did not go unnoticed, indicated by the Portuguese official reports that described a Felupe woman prophet who began to teach about a new spirit shrine of Emitai called Kasara.[28] French colonists of the Casamance area also reported on the strong presence of religious women who "played a central role in Diola resistance."[29] Baum asserts that the role of the prophetic women helped to mitigate the "spiritual challenges of the Diola's loss of political and economic autonomy."[30] During the time of WWII, a woman named Alinesitoué Diatta claimed to experience visions from Emitai that empowered her to receive a spirit shrine and teach in ways that restored "community identity and control over people's lives," during occupation by the French and the "growth of invasive new religions" (Islam and Christianity).[31]

---

25   Baum, *Shrines of the Slave Trade*, 40.
26   Ibid., 48.
27   Ibid., 48.
28   Baum, *West Africa's Women of God*, 69.
29   Ibid., 81.
30   Ibid., 61.
31   Ibid., 126.

These examples of female religious agency in the public sphere are reflections of the empowering and legitimizing effects of D/V experiences, a characteristic already mentioned in Chapter 2 in relation to dreams in Islam and their socio-political role in Islamic history. Similar links between Pentecostal D/V experiences, religious call and directives leading to engagement in the public sphere will be brought out in the analyses of case studies in Chapter 6.[32]

1.3 Islam and Dreaming among the Tukolor Weavers

The dream lore of the Tukolor of Senegal and Western Mali is distinctive due to the influence of Islamic oneiric beliefs and practices. It has already been established in Chapter 2 that Islam has carried forward institutionalized and positive attitudes toward the virtue and usefulness to be found in certain dreams. As Professor of Social Anthropology at the University of St. Andrews, Roy M. Dilley points out, marabouts (Muslim clerics) among the Tukolor follow oneric traditions regarding dream interpretation which involves using dream manuals. Marabouts are also prepared with prescriptions for instructing on how to respond to certain dreams or may engage in mediation by seeking the counsel of Allah. Allah can be expected to give revelation to the marabout in a dream regarding the client's dream. Another type of grand marabout, a *sir-ruyankoobe*, can be hired to go into seclusion on behalf of a client in order to evoke special dreams that give special knowledge on behalf of a client. Dilley reports that distinctions between popular assessment of dreams and Islamic assessments exist, but that Islamic interpretations are still weighty, if enough trust has been built to overcome concern "whether a particular marabout or diviner is a charlatan or not."[33]

---

[32] It should be noted here that tracing dream lore from pre-Christian to Christian thought and praxis should be attempted with care. For example, Simon Charsley challenges "a necessary connection between pre-Christian and Christian concern with dreaming" and pushes for steering away from "aggregations" toward research that documents distinctions in dream narratives and their implications. See M. C. Jędrej and Rosalind Shaw, eds., *Dreaming, Religion & Society in Africa* (Leiden: Brill, 1992), 17, 156. Also, Charsley challenges Bengt Sundkler's suggestion that dream "preoccupation was one of the factors making for the departure ... of African Christians from missionary churches." In support of Sundkler, though, Umar Danfulani (Chapter 4) considers negative attitudes from Western missionaries as a possible factor as per our interview, Aug. 22, 2017. Also, data from Nelson O. Hayashida's work in Zambia notes the apparent disparaging of D/Vs felt by Zambians of mission churches. See Nelson Hayashida, *Dreams in the African Church: the Significance of Dreams and Visions Among Zambian Baptists* (Atlanta, GA: Rodopi, 1999) 79, 137, 308–309.

[33] Roy M. Dilley, "Dreams, Inspiration and Craftwork Among Tukolor Weavers" in M. C. Jędrej and Rosalind Shaw, editors, *Dreaming, Religion & Society in Africa* (Leiden: Brill, 1992), 74.

Dilley researched the dream phenomena associated with creative inspiration in the lives of Tukolor weavers. He found that a distinction was made between *gandal danewal* (Islamic dream lore considered "white lore") and *gandal mabube* (indigenous or "black lore") when it comes to referencing the dreams of craftsmen. That is because craftsmen and musicians acknowledge the source of their dreams and inspiration to be the *jinneeje* (jinn) rather than Allah or one of his angelic host. The *jinneeje* are local spirits associated with the mythical ancestor of weavers and his son, Beram, who was granted knowledge of the loom frame through the *jinneeje* associated with his father. Consequently, Tukolor weavers attribute insightful, inspirational dreams of new designs and problem solving techniques to spirit visitation during the night.[34]

A noteworthy aspect of Tukolor weavers' understanding of their dream experiences is their assessment of them as direct communication that needs no mediated interpretation. Dilley observes, "[t]o the weaver the dream is an explanation in itself: it is a spirit communication which has relevance to his craft." Dilley suggests that Muslims are taught to value the dreams that give indications of interaction with "an outside reality" and that, likewise, Tukolor weavers "reject" the validity of dreams that give no indication of interaction with spirit agency. Rather, they find useful the dreams of a "practical/artistic nature" which can assist in sharpening their own skills or which inspire mystical incantations, songs, or tropes, some aimed at diminishing the success of another weaver.[35]

2 Dreams and Visions in the AICs and among Zambian Baptists

Scholar of African Pentecostal studies, Allan Anderson, published on the AICs (African Initiated Churches) in 2001. At that time he observed, "[t]he many thousands of AICs today, including the most recent varieties, have become the dominant and fastest growing expression of Christianity on the continent."[36] He concurs with certain other scholars about the nature of the movement from mission churches to the establishment of independent churches.[37] It was not secession but rather an act of "conversion" compelled by the desire to heed the Holy Spirit who was perceived as often neglected or suppressed in Western

---

34   Dilley, "Dreams, Inspiration and Craftwork Among Tukolor Weavers," 76–78.
35   Ibid., 80.
36   Allan H. Anderson, *African Reformation: African Initiated Christianity in the 20th Century* (Trenton, NJ: Africa World Press, 2001), 10.
37   Ibid., 32–33. He refers to M. L. Daneel and Adrian Hastings.

Christianity. On the other hand, Anderson asserts that the phenomena represent continuity with the former mission church due to the desire to reproduce "what they saw as important in missionary Christianity." In the process, they found their voice as agents and subjects and would no longer be seen only through the European lens as objects of mission.[38]

Also, of major significance was that AICs met the felt needs of congregants by attending to issues related to poverty, witchcraft, illness, and exorcism. Referring to M. L. Daneel's work among the Shona of Zimbabwe, Anderson notes that Christianity which offers the power of the Holy Spirit is good news. "This was a religion that offered solutions to all of life's problems and not only the so-called 'spiritual ones.'"[39] Christian bishops, prophets, pastors, and evangelists are understood as those who have the authority from God to impart healing, doing so in continuity with biblical tradition. Anderson writes, "African prophets have arisen in the situation of the felt needs of the African people, and provide an innovative alternative to traditional healers."[40]

It will become evident how dreams and visions played an important role in birthing some of the new movements among the AICs, as told, for example, in the stories of William Wadé Harris of Liberia and Johane Marange of Zimbabwe. D/Vs are also part of Christian spirituality in the experience of Zambian Baptists who remained in mission churches. In regard to dreams among congregants of mission churches, Bengt Sundkler, who researched the AICs of the Zulus (of the Bantu people) noted that the study of dreams in the AICs harks back to their significance in mission church experience. He observed, "[t]he importance of dreams in the crisis of conversion is well established from the experience of missions in Africa."[41] A closer look at D/Vs in the mission churches and AICs follows.

2.1   *Dreams and Visions in New Movements of West Africa*
The emergence of independent or African-initiated movements is an important part of West African religious history in the early portion of the 20th century. This section surveys a few of the individuals instrumental in the rise of the Aladura churches in Nigeria, and then reports on the lives of William Wadé Harris and Garrick Braide and their role in new movements in West Africa. All of these were initially connected to some degree with mission churches.

---

38   Anderson, *African Reformation*, 34.
39   Ibid., 36.
40   Ibid., 224.
41   Sundkler, *Bantu Prophets in South Africa*, 267.

The Aladura churches of Nigeria are traced back to a significant prayer group that was held at Ijebu-Ode at People's Warden of St. Saviours' Anglican Church. It was led by J. B. Shadare and attended mostly by Anglicans, with some attending also from the city of Lagos. It was a time of distress due to the sluggish economy, famine and poverty, but also due to the influenza epidemic which prompted the governmental shut down of schools and churches. A young woman named Sophia Odulami had a vision in which she saw that using water only would bring relief from the influenza. According to Nigerian scholar of Religious Studies, Matthews A. Ojo, it was about 1918 and the first time that the connection between prayer and healing was publically announced. It caused a stir in the community. The group, referred to by the name of the Precious Stone Society or Diamond Society, was opposed by the Anglican Bishop and therefore disconnected at that point from the mission church. About or at the same time, connection with the Faith Tabernacle Congregation of the US energized the movement.[42]

The Aladura churches are perhaps most well known for the rise of the prophet Joseph Ayo Babalola. Babalola was employed in the Public Works Department and repaired the roads. He experienced a vision in which he was commissioned by Jesus Christ to minister healing to others. Ojo records that a series of revival meetings ensued and attracted many who needed healing and that many came from the Anglican churches. Babalola had revival meetings in Ilesa and Ekiti and influenced thousands to abandon traditional beliefs and embrace Christianity. Another Nigerian visionary and former Anglican, Josiah Ositelu, recorded ten thousand visions over a period of nine years. He was also dismissed from the Anglican fold and founded a church in 1930.[43]

William Wadé Harris is considered the first major Pentecostal revivalist of the Ivory Coast and the Gold Coast of West Africa. He had been raised in the Methodist tradition in his homeland of Liberia. In 1910 he had a vision while in prison for his part in a public protest of government policies. In the vision the angel Gabriel appeared to commission him in the role of a prophet.[44] He also experienced speaking in tongues while the Spirit reportedly descended upon him three times.

---

42 Matthews A. Ojo, *The End-Time Army: Charismatic Movements in Modern Nigeria* (Trenton, NJ: Africa World Press, 2006), 32–33. See also Elizabeth Isichei, *A History of Christianity in Africa: from Antiquity to the Present* (Lawrenceville, NJ: Africa World Press, Inc., 1995), 280–281.
43 Isichei, *A History of Christianity in Africa,* 282.
44 Anderson, *African Reformation,* 70.

Harris proceeded to evangelize upon his release from prison in Liberia, but had the most success in Ivory Coast. He is reported as having baptized about 120,000 converts. Scholar of Religious Studies Elizabeth Isichei observes, "[h]is vision led to a quantum leap in his own religious experience, and in that of hundreds of thousands of others. He was to be, without a doubt, the most successful missionary who has ever worked in West Africa."[45]

Harris was eventually driven away by French authorities. Harris directed his converts located closest to Catholic missions to be nurtured in Christian faith there. When the Methodist Church arrived in 1924 to the coast, they discovered an abundance of Harris Christians who lived a distance from Catholic missions and had been instructed by Harris to await the arrival of Bible teachers. The Methodists, therefore, pre-date Christian missions to the time of 1914 in honor of Harris' extraordinary ministry.[46]

About the same time that Harris was ministering, farther east, Garrick Sokari Braide rose up in his area of the Niger Delta to minister in a similar prophetic calling. He had worked paddling canoes but later in the fishing industry. Braide experienced a vision while taking communion in the Anglican church in 1912. While Harris' ministry was to non-Christians, Braide's influence was strong among the local people of mission churches and his ministry effected many healings. He also took a strong stance against traditional religions. By 1916, he had become known as Elijah II and had lost the favor of the Anglican Bishop. He and his followers therefore left the Anglican church, but only to confront the suspicion of the British authorities. He was finally imprisoned, but only after succeeding in bringing many to the Christian faith. He died in either 1916 or 1918, possibly of influenza.[47]

2.2 Dreams and Visions and the Bantu Prophets

Swedish scholar Bengt Sundkler is considered one of the premiere Africanist missionaries of his day. In 1937, he took a position in South Africa with the intention of teaching at Rorke's Drift Theological Seminary in Zululand (Empangeni). Circumstances, however, led him to spend the majority of his time in pastoral field work in the coal mining towns (Dundee, northern Natal, and Ceza) among the Zulu. It was undoubtedly the most propitious arrangement for one destined to share so illustriously regarding Zulu culture. His first

---

45 Isichei, *A History of Christianity in Africa*, 284.
46 Ibid., 285.
47 Ibid., 278, 286–288. See also Ojo, *The End-Time Army*, 7, 31, 200–201.

work on African Christianity appeared in Swedish and was published 1938/ 1939, a sixty-eight page account of life in a Zulu Christian congregation.[48]

It was his later work, though, that has distinguished him as a major contributor to religious history. *Bantu Prophets in South Africa* was published in English in 1948 (republished 1961) and offers one of the first detailed expositions of Christian movements in South Africa.[49] In regard to oneiric traditions, he offers a more comprehensive view than Rattray was able to bring forth about Ashantis in West Africa. Sundkler cites access to about fifty dreams as recorded by himself or an assistant, and the hearing of hundreds of Zionist dreams.[50] He gives a sense of the value of D/Vs among the Zulu of mission churches and Zionist AICs.

Missionary enterprise among the Zulu took place as early as 1823 with the first survey of the area of Cape Province by Wesleyan William Shaw. Dutch colonial presence was already challenging Zulu political strength by 1838 with the Bantu-Boer conflict. Thereafter, the climate for newly arriving Anglican and American Congregationalist missions was not conducive and work for these missionaries proceeded with difficulties. The Norwegian HPS. Schreuder succeeded in receiving permission to build a mission station at Empangeni (Zululand) due to providing King Mpande with medicine. Following these beginnings, Lutheran Societies from Denmark, Sweden, and Germany arrived between 1850 and 1878. The influx of diverse mission agency continued to the point that, by the time the World Missionary Conference had convened in Edinburgh in 1910, the issue brought out regarding South Africa was the extent to which mission work had overlapped, and with negative consequences.[51]

Sundkler situates the Zulu Zionists as Separatists who consciously broke from mission churches or who simply founded churches beyond the auspices of the missionaries. There were undoubtedly various reasons for the secessions. The fact that the affirmation of the self-supporting, self-governing, and self-propagating church by Europeans and Americans was proving only theoretical was certainly one of them, according to Sundkler.[52] He also notes that the Christianity of the mission churches was perceived as somewhat anemic.

---

48   Eric J. Sharpe, "The Legacy of Bengt Sundkler," *International Bulletin of Missionary Research* (April 2001) 58–63.
49   Sunkdler mentions Allan Lea's work on "the Separatist movement in South Africa" published in 1926 as a preliminary survey which does not share much about Bantu Independent Churches. See Sundkler, *Bantu Prophets in South Africa*, 5, 375.
50   Ibid., 265.
51   Ibid., 25–28.
52   Ibid., 29–30.

For example, missionaries were not, for the most part, in favor of the emphasis put on D/V experiences by converts. Sundkler comments, "[t]he material of dreams from Mission Churches would probably have been even more extensive than it is now ... if it had not been for the fact that some missionaries have felt humiliated and even scandalized because of stress on dreams by Africans."[53] Sundkler posits that this contributed to driving some from mission churches to join the Zionist Church. For example, a man named Mafuzula left the Presbyterian church because he felt he could not share his dreams.

Sundkler was able to locate the "call" dream within Zulu culture as a dream type within traditional epistemology as well as within Christian spirituality. These types of dreams indicate a call to new vocation by means of the appearance of an ancestor in the dream, or, as in the case of Saula Mthembu, the appearance of an herbalist. Another man, Ndlulangaye Ngcobo, who was esteemed in Sundkler's day as a "famous diviner," reported a dream in which his father and the spirit of an old diviner instructed him to be initiated. According to Ngcobo, diviners must also continue to receive revelatory dreams in order to maintain the reputation of a "real diviner."[54] Call dreams are found in Christian spirituality, as well. Sundkler reports on the stories of J. N. and Lazarus M. The farmer named J. N. belonged to the Norwegian (Lutheran) Missionary Society in Central Natal.

In a dream in which he saw two pools of water, one belonging to the Lutheran and one belonging to the Zionists, a man in white appeared who stirred the waters of the Lutheran pool. Zionists who heard his dream gave interpretations that favored him leaving the Lutherans, and supplemented his dream with other dreams they claimed to experience in which J.N. appeared to them as one who had the Holy Spirit. They suggested he leave the Lutherans to join the Zionists, where his own father had already planted himself. A course of action he did take.[55]

While still affiliated with the Methodists, Lazarus M. dreamt of approaching a city atop a hill which only those who had repented could enter. He saw the people in the city wearing white robes and heard the choir singing. Then a man in white instructed him to rebuke the evangelist Makhaye: "You must ask him why he has turned the day of the Lord into a working day." When he shared the dream with Methodists of his church he was scoffed at. Thereafter, a Zionist approached him one day reporting that he had dreamt that Lazarus was in need of prayer. Lazarus accompanied him to the Zionist church and upon

---

53   Sundkler, *Bantu Prophets in South Africa*, 267.
54   Ibid., 266–267.
55   Ibid., 268–269.

entering he recognized the white robes and the songs as those shown him in the dream.[56] Call dreams are also one of the dream types recognized among congregants of Baptist churches further north in Zambia. Nelson Hayashida reports similar stories gathered there of tension felt by Zambian visioners who saw D/Vs overlooked or devalued in their mission churches.

2.3 Dreams and Visions among Zambian Baptists

A unique resource for its intentional focus on dreams and their value in African Christianity is the work of Nelson O. Hayashida titled *Dreams in the African Church* (1999). Hayashida traces the significance of dreams to African Christianity as brought out by select scholars, yet his is the first systematic use of data gathered from Zambian Baptist congregants. He writes about his work, "[i]t is to my knowledge the first treatment of African Christian dreams and visions on a systematic scale utilizing data from a mission church."[57]

Therefore, he wrote expressly to address the lacuna of the lack of attention to dreams for their role in African societies first noted by Kenyan scholar John Mbiti.[58] Hayashida also writes, "[t]here are few substantial works on dreams ... This study is a small attempt to diminish the imbalance."[59] His volume is a comparative study among Baptist churches in Zambia drawing subjects from rural Manyika, from urban Lusaka, and from urban English-speaking congregations of Lusaka, Kafue, and Copperbelt. Hayashida reports on the content of dreams and the themes which emerged, but also on the dynamics affecting D/V valuation in the epistemic milieu of the mission church. He was also intrigued with the differences between dreaming in the AICs as compared with dreaming in the Baptist churches. He refers frequently to Bengt Sundlker's work among the Zulus along these lines, and also to the work of M. L. Daneel.

Hayashida concludes that Zambian Baptists demonstrated attention to D/V experiences in spite of the influence of Euro-Western mission epistemology. He compares his own data with that of Daneel, in regard to dreaming in the mission churches. Daneel studied the dream lives of the Shona of Zimbabwe, comparing dreaming among congregants of the mission churches, "Ethiopian-type churches," and "Spirit-type" churches.[60] He observed that within the

---

56 Sundkler, *Bantu Prophets in South Africa*, 269–270; quotation from 269.
57 Nelson O. Hayashida, *Dreams in the African Church: the Significance of Dreams and Visions Among Zambian Baptists* (Atlanta, GA: Rodopi, 1999), 2.
58 Ibid., 2. See also John Mbiti, "God, Dreams and African Militancy," in *Religion in a Pluralistic Society*, ed. J.S. Pobee (Leiden: Brill, 1976), 38–47.
59 Hayashida, *Dreams in the African Church*, 2.
60 Ibid., 90. See also M. L. Daneel, *Old and New in Southern Shona Independent* (The Hague, the Netherlands: Mouton, 1974). It is helpful to see Sundkler for an explanation of the

population of his study 48% of the mission church, 54% of the Ethiopian-type church and 50% of the Spirit-type church considered dreams as a vehicle for messages from God. Referring to Daneel's work, Hayashida observes the similarity in his own findings. As in the case of Daneel's mission congregants, many Baptists of the Zambian mission churches believed that God uses dreams, reflecting percentages that approximated the findings among the AIC members of Daneel's study.

What Hayashida laments was the lack of support for Baptist visioners indicated in the data. He notes the dissonance between the dreaming community and church ministry philosophy since there was the lack of "a framework or formal mechanism" to assist congregants with the process of reflection on their dreams. He observes that the Baptist church "is unwilling or unable to provide the context and encouragement to help their members adjust to what they see as intrusions from the spiritual realm—divine or demonic—in their lives through their dreams and visions."[61] Hayashida suggests that the visionary lives of congregants should have prompted pastoral counseling, especially for individuals whose dreams point to preoccupation with death. He notes that many visioners refer to "coffin," "dead bodies," "hell," "black angel," "grave," and "bombs," for example. For Hayashida, such indicators reveal that there are "enormous opportunities for pastoral counseling." He also offers that visioners can be helped not just to comprehend their visions but to reflect on how a dream can be made useful for the "task of integrating it with real life issues."[62]

While D/Vs and their valuation showed up as a significant aspect of spirituality, Hayashida concludes that missionaries negatively impacted the attitudes of congregants toward dreams. Conversion dreams were affirmed by missionaries leading mission churches, as Sundkler also observed, but missionaries associated with the Baptists were not convinced of the value of dreaming in the lives of congregants. Hayashida writes, "[b]ecause missionaries set less

---

difference between the Ethiopian-type and Spirit-type churches. Sundkler notes the former as motivated by a racial and nationalistic outlook. He explained the Zionists (Spirit-type church) as historically referencing the movement in the US at Zion City, IL, ideologically referencing Zion as Jerusalem, and theologically "syncretizing" healing and speaking in tongues with Old Testament and indigenous elements. See Sundkler, *Bantu Prophets in South Africa*, 53–59.

61   Hayashida, *Dreams in the African Church*, 304.
62   Ibid., 306. Along this vein, Esther Acolatse, who appears in Chapter 4, suggests that biblical realism is a hermeneutical approach that allows for registering the awareness of ontological realities (evil beings) as they are depicted in Scripture. Pastoral care can follow, funded by a biblical worldview which personifies evil. Conversely, a truncated worldview can affect pastoral care.

store by dreams and visions as channels of divine revelation, African believers did not share their dreams with missionaries, nor ... did they treat their dreams with the significance comparable in the traditional religious context."[63] As one respondent reported, "[m]any missionaries do not tell us that dreams are of use even at this time ... They concentrate very much on the Bible and you have the sense that we should use only the Bible, not in dreams coming in any way."[64]

On the other hand, Hayashida finds a certain report of positive Pentecostal influence on Baptist congregants to be intriguing. For example, Leonard Mombanya was an interviewee who had attended a Pentecostal church of Lusaka, Zambia, where pastors taught the significance of dreams. The man recalled, "[h]e said God can talk to you in dreams."[65] Hayashida follows that section with an observation, "[i]t would be interesting to discover to what extent Pentecostal churches in Africa not affiliated with any independent church uses dreams or visions as means of revelation and if they provide a church sanction or testing mechanism."[66]

It is unclear what point he is making in excluding the "independent" Pentecostal church in his purview. It appears that his curiosity is in regard to the protocol with D/Vs in Pentecostal churches derived from Pentecostal missions and that he would like to know the nature of the approach to D/Vs as it contrasts with that of other Protestant missions. Again, Hayashida's concerns are pastoral, as is evident in one of his closing statements, "I postulate that unresolved or misinterpreted dreams, even ignored dreams, or dreams without appropriate response in behaviour, may lead to spiritual regression."[67] The Pentecostal approach of the Church of Pentecost of Ghana might be of great interest to Hayashida. The discussion turns now to understanding their epistemological stance toward D/Vs and how they are seen as vital to pastoral counseling.

3 Opoku Onyinah on Pentecostal Dreams, Prophecy, and Angels

The significance of D/V experiences in everyday life in West Africa was brought to light as early as 1927 in R. S. Rattray's survey of Ashanti thought and culture. This section turns now to the theology and praxis of the Church of Pentecost

---

63   Hayashida, *Dreams in the African Church*, 280.
64   Ibid., 137.
65   Ibid., 139.
66   Ibid., 139.
67   Ibid., 307.

in Ghana. It will bring into focus the appreciation of D/Vs in Ghana now, almost one hundred years later, in the contemporary setting of a Pentecostal denomination.

The denomination began as a movement sparked by the influence of a magazine published by the Faith Tabernacle Church of Philadelphia in the US. In it, teaching on healing and renewal was the topic. That spark ignited an enthusiasm which has precipitated the Church of Pentecost, now a rapidly growing transnational West African denomination.[68] Former Chairman of the denomination, Opoku Onyinah, refers to the Church of Pentecost as one of the classical Pentecostal movements, along with the Assemblies of God, which originated in the first decades of the 20th century.

In 1917, Ghanaian Peter Anim read the magazine and its message regarding the link between faith and healing and thereafter experienced a personal healing from guinea worm. Thereafter, contact with the Scottish missionary James McKeown and the Apostolic Church of Bradford in the UK came about in 1937. McKeown was sent to Ghana at Anim's request to guide the movement into a fuller understanding of the baptism of the Holy Spirit. Onyinah notes that the CoP link their beginnings to the mission work of McKeown and the branch he helped develop after a split with Anim in 1939.

Thinking back to Hayashida's curiosity, observing the use of D/Vs in the CoP could satisfy Hayashida's curiosity about the policies and procedures for their incorporation into the life of the church. On that point, Onyinah contributes to this discussion by recontextualizing traditional epistemology (ways of knowing, and ways of thinking about knowing) in regard to dreams, visions, and sleep experiences on Pentecostal terms.

3.1 The Role of Dreams and Visions in Abisa

Onyinah explains the recontextualization of *abisa* within its relationship to the practice of exorcism. *Abisa* is the Akan practice of divinatory consultation and is an appropriated traditional practice that is now part of the stewardship of the prophetic gifts of the Spirit for revelation in the CoP. The process is explained in his seminal work focused on the theology and practice

---

68 At the close of 2007, CoP (Church of Pentecost) worldwide membership had reached 1,695,412 with 10,634 congregations in Ghana alone. Ghanaian scholar Joseph Quayesi-Amakye shares that it is the largest and fastest growing Pentecostal church in Ghana. See Quayesi-Amakye, *Prophetism in Ghana Today*, 49. Girish Daswani reports worldwide membership to be two million in 2008. See Girish Daswani, *Look Back, Moving Forward: Transformation and Ethical Practice in the Ghanaian Church of Pentecost* (Toronto, Canada: University of Toronto Press, 2015), 15.

of the Church of Pentecost of Ghana contained in the volume *Pentecostal Exorcism: Witchcraft and Demonology in Ghana* (2012).[69] The volume is significant as a theological (and confessional) treatment of the practice of exorcism within a particular local, denominational context and therefore is offered here as a much-needed sample of Pentecostal microtheology sourced in Pentecostal epistemology.[70] As such, it is fit to either challenge or champion conclusions being drawn in the anthropological, sociological, or missiological sectors, including the regnant (often "outsider") views.

Onyinah, for example, is in disagreement with the idea that exorcism is motivated by a modernising project. Rather, he asserts, that assumption is superimposed onto African rationale by Western anthropologists such as Birgit Meyer who interpret exorcism as part of Pentecostal disdain of things traditional.[71] Instead, exorcism takes its cues from the long history of traditional anti-witchcraft efforts. Furthermore, it is brought forward into the Pentecostal context and is guided by "biblical concepts of prayer" so that divinatory consultation (*abisa*) for exorcism is "an inquiry into the sacred and the search for meaning."[72] Therefore, scholars of the social sciences have over emphasized the break with the past in favor of modern ideals such as prosperity, instead of recognizing the traditional Akan "quest for wholeness" and the desire for hidden knowledge about true causes which give impetus to deliverance ministry.[73] These ideals fuel the Pentecostal practice of deliverance, according to Onyinah. The experience of wholeness and the search for knowledge of the true state of things also point back to the metaphor of "piercing the veil" introduced at the outset of this project. Spiritual knowledge is important for Pentecostal exorcism, since it is a practice that cannot be appreciated without a deeper understanding of witchdemonology and a "theological analysis of the "demonic" to complement it."[74] Therefore, ascertaining spiritual knowledge, that is, piercing the veil, is embodied in the traditional practice of *abisa*.

The practice of *abisa* is embedded in Akan epistemology as a valid source of knowledge. The word *abisa* is the infinitive form of the verb *bisa* which Onyinah renders as "the act of consulting a traditional priest, a sorcerer, a

---

69 Opoku Onyinah, *Pentecostal Exorcism: Witchcraft and Demonology in Ghana* (Dorset, UK: Deo Publishing, 2012), 268–275.
70 Ibid., 4. Onyinah notes that classical Pentecostalism is "under-researched" since most attention has gone to the AICS.
71 Ibid., 286.
72 Ibid., xii, 286.
73 Ibid., 219.
74 Ibid., 231.

prophet, a prophetess or "any powerful person" who appears to have supernatural solutions or explanations for one's inexplicable problems."[75] Onyinah reports that those who practice *abisa* expect solutions through "the mediums of prophecies, dreams, visions, words of knowledge, words of wisdom or divination."[76] He explains that the CoP have recontextualized *abisa* as an epistemological form. Onyinah uses a biblical approach to evaluate the prophetic *content* of *abisa*, which is understood to have its origins in the Holy Spirit or an angel of God, for a Pentecostal epistemology.[77] Prophetic knowledge is especially crucial for ministering exorcism within a social context where witchdemonology poses a constant threat.

Witchdemonology is Onyinah's preferred term to explain the blending of human agency with the demonic. The worldview that accepts that possibility understands the activities of witches as a major source of disharmony.[78] Onyinah sees witchdemonology as a concretization of the ideology regarding Satan and devils brought to the Akan by missionaries and fanned by proponents of Pentecostalism and Charismatic Renewal in more recent years.[79] Due to the realities of spiritual oppression, Onyinah resonates with the pastoral concerns of Hayashida reported above. Onyinah sees the need for pastoral counseling (which may include exorcism) as warrant for recontextualizing *abisa,* and, consequently, for placing value in the knowledge to be ascertained from D/Vs. Providing pastoral training for counseling is important, he asserts, but it should be from a standpoint which takes the Akan worldview into consideration.[80]

According to Onyinah, it is important that *abisa* be assessed within a Pentecostal reframing of the gifts of the Holy Spirit at work within the Church. That is because the Old Testament as well as the New Testament indicate the divine sanction of D/Vs for "the prediction of future events, to give specific directives, to warn of dangers ahead, " and as "a reminder of God's faithfulness or promises."[81] Also, Onyinah cites Luke's report of the happenings on the day of Pentecost and Peter's understanding of the Spirit's outpouring as connecting

---

75 Onyinah, *Pentecostal Exorcism*, 19.
76 Ibid., 19.
77 Ibid., 268–272. On the topic of recontextualization of this type, see also Allan Anderson's assertion that distinguishing *form* from *content* is essential for understanding "pneumatological manifestations in African Spirit-type churches." This is in Allan Anderson, *Moya*, 39.
78 Onyinah, *Pentecostal Exorcism*, 171–231.
79 Ibid., 176. He mentions Derek Prince as a more recent influence, 182.
80 Onyinah, *Pentecostal Exorcism*, 273.
81 Ibid., 238.

D/Vs with the prophetic life. He writes, "*Abisa* needs to be contextualised into the framework of the NT concept of the prophethood of all believers."[82] Therefore, *abisa* is not considered contradictory to a biblical understanding of God's desire to communicate and to the role of the Spirit, or an angel, in the impartation of revelation. Retaining *abisa* and the value of D/Vs for spirituality speaks to continuity for the sake of reframing cultural practices for Pentecostal spirituality.[83]

Onyinah also comments that there is a need for "corporate discerning" of the prophetic within the Church.[84] That is because it is possible for the communicator to "misunderstand or misinterpret a given revelation."[85] Therefore, prophetic counsel is made subject to testing by the Church. Onyinah asserts that it is by means of encouraging all believers to prophesy, rather than stifling the operation of the prophetic, that a climate of openness is cultivated and these utterances can be brought out in the open and be made subject to the discernment of others.

3.2   *The Sleeping State and the Diagnosis of Witchdemonology*

Onyinah defines *abisa* as existing at the core of Akan religiosity as "the act of consultation to find out the supernatural causality of one's problem and knowing how to combat it."[86] Therefore, when dreams and visions are experienced by the afflicted or those counseling them, they are noted as diagnostic. The D/Vs are important for addressing spiritual needs, especially for those with

---

82 Onyinah, *Pentecostal Exorcism*, citation on 272, see also 273.
83 In *Moya: The Holy Spirit in an African Context* (Pretoria: University of South Africa, 1991), 123, Allan Anderson comments, "The Holy Spirit has sanctified for his use religious expressions which are found in traditional Africa!" Also, anthropologist Girish Daswani observes that a "new quality" is created when the "translation of the Christian message" results in an amelioration of rupture and continuity. In that instance, official religion and lived religion coexist in a "single interpretive framework." See Daswani, *Looking Back, Moving Forward*, 19. I think that Onyinah would agree that the practice of *abisa* falls into that category, as long as due recognition is given to biblical precedence of the practice, and to awareness that "official versions of the religion" as interpreted *outside* the Akan culture are themselves interpretations.
84 Onyinah, *Pentecostal Exorcism*, 273. The real concerns regarding prophetic accountability within the church were driven home by feedback I received after presenting "Pentecostal Dreams and Visions and Social Engagement in African Contexts" at a conference of the Society for African Life and Thought at Stellenbosch University, Sept. 8, 2018. An incident regarding a false prophet claiming visions in Uganda which led to the death of many people was brought up. A participant in this study also referred to the same incident.
85 Ibid., 273.
86 Ibid., 87.

emotional disturbances, bondages through witchcraft, and addictions.[87] But it is at this point that the visionary experience becomes ambiguous, requiring that the reference be made more broadly to the sleeping state. That is because the sleeping state is sometimes reported by the visioner to be literal and not a dream experience or metaphorical in nature.

Sometimes individuals report traveling out of the body to activities in a mystical realm (see Danfulani's cosmology in Chapter 4). When that is the case, the experience in the sleeping state is treated as knowledge regarding the true state of things, or, in the language provided by Nimi Wariboko (Chapter 4), as a piercing of the veil to see the true state of things in the noumenal realm. Therefore, *abisa* may come by means of transport to the realm where what is normally hidden to human perception can be perceived.[88]

Onyinah shares about the CoP prayer camps where clients may come seeking relief from some malady. These camps began as a trend whereby a gifted prophet exercised his/her gift of intercession and deliverance for others, under the auspices of CoP supervision. Many individuals who are not part of the CoP have come to be ministered to at the camps, including those not professing Christianity. At the camps, persons seeking spiritual deliverance are required to fill out a questionnaire which includes questions regarding any strange phenomena being experienced, or the experience of a "peculiar dream state."[89] In some situations, the afflicted may be prescribed a certain amount of days of fasting and then granted a place to sleep on the premises. Onyinah writes, "[a]fter the diagnosis and prescription for fasting, the client is allocated a place to sleep and later consults the leader for the interpretation of any dreams s/he may have."[90] This practice reflects the tradition of incubation recontextualized for Pentecostalism.[91]

Onyinah reports on the experiences of two clients, Ferkah and Abena, who each received help at the CoP prayer camps. In both cases, dreams were key to diagnosing the true hidden issues at work in their lives. Also, in both instances, the individuals were enticed with food in a dream state by family members involved in a witchcraft cult. Enticement with food is indicative of initiation into a witch cult. The leader at the camp who ministered to Ferkah played an

---

87   Onyinah, *Pentecostal Exorcism*, 197.
88   Wariboko does not, himself, designate discernment or knowledge of this type as necessarily associated with soul/spirit transport. He does point out that Pentecostal discernment of this type is not dependent on perceptions using the normative human senses.
89   Onyinah, *Pentecostal Exorcism*, 192.
90   Ibid., 193.
91   Incubation was mentioned in Chapter 2 as an ancient practice.

important role by interpreting dreams and bringing awareness about the situation, while in the case of Abena, she also became aware of her own involvement in witchcraft through help given to her at the Agona Wassa Prayer Camp.[92]

In another of Onyinah's volumes, *Spiritual Warfare* (2012), he reports on the dreams of a young man named Bobby Essel. He experienced many peculiar dreams. "In a series of dreams, I saw that I had entered a different world where I met a man ... What he instructed me in dreams, I should do in the physical without divulging such secrets to anyone. That man ... helped me to appease all the witches around in that area."[93] Among data gathered for the Dream and Visions Project there are similar reports of insight given through dreams regarding witchcraft activity. That will be taken up in Chapter 6.

3.3 The Sleeping State and Angelology

Onyinah contributed to the Dreams and Visions Project with a personal interview.[94] When asked about whether he had a significant dream he could share, he relayed an experience that is also recorded in the volume *Myth or Mystery: the 'Bio-autobiography' of Apostle Professor Opoku Onyinah* (2016) by Gibson Annor-Antwi. It exemplifies epistemological coordinates that stretch beyond the normative in Western Pentecostalism. It also reinforces how important it is to locate dreams and visions within a genre of experience associated with the sleeping state, and to delineate the nuances. Dreams are not the only phenomena associated with sleeping that count in CoP Pentecostalism.

In 1976, Onyinah was appointed as the new Overseer of the Wa District. One of the first events he arranged for was a week of fasting and prayers for the churches. The setting of his sleep experience that week was the mission home where he and his family were living. At the time, he had a visitor named Brother Kenneth Impirim in their home. Onyinah invited Kenneth to spend the Tuesday night of that week with him in all-night prayer. As Onyinah recounted it, he fell asleep a few hours into their vigil, while Kenneth remained awake. To Kenneth's surprise, Onyinah began to speak while asleep. Kenneth reported to Onyinah, "I realised that a voice was speaking through you in English. The voice sounded like another entity was speaking through you, 'I am the Arch Angel Michael. Three times have I been sent to reveal the mysteries of God to

---

92 Onyinah, *Pentecostal Exorcism*, 202–203.
93 Opuko Onynah, *Spiritual Warfare: A Centre for Pentecostal Theology Short Introduction* (Cleveland, Tennessee: CPT Press, 2012), 75.
94 The interview took place on July 19, 2017 in Ghana.

you, but I could not get the opportunity.'"[95] Kenneth reported these words and the whole message to Onyinah the next morning.

That afternoon they began prayers again, this time in obedience to instructions given by the angel. During that prayer time, both Onyinah and Brother Kenneth experienced the same vision and later shared it with each other. In that vision an angel brought a sealed book which had the inscription "Mystery Book," along with the key to open the book, to Onyinah. He was instructed to preach from the book to the large crowd that gathered. Onyinah and Kenneth later shared their visions with each other and were astounded at the fact that they were identical. They both realized that the vision affirmed Onyinah's call to ministry and leadership. Kenneth was careful to keep the vision a private matter, especially since the angel Michael had specifically directed him not to write down the specifics of the instructions he heard on Tuesday night. Onyinah was also circumspect. Annor-Antwi writes, "[f]or an overseer that young in the ministry, it was a scary and delicate encounter ... it could perhaps have been very disastrous for him to have bandied such mysterious messages within the church community."[96]

The indication that angel possession is a recontextualization of an aspect of religious interaction with the spirit world seems clear. West African spiritualism has been reported on from within and without the context. As Robert Baum wrote in his report of the customs among the Diola of Senegambia reception of the "spirit shrine" is a source of power and knowledge. Anthony Ephirim-Donkor explains spiritism in the phenomenon of a spirit alighting on a woman for possession in Akan spirituality (Ghana). He reports that possession is indicated by a change in the participant. He writes, "[w]hen that happens [possession] the entire disposition of the possessed changes as she or he begins to sway from side to side."[97] Anthropologist David Tait reports on the spirit possession of a dancer during the burial ceremony of the Konkomba of northern Ghana. In that case the spirit of the deceased is understood to be present in the human host. "The spirit of the dead woman is bidding farewell to the women among whom she lived."[98]

It appears that angel possession according to Onyinah falls into the general category of spirit possession such as that described above, yet contextualized and reframed biblically for Pentecostalism. Since the interview with Onyinah,

---

[95] Gibson Annor-Antwi, *Myth or Mystery: The 'Bio-autobiography' of Apostle Professor Opoku Onyinah* (UK: Inved, 2016), 150.
[96] Ibid., 153.
[97] Ephirim-Donkor, *African Spirituality*, 50.
[98] Tait, *The Konkomba of Northern Ghana*, 139.

his experience has evoked several questions. Is Onyinah's experience considered acceptable Pentecostal practice within the CoP, or among other Classical Pentecostals such as the Assemblies of God, or for Ghanaian Charismatics? Was the experience ever brought out in the open and made subject to the discernment of others, as in the case of the prophetic utterances of other types of *abisa*? Does Onyinah offer, elsewhere, theological support for angel possession? These are some of the questions that arise on this quest in search of the pneumatological imagination of West African Pentecostalism and which invite more research.

4 Conclusion

In the concluding remarks of Nelson Hayashida's text, he summarizes the task at hand as he saw it over twenty years ago. "The task is to know not only the long past, but the recent past, and the changing present, to better understand the dream, and the church, of today and tomorrow."[99] This chapter has concerned itself with the long past as well as the recent past in a survey of D/V valuation in some African contexts. A trajectory of dream valuation has been traced from the spirituality of the Akans through to today's expression of D/V appreciation in the Church of Pentecost. Also, examples of D/V valuation among peoples of other West African contexts and in Zambia were presented. It becomes evident that in the lives of West African Pentecostals as well as Baptists of Zambia in South Africa, D/Vs have been elements with significance for Christian spirituality.

In Chapter 4, the epistemological soundings of African scholars will weigh in to help provide a clearer sense of how dreams and visions fit into the contemporary epistemic landscape. It takes us a step closer to grasping their significance as elements of pentecostal epistemology according to the sub-Saharan horizons of the pneumatological imagination.

---

99 Hayashida, *Dreams in the African Church*, 309.

CHAPTER 4

Epistemology: African Perspectives

> According to elders from northern Uganda,
>   knowledge of medicine was revealed through dreams.
>   WILFRED LAJUL[1]

∴

> God is looking for someone to talk to.
>   Tonia Osineh Agu, Enugu, Nigeria[2]

∴

> Theology's cross-border promises are greater than
>   the boundary-fixed rule for it as a domesticated activity of the mind.
>   LAMIN SANNEH[3]

∴

This chapter describes something of the philosophical context in which the discussion of rationality (how one thinks) and epistemology (how one knows) has come to the forefront among African scholars. As an example, Kwame Anthony Appiah, a British-born Ghanaian philosopher, has continued an important vein of critique begun by statesman J. B. Danquah decades earlier, one which corrects the inauthentic conclusions of some writing on African studies. Danquah (b. 1895) set out to prove that the knowledge of the Supreme God among Akan religious was a fact, contrary to Western assertions. Danquah also posited the possibility of direct relationship with God through the ɔkra (the soul, inner

---

1 Wilfred Lajul, *African Philosophy: Critical Dimensions* (Kampala, Uganda: Fountain Publishers, 2013), 139.
2 "Dreams and Visions Transcription," 98.
3 Lamin Sanneh, *Whose Religion is Christianity?: The Gospel Beyond the West* (Grand Rapids, MI: William B. Eerdmans Publishing Co., 2003), 57.

ego, or self) given by God. Appiah, likewise, locates the Western penchant for interpreting African religions as resting on symbolic themes as plain misrepresentation. "Symbolists," according to Appiah, "deny that traditional people mean what they say."[4]

It is in this spirit of philosophical reflection that this chapter offers a sense of the epistemological milieu of D/V experiences and their interface with the ontological realities of African life and thought. There are two sections ahead. The first presents relevant epistemic categories funded by postcolonial as well as religious sentiments, and the second features Nigerian Pentecostal perspectives that help to frame the analyses of D/Vs ahead.

1 Knowledge, Ontology, and the Holy Spirit

While these paragraphs by no means do justice to introducing the complex epistemologies embedded in African philosophies, the survey at least frames how dreams and visions can be discussed in relation to the turn toward indigenous knowledge and other realities. To set the scene, attention to the issue of epistemology in non-Western contexts has continued from colonial times until today, energized by the postcolonial project of evaluating and deconstructing the vestiges of Western foreign impositions. It is argued here that holding to the spiritual value of D/Vs is integrated, whether instinctively or intentionally, with the resistance to endorsing all Western criteria for valid knowledge. Also, the deconstruction of Western colonial paradigms has been a subject of key significance worldwide for those addressing oppressive class systems through liberation theology or for those seeking to dismantle Western narratives such as the constructs of racism, patriarchy, or globalization. For African philosophers, reflection is bound together with the issue of matters of identity, the critique of Western democratic ideals of multi-party politics as a one size fits all system, and the turn toward the postcolonial re-evaluation of indigenous resources, epistemological and otherwise.[5]

---

4 See J. B. Danquah, *The Akan Doctrine of God*, second edition (NY: Routledge, 1968), xxiv. See also Kwame Anthony Appiah, "African Studies and the Concept of Knowledge" in *Knowledge Cultures: Comparative Western and African Epistemology*, Bert Hamminga, ed. (NY: Rodopi, 2005), 34. Bert Hamminga also reiterates a distinctive epistemological milieu by pointing out that rationale in African cultures is derived from sensory knowledge in a world where "there is no need for a borderline between this world and the 'transcendental.'" See "Language, Reality, and Truth: The African Point of View" in Hamminga, *Knowledge Cultures*, 104.

5 As an example, Ghanaian Kwasi Wiredu drew from K. A. Busia's description of Ashanti governance (*The Position of the Chief in the Modern Political System of the Ashanti*, 1951) written

This section explains how the value of D/Vs within African Pentecostalism plays a part in the indigenous critique of Western modes of thought. It acquaints the reader with contemporary themes being discussed by scholars in and outside of religious studies, moving from the most prominent voices of African studies, to those representing Christian perspectives, and then to scholars who press into Pentecostal emphasis of Spirit. The flow begins, therefore, with the emphasis on the turn toward indigenous thought, moves on to Christian perspectives on knowing in African terms, and onward to what scholars make of the Holy Spirit and epistemology in the African context.

1.1   Voices from African Studies

In this section, scholars present comments from various vantage points of academia and emphasize different concerns, all of which interface with epistemic realities in African contexts. Kwasi Wiredu challenges Western ideas of religiosity in favor of a Ghanaian emphasis on ethics in Akan interaction with deities. Kwame Anthony Appiah affirms belief in unseen beings as he dismantles notions of a dichotomy between science and African pragmatism. Abdul Karim Bangura offers crucial input from both Toyin Falola and Dani Wadada Nabudere on the need to challenge Western assumptions for the sake of knowledge generation in African contexts. Lastly, Anthony Ephirim-Donkor, who could have served just as well among Christian voices up ahead, is featured here because of his strong championing of Akan cosmology for epistemology.

Kwasi Wiredu is one of the pillars of West African contemporary philosophy who was educated at University College in Oxford during the era of Ghana's political infancy. He is noted for addressing major themes such as the analysis of "conceptual decolonization" and the comparison of Western democracy with African traditional consensual governance.[6] His writings portray special

---

before the break from British rule, to point out the dissonance between Ghanaian governance and the Western democratic system. He stresses what Busia pointed out, that the chief was not an autocratic leader but rather consensus was in operation at all levels in a system in which representative councils functioned. Wiredu contrasts that governance with the "majoritarian," multi-party democracy which he asserts has not been seamlessly adapted into Ghanaian politics. Wiredu also illuminates on the fact that multi-partisanism was already organically in effect in the "one-party" governance of the chieftancy. Wiredu poses the question, "[h]ow substantial have these [gains in freedom] been and to what extent have these developments built on the strengths of the indigenous institutions of politics in Africa?" See Kwasi Wiredu, *Cultural Universals and Particulars: An African Perspective* (Indianapolis, IN: Indiana University Press, 1996), 184–185, citation 188.

6   Kwasi Wiredu, ed., *A Companion to African Philosophy* (Malden, MA: Blackwell Publishing, 2006), 14–21.

concern for the political transformation of his home country since its rise to independence as a republic in 1957.[7]

Wiredu touches on how the epistemological category termed "objectivity" implies the superiority of abstract knowing. He writes, "[t]he mind is not the brain but rather a certain complicated set of aspects of its states," and "[a] very prevalent error in philosophy, which is committed by the realism in respect to meanings ... is the idea that for something to be objective it must exist independently of the mind."[8] Wiredu, therefore, challenges the Western suspicion of subjectivity, and he is not alone in his concerns. The critique of Western epistemology is taken up similarly by some Westerners, for example, those in the stream of American pragmatism. Pragmatists are part of the philosophic trend toward reforming Enlightenment notions of a stark duality in subject-object dynamics by shining the light on complex processes of hermeneutical engagement with the metaphysical (ontology).[9]

Kwasi Wiredu also challenges assertions about religiosity as an inherent epistemic category in African life and thought. The ontological reality of beings included in the Ghanaian lifeworld is an important component of the cultural mindset, which Wiredu prefers to express in terms of ethics. He remarks that Western observers have naïvely imposed the concept of "religious" and concocted other inventions to project onto African conceptualizing. He refutes Western assessments of African epistemological intuitions by referencing the Akan culture of his own family heritage, arguing that, actually, ethical motivations are at the bedrock of what the West has construed as "religious."[10]

In regard to the topic of mysticism, Wiredu resists the idea of mysticism as a descriptor of the indigenous Akan spirituality he is familiar with. His

---

7 See Kwasi Wiredu's chapter "What Can Philosophy do for Africa?" in *Philosophy and an African Culture* (New York, NY: Cambridge University Press, 1980), 51–62.
8 Wiredu, *Cultural Universals and Particulars*, 18.
9 The pragmatist C. S. Peirce has influenced Pentecostal Amos Yong who draws from Peirce for the concept of semiotics in Pentecostal theology. See Amos Yong, *Spirit–Word–Community: Theological Hermeneutics in Trinitarian Perspective* (Eugene, OR: Wipf and Stock, 2002), 100–101.
10 See Wiredu, *Cultural Universals and Particulars*, 45–60. Yet, African scholars from other sectors use "spirituality" and "religious"—accompanied by their qualifications—quite freely. See Kwame Bediako, *Jesus and the Gospel in Africa: History and Experience* (Maryknoll, NY: Orbis Books, 2004), 4; Anthony Ephirim-Donkor, *African Spirituality*, 3; *African Religion Defined*, vii; *The Making of an African King: Patrilineal and Matrilineal Struggle among the Āwutu (Effutu) of Ghana* (Lanham, MD: University Press of America, Inc.), 90; *African Personality and Spirituality*, 44; Wariboko, *Nigerian Pentecostalism*, 24; and Ogbu Kalu, *African Pentecostalism: An Introduction* (Oxford, UK: Oxford University Press, 2008), x-xi.

reasoning is that the focus of Akan engagement with deities is mundane and empirically oriented. And ontologically speaking, the immaterial or quasi-material beings are not spiritualized as in the Western concepts that speak of "ghosts," "apparitions," or "poltergeists." The criterion of the "transcendence of sensible experience" in the Western definition of mysticism seems to him to contradict Akan beliefs about reality, a conclusion he makes in reference to mysticism à la Meister Eckhart, the 13th century European medieval theologian/mystic.[11] Interaction with the immaterial is not a matter of attaining to some elevated mystical height or of having contact with the "supernatural," according to Wiredu, but rather, "[b]y the Akan definition of the universe, everything is a regular part of the system of reality."[12] The question emerges regarding how Wiredu would approach a definition of mysticism reframed according to Nigerian sensibilities, as in the case of Umar Danfulani's pragmatic mysticism that appears later in this section. Nevertheless, the significant point Wiredu brings to the discussion is that Akan epistemic engagements with unseen beings rests on the premise of causality, which he locates as a notion similarly embedded in projects of Western science.

The occupation with spiritual agency in the theories of cause and effect embedded in African religious thought is also commented on by Kwame Anthony Appiah. He states that the logic of it, while it involves interaction with invisible agents, is not unlike the logic running through scientific theories. He writes, "[t]raditional religious theory is in certain respects more like modern science than modern religion—in particular, that it shares the purposes of modern natural science, which we may summarize in the slogan 'explanation, prediction, control.'"[13] Appiah locates the same concept of efficient causality that operates in traditional African thought in Aristotle's philosophy of causation, but adds that in African contexts cause and effect epistemology also works in tandem with functional explanations. He cites the Zande in their reasoning for the meaning behind the destruction of the granary supports by termites, an account reported by English anthropologist E. Evans-Pritchard.[14]

Appiah's observations seem to resonate with the awareness of mystical agents of Pentecostal thinking, agents who seek to "control forces" and promote

---

11 See Wiredu, *Philosophy and an African Culture*, 104–105.
12 Wiredu, *Cultural Universals and Particulars*, 124.
13 Appiah, *In My Father's House*, 120.
14 See Appiah, "African Studies and the Concept of Knowledge" in Hamminga, *Knowledge Cultures*, 40–44.

opportunities for demonstrations of the functionality of the power of the Spirit. Additionally, the observations do not seem prohibitive of a welcome of dreams for the spiritual meaning that might be derived from them. It is within this orientation toward meaning-making which addresses the "why" of events, as well as the "who," that Pentecostal knowing is situated. Appiah's insights help to locate the bias present in Western critiques of that type of knowing. Those critiques resist a knowing that is derived from living holistically in relation to others in a universe of many beings, but they also imply Western naiveté in regard to the "scientific principles" of African epistemology. Drawing from the perspectives of Appiah and Wiredu, it is Western epistemology that does not recognize the importance of understanding the metaphysical and interrelational aspects of existence and what it means to live in light of them.

The need for a decolonized epistemology is one of the themes in a recent volume by West African Abdul Karim Bangura of Sierra Leone. He is Professor of Research Methodology and Public Policy at Howard University in Washington, D.C. His text interacts with Nigerian historian Toyin Falola's contributions to postcolonial African thought. Falola champions a return of "African-centered conceptualization" whereby Eurocentric frameworks can be circumvented as necessary.[15] For example, as Bangura points out, Falola's works make use of African concepts and their meaning for explaining African phenomena. Also, Falola challenges Eurocentric standards of economic and technological progress as indicators for judging "a lack of civilization or cultural inferiority."[16] To counter that rhetoric, Falola emphasized the "literary works of great black thinkers on the continent and in the diaspora, postcolonial history, the interaction between culture and politics, the ethnicity for politics and the modern educated elite, and the political strategies and tools developed by the elite."[17] Additionally, Falola exposed the "colonization of memory" and reported that there should be a resistance to the Eurocentric image of Africans and especially to the distortions of representation in regard to the slave trade and experience of Africans in the West.[18]

Bangura also brings out the suggestions of Ugandan academic Dani Wadada Nabudere for a pluridisciplinary methodology for African-centered researchers. Nabudere calls for a turn away from oppressive and deprecatory categories

---

15   Abdul Karim Bangura, *Toyin Falola and African Epistemologies* (New York, NY: Palgrave Macmillan, 2015), 43.
16   Ibid., 164.
17   Ibid., 164.
18   Toyin Falola, "The *Amistad's* Legacy: Reflections on the Spaces of Colonization," *Africa Update* 2:14 (2007) 1–38.

of Western thought.[19] He also suggests that the turn toward African spirituality "leads to enlarged humanity and recaptures the original meaning of humanity that Western scholars, beginning with Plato, in their hollow and lopsided search for material progress, have abandoned."[20] The turn toward African epistemology and cosmology is essential and would "imply the development of an all-inclusive approach that recognizes all sources of human knowledge as valid within their own contexts."[21] Also, on the subject of the spiritual realm, Nabudere writes, "[t]he Western scholarly approaches have separated the body from the mind, and through this gimmick they have explained away the existence of the spirit world from its ontological embeddedness in the human condition."[22] The contributions of these interlocutors echo the turn away from Western epistemology emphasized by Wiredu and Appiah. The critiques resonate with what some theologians and scholars of African studies are also expressing, as will be demonstrated in the next few sections. But first, the voice of Anthony Ephirim-Donkor brings a view so profoundly invested in Akan cosomology that his Christian perspective provides a seamless transition between African studies and other theological perspectives up ahead.

Anthony Ephirim-Donkor from Ghana provides scholarship that blurs religious boundaries between Christianity and traditional beliefs of the Akan of West Africa. He himself fills the role of king (chief) in his locale in Ghana while also ordained as clergy in the US. His contributions to the conversation are helpful for his detailed reports of the Akan cosmology, the nature of Akan epistemology, and his staunch resistance to abandoning that worldview. He claims that non-Africans embrace only a caricature of the spiritual realm, one of empty space, and that in the case of traditional veneration of ancestors, Africans have been intimidated into compliance with Western ideology. He writes, "[t]herefore, the hypocritical disdain for African rites and symbolism by some Ghanaian clergy reflect on their own ignorance and inferiority complex … Africans and Ghanaians in particular are the ones ashamed of practicing ancestor worship for fear of angering their European and Arab (for African

---

19   Bangura, *Toyin Falola and African Epistemologies*, 105–106.
20   Ibid., 105.
21   Ibid., 106. Nigerian scholar, Nimi Wariboko, who is featured more extensively up ahead, makes a similar assessment, "[s]o for Nigerian Pentecostals epistemology and subjectivity are not ordinary matters or mere debates but matters of life and death, being and existence. Their spirituality is a critique of the modernist notions of epistemology, subjectivity, and truth." See Wariboko, *Nigerian Pentecostalism*, 264.
22   Dani W. Nabudere, *Afrikology, Philosophy and Wholeness: An Epistemology* (Pretoria, South Africa: Africa Institute of South Africa, 2011), 45.

Muslims) masters."[23] He also offers that the spiritual epistemology of the Akan is rooted in "awareness of "others" that cause people to blame their misfortunes on spiritual forces believed to inhabit every inch of the so-called space watching every endeavor of human beings."[24] He reports that invisible beings from the spiritual realm materialize from time to time "just enough to remind people they are still around."[25] For Ephirim-Donkor, dreams are vehicles for revelation in Akan spirituality where children often "see" beings in dreams and where predictive dreams are not uncommon.[26] Spirituality from within that awareness of a populated invisible realm "is understood as a here-and-now phenomenon because people seek treatments for what they believe to be spiritual causalities of their illnesses."[27]

The relevance of Ephirim-Donkor's contribution to this discussion pertains to how it so vividly illustrates West African epistemology in a populated cosmology. For example, his interpretation of Paul's discussion of head covering for women in 1 Cor. 11:4–10 includes commentary on the propensity of the Abosom—deities who operate in a degree of authority invested them by the Supreme being, God—to "alight" (for spirit possession) women whose heads are uncovered. It is a distinctly pentecostal line of thought in that the realm of the spirit is brought to the forefront.[28] Ephirim-Donkor's vantage point makes explicit the *polis* (the public sphere) in which the Akan conceptualize the lifeworld.[29] His work reflects biblical reading through the lens of African

---

23   See Anthony Ephirim-Donkor, *The Making of an African King: Patrilineal and Matrilineal Struggle among the Awutu (Effutu) of Ghana*, 165–166. Undoubtedly, many West African Pentecostals would contest Ephirim-Donkor's assumptions on a theological basis. But Mercy Amba Oduyoye expresses a similar lament about the prejudice acquired against indigenous religion and African thinking by "African dogmaticians." She cites the case of theologian Byang Kato who she says holds to a Euro-American Christian ideal that rejects "Africanness." See Mercy Amba Oduyoye, *Hearing and Knowing: Theological Reflections on Christianity in Africa* (Maryknoll, NY: Orbis Books, 1990), 61–62.
24   Ephirim-Donkor, *African Personality and Spirituality*, 3.
25   Ibid.
26   For an example of similar perspectives outside of African contexts, the volume edited by Roger Ivar Lohmann titled *Dream Travelers: Sleep Experiences and Culture in the Western Pacific* (NY: Palgrave Macmillan, 2003) reports a spiritual world where witches, spirits of the dead and other spirits traffic in the realm accessed by dreamers in Papua New Guinea and other regions.
27   Ephirim-Donkor, *African Personality and Spirituality*, 3. See also his other volumes *African Religion Defined: A Systematic Study of Ancestor Worship among the Akan*, 2010 and *African Spirituality: On Becoming Ancestors* (Trenton, NJ: Africa World Press, Inc., 1997).
28   Ephirim-Donkor, *African Personality and Spirituality*, 125–126.
29   The term "lifeworld" is borrowed from theologians Mark J. Cartledge and Paul S. Chung. "Lifeworld" (*Lebenswelt*) was used first by Edmund Husserl in his concept of social schema. Cartledge uses it to elucidate the work of practical theology. See *Practical Theology*, 28, 82.

spirituality and is especially important for understanding the D/Vs of those in this study. That is because, for the visioners of this project, dreams and visions represent a sphere of existence where experience with proponents of the African lifeworld is possible.

1.2 *Voices from African Christianity*

The concepts brought forth by Gambian Lamin Sanneh, Ghanaian Esther Acolatse, and Nigerian Umar Danfulani are situated here as exemplars of distinctive epistemic stances from the Christian sector. They either explicitly or implicitly challenge Western constructs in favor of concepts of rationality or knowledge generation authentic to African thinking. At the same time they prepare the discussion for its turn toward the Pentecostal-Charismatic intuitions brought out in the following section which features the Spirit as a major protagonist in Pentecostal epistemology.

Lamin Sanneh, originally from the Gambia, was D. Willis James Professor of Missions and World Christianity at Yale Divinity School and Professor of History at Yale University. Sanneh's doctoral work explored the field of African Islamic history and his attention extended throughout his lifetime to address Christian-Muslim relations and the topic of interreligious dynamics. Regarding epistemology, Sanneh makes an appeal to experience and alludes to it as an epistemic category that can challenge Enlightenment rationality.[30] Sanneh also explains the robust Christian momentum moving outside the West as the result of the "indigenous discovery of Christianity" linked to the acquisition of Scriptures in the dialects of the people.[31] In regard to non-Western impact on the West, he makes a statement about what the worldwide Christian resurgence going on outside the West can mean for revitalization. He writes, "[t]he West can encounter in the world Christian movement the gospel as it is being embraced by societies that had not been shaped by the Enlightenment."[32] That encounter can lead to a deeper understanding of the culture "that shaped the origins of the NT church."[33] Therefore, Sanneh points implicitly to Enlightenment thinking's ambiguous outlook on the value of religious experience as an impediment to engagement with the New Testament. He also posits that the West in its state of secularization is poised to receive now from the vibrancy of non-Western Christianity.

---

30   Sanneh, *Whose Religion is Christianity?*, 82, 115–116.
31   Ibid., 10–11.
32   Ibid., 26.
33   Ibid.

Esther Acolatse offers a penetrating theological critique of Western (North Atlantic) readings of Scripture and suggests that "biblical realism" is the hermeneutic remedy. She is Associate Professor of Pastoral Theology and Intercultural Studies at Knox College, University of Toronto.[34] Her book *Powers, Principalities, and the Spirit: Biblical Realism in Africa and the West* (2018) speaks cogently to the issue of the epistemic dissonance characterizing Western and African theologizing. Her concerns lie at the heart of this book as well, that is, she shares the strong sense that biblical readings and theologies of those in the southern hemisphere of global Christianity are needed at the theological table. Acolatse is also a special interlocutor because of her investigation into the problems associated with demythologizing and depersonalizing the New Testament concept of "powers and principalities." The concept of powers and principalities is part and parcel of the epistemic milieu in which D/vs of African Pentecostal-Charismatics are situated. Acolatse is, therefore, important to a conversation on the validation of ontological realities which populate the biblical worldview, but also the African worldview, and specifically, the ontological sensibilities found in African Pentecostal biblical readings.

Acolatse begins her text by introducing the scholarship of one of Ghana's most esteemed educators, Methodist Kwesi Dickson, who articulated the intricacies of theology, culture and identity for post-colonial Ghanaians. Dickson took the task of articulating African Christian theology and philosophy of religions as crucial for addressing Western assumptions regarding African religions and African Christianity. Dickson, for example, critiqued the Western suggestion that African religiosity was animistic or a "nature religion." Rather, Dickson pointed out how the reductionist treatment of African epistemology overlooked the holistic treatment of beings that makes up the "interpenetration of the two worlds" as is most noted in "the working of this interrelatedness … especially regarding the causes of disease and death."[35]

As Acolatse reports, Dickson pointed out that the descriptors "primitive" and "pre-logic" applied to African epistemology were actually indicators of a Western invention and the projection of "a measuring standard foreign to it."[36] Dickson also brought awareness regarding the important interfaces between African life and worldview and the biblical worldview which impacted positively for a contextualization of the biblical texts. Acolatse explains that what has resulted is a hermeneutic funded by biblical realism. An approach that

---

34   I appreciate Nimi Wariboko for steering me to her work.
35   Esther Acolatse, *Powers, Principalities, and the Spirit: Biblical Realism in Africa and the West* (Grand Rapids, MI: William B. Eerdmans Publishing Co., 2018), 34.
36   Ibid., 36.

involves being willing to appropriate the biblical worldview is what southern readings demonstrate. Acolatse notes that this biblical hermeneutic (realism) employed by Dickson was in opposition to the regnant interpretations of Scripture in the North.

Acolatse's compelling examination of the treatment of the powers and principalities (Eph. 6:10) as refracted by the great theological thinkers of the centuries also yields important conclusions. While Clement, Origen, and Tertullian all recognized the existence of personified evil as Paul described it, the more recent interpretations of Bultmann and Barth, as well as those of theologians Walter Wink and John R. Levison veer from the earlier readings. While the techniques for resisting taking Paul's words at face value vary, the implications for not ascribing to the biblical worldview are crucial to note, according to Acolatse.[37] For her, a hermeneutical approach which embraces biblical realism allows for embracing the biblical worldview and drawing from Scripture for accomplishing the work of the church. A different approach can only result in thwarting the purposes of the church.

Acolatse's concern is undoubtedly fueled by her own inclinations toward pastoral care and counseling and concentration on those fields in her studies. It seems apparent that to champion Paul's rendering of the influence of evil spiritual beings is also to champion ministry to those who are oppressed by them. For example, in regard to the end result of readings of Scripture which are affected by bias, she writes, "[t]he result is usually an interpretation that does not serve the church and its mission in the world because part of its identity ... is lost."[38] Acolatse resonates perfectly with the ideas of Hayashida (Chapter 3) who researched dreaming among Zambian Baptists. He also brought out the need for pastoral counseling for visionaries, especially for those reporting the impingement of evil as detected in their dreams. Accordingly, Acolatse suggests that biblical realism offers the best "epistemological fit" as a method for the global church to exegete and interpret the Scriptures, not only for the sake of remaining faithful to early church theology, but for the sake of the mission and health of the church.[39]

---

37   Acolatse, *Powers, Principalities, and the Spirit*, 56, 89, 143, 216. Acolatse mentions various theologians. For Bultmann, the concern is for trimming myth from what can be utilized for effective contextualizing of Scripture. For Barth, evil has no ontological substance but is "nothingness." For Wink, the powers and principalities are representations of social structures, and are therefore depersonalized. In Levison's case, Acolatse notes that his pneumatology amounts to the conflation of the Holy Spirit with the human spirit and posits, in Acolatse's terms, "an impotent image" of the Spirit.
38   Ibid., 216.
39   Ibid., 221.

To close this section, and to complement the preceding emphasis on the ontological, Umar Danfulani offers a particular, Nigerian cosmology. He took part in the Dreams and Visions Project and offered his understanding of the metaphysical world of beings. He is a long time lecturer at the University of Jos, Nigeria, having earned a PhD in the History of Religions at Uppsala University in Sweden. He has been lecturing in Jos and globally for the past 34 years. His scholarship has been presented at numerous conferences on issues of Muslim-Christian relations and peacekeeping, African Christianity, holistic ministry, and the interface between African religion and scholarship. He also took part as a researcher in collaboration with the work of sociologists Donald Miller and Tetsunao Yamamori in their investigation of Pentecostalism in Nigeria.[40] Danfulani serves in a pastoral role at God's Grace Divine Mission where he reported that many desiring to be set free from witchcraft are being ministered to in the power of the Holy Spirit.

During the interview on dreams and visions in which he expounded on the phenomena from his cultural context among the Mupun people of Nigeria, Danfulani shared from a model he uses which depicts the seen and unseen realms.[41] It describes the physical realm and the spiritual realm joined by the mystical realm—or spiritual earth—which overlaps between the two. As Danfulani put it, "I talk about the solid earth, I talk about the spiritual earth, and I talk about the earth in between the spiritual and the physical. The lines that divide are not that very clear. They actually dovetail into each other."[42] It is interesting to note that the physical realm is situated above, with the spiritual realm placed below, drawn, perhaps, from the intuition that the underworld is a populated world of spirits, as was reported to me by a woman who claimed to traffic between the two.[43] The belief that harmful, negative things are being done via the mystical realm is crucial, as Danfulani states, "[t]he people that are controlling these [negative] forces, so to speak, live in the physical world and for them, really, to get things happening in the spiritual world, they have to go through the mystical."[44] Yet, Danfulani asserts, the mystical realm is also the place of the powerful prayers and declarations of Christian prophets and pastors. This assessment of the cosmological lifeworld informs for an understanding of Spirit-orientation in Christian faith and practice. Pentecostal spirituality

---

40 See Chapter 1, fn. 8.
41 The interview with Danfulani took place in Jos, Nigeria on Aug. 22, 2017.
42 "Dreams and Visions Transcription," 33.
43 This conversation took place in Cameroon in 2015 with a Christian woman who had come out of the Mami Wataa cult. See also Chapter 3, fn. 12.
44 "Dreams and Visions Transcription," 33.

is understood as a form of divine mysticism and the power of the Spirit as the agency animating ministers.

Reflecting on how Danfulani might interact with Kwasi Wiredu's empirical philosophy of engagement with deities discussed earlier in this chapter, it seems that there is congruence. Wiredu holds to tenets similar to those driving Danfulani's pragmatic mysticism. Danfulani's mysticism is equally concerned with mundane effects, whereas the thrust of what he offers a discussion on epistemology from the Nigerian context is his assertion about the capacity of human beings to operate in the mystical realm. In other words, what he brings out reflects ontological assumptions about human beingingness, but also about the agency of the Spirit. For Danfulani, those mundane effects of navigating the spiritual realm can include the deliverance of individuals from witchcraft ties, or the wisdom imparted through divine messages in dreams, which Danfulani claims can come from God to lead people safely through spiritual warfare.

As the discussion turns now more intentionally to the Holy Spirit and knowing, it is helpful to reflect on Acolatse's admonishment that the praxis of the church suffers from a truncated epistemology. She highlighted the important impact of theory (theology) on practice and of knowing on doing. In the next section, the phenomenon of practice will be linked expressly to pentecostal epistemology through the person of the Spirit.

1.3   The Holy Spirit and Knowing

Two scholars contribute articulations of Pentecostal epistemology here and in doing so provide a bridge to engagement with the self-awareness—in terms of theology and practice—of the visioners who participated in this study. Ghanaian Methodist scholar J. Kwabena Asamoah-Gyadu points out the neglect of Spirit emphasis in non-African Christianity as compared to African experience. He serves as the Baëta-Grau Professor of Contemporary African Christianity and Pentecostal/Charismatic Theology at Trinity Theological Seminary, Accra, Ghana. He was interviewed for the Dreams and Visions Project and was also influential in securing permission for students of the seminary to take part in the project, as well.[45] He voices admission to the value of D/V experiences for Christian spirituality. In fact, he laments the academic theological approach in the Euro-Western institutions which divorces theology from "the active presence of the Spirit."[46] Consonant with Sanneh's perspective, he

---

45   This interview took place on July 28, 2017 in Legon, Ghana.
46   J. Kwabena Asamoah-Gyadu, *The Holy Spirit Our Comforter: An Exercise in Homiletic Pneumatology* (Accra, Ghana: Step Publishers, 2017), 247.

sees non-Western Christianity as that force leading the way into renewal in the West, and Asamoah-Gyadu's commitment to fanning the flame of African Christianity can be seen in his dedication to investing in West African scholars. As theologian Clifton Clarke notes in a recent publication, it is not for lack of offers to teach in Europe and America that Asamoah-Gyadu has held to his post at the seminary in Accra.[47] Therefore, Asamoah-Gyadu exemplifies more than just philosophic optimism regarding African contributions to the revitalization of the Church and academia. He also represents real commitment to sustaining and increasing the fruit of it.

British-born South African Allan H. Anderson published almost three decades ago of his concern for the study of "Spirit-type pneumatology" and "the work of the Holy Spirit in relation to African power concepts and to the African spirit world."[48] He has been vocal for many years regarding the deficiency of Western epistemology for accommodating the knowing associated with the presence and activity of the Spirit in Africa. With a depth of exposure to African cultures and a long concentration on manifestations of the Spirit, or *moya*, in African contexts, Anderson pinpointed the issue of revelation in a lecture presented in 2011 when he stated:

> The emphasis on the power and provision of the Holy Spirit in African Pentecostalism means that we should consider whether traditionally Western concepts of revelation are adequate. What theological value should be given, for example, to direct "revelation" (prophecy) given to individuals or to visions and dreams?[49]

He also offers, "[t]he widespread use of dreams and visions as a vehicle of revelation in AICs (African Initiated Churches) is also a biblical practice, but one regarded of little significance in western Christianity."[50] And in regard to the Western theological approach to understanding African Christianity he writes, "[r]ather than occupying ourselves with speculation as to who the Holy Spirit is in academic and rather Western theological terms, we should be concerned

---

47   Clifton R. Clarke, *Pentecostalism: Insights from Africa and the African Diaspora* (Eugene, OR: Cascade Books, 2018), e-book, loc. 74.
48   Anderson, *Moya*, vi.
49   This quote from Anderson was first presented in a lecture at the University of Hamburg, Germany, 2011. See also Allan Anderson, "The Pentecostal Gospel, Religion, and Culture in African Perspective," in Clifton R. Clarke, ed., *Pentecostal Theology in Africa* (Eugene, OR: Pickwick Publications, 2014), 169.
50   Anderson, *African Reformation*, 248.

to postulate what the Holy Spirit *does* in interacting with the existential spirit world of the African."[51] Anderson's concerns line up with the intentions of this project since this book argues that D/Vs, as experienced and then interpreted by visioners, are samples of Pentecostal understanding of Spirit agency rendering a distinctly pentecostal epistemology.

Anderson picks up the theme of Western disinterest with or negativity toward the realities of Christian experience in African contexts on the issue of understanding the concept of power. He sees Western bias at the root when he writes, "[t]he negative evaluations again stem from an overemphasis on theological theory (as Westerners see it), and a disparaging of the real-life situation as the African experiences in the world of the Spirit."[52] Anderson also cites the failure of Western theologians and scholars to differentiate what is Christian from what is "audacious ethnocentrism" in favor of "Western society and its cultural pattern."[53] Western assumptions are imposed on the understanding of the Holy Spirit, and to the degree that African assessment of traditional ideas has been affected, as Anderson argues, "[o]ne gets the impression that some African theologians have downplayed the importance of the spirit world in African traditional life out of deference to the Western rationalistic world to whom such descriptions would be 'unscientific'."[54]

An example of dissonance of epistemic views is found in the understanding of power for life. The understanding of power as "vital force" or "life force"—as Anderson notes is conscientiously articulated in the work of Placide Tempels in regard to the Bantu people—is, according to Anderson, not congruent with Western assessments of how the Holy Spirit is understood by Africans.[55] Anderson argues that the Spirit is not depersonalized nor commoditized as a manipulable force among forces as some suggest.[56] He also offers that the force or power of the Holy Spirit is not understood as a mysterious, impersonal force, but rather, the *dunamis* that comes through the Spirit gives "dignity,

---

51 Anderson, "The Pentecostal Gospel, Religion, and Culture in African Perspective," 24, italics belong to Anderson.
52 Anderson, *Moya*, 59. Also, Henning Wrogemann restates a similar sentiment more recently when he writes, "[i]n my opinion, one of the important tasks of intercultural theology is to reflect on the true state of affairs, on what is done in practice … many … depict a very limited selection of the theologically acceptable positions of the theological elite." See Henning Wrogemann, *Intercultural Theology: Intercultural Hermeneutics*, vol. 1, English edition (Downers Grove, IL: IVP Academic, 2016), 331.
53 Anderson, *Moya*, 59.
54 Ibid., 78.
55 Ibid., *Moya*, 58–59.
56 Ibid., 58–59. He references Peter Beyerhaus and M. L. Martin.

authority, and power over all types of oppression."[57] Therefore, the Spirit is readily received as God who expresses love on behalf of those with tangible, existential needs since, as Anderson writes, "[a] person who is oppressed, who must daily face injustices and affronts to his personal dignity, is a person who lacks power."[58]

The African concept of power is inherent to understanding survival in a spirit-filled world. In light of the concepts already offered by Anthony Ephirim-Donkor and others about the world of immaterial beings, along with the admonitions of Umar Danfulani regarding transactions of the mystical realm, Anderson's explanation of power dynamics reiterates and also clarifies the importance of the role of the Holy Spirit. Anderson writes, "[t]he universe and all it contains is permeated with 'power', which may be appropriated by a person in varying degrees, and may be applied with good or evil consequences."[59] The African social world, therefore, includes the possibility of confrontations with the powers of ancestors, witches, and other agencies since the fact of being in African epistemology is the fact of interrelatedness. Anderson notes this as the context into which Christianity has spoken and in which the Holy Spirit animates the Spirit-type churches.

Armed with this understanding, Anderson critiques certain scholars of African studies such as Bengt Sundkler, who brought the spirituality of the Bantu Zionists of South Africa to light as early as 1938. Rather than siding with Sundkler in representing AICS as unorthodox in practice, Anderson drew from the work of M. L. Daneel who reported that prophets of the Spirit-churches were careful to minister in spiritual power in a discerning way as led by the Spirit and in adherence to a sense of Christian morality.[60] Anderson does add a consideration, though, in regard to emphasis on power to the neglect of understanding a theology of the cross or the qualities of the Spirit such as humility, patience, and peace. Anderson suggests that Pentecostals must embrace a pneumatology that brings a balance of emphasis on trials as well as successes in Christian living.

The inherent link between the work of the Spirit and the office of the prophet in African Christianity is important in Pentecostalism. Relevant to this book, that link also explains the agency of the Spirit in the prophet's reception of dreams and visions. Anderson shares that the role of the traditional diviner has always functioned similarly for the diagnosis of sickness and problems, but

---

57   Anderson, *Moya*, 63.
58   Ibid., 63.
59   Ibid.
60   Ibid., 71–72.

that the source of inspiration for Christians is distinct. Anderson writes, "[t]he prophet invokes and speaks on behalf of the Holy Spirit exclusively."[61] The dynamics of recontexualization involved in retaining the mode of gaining hidden knowledge—as through diviners, yet now through Christian prophets—come to the forefront as operating by means of the Christian re-assessment of the importance of foretelling or forth-telling through revelations of spiritual knowledge. As Anderson writes, "The Holy Spirit has sanctified for his use religious expressions which are found in traditional Africa!"[62]

All of this is reiterated in Anderson's most recent work, *Spirit-Filled World: Religious Dis/Continuity in African Pentecostalism* (2018) where he explains, "Pentecostalism, through its experiences of the Spirit, often unconsciously taps into deep-seated religious and cultural beliefs. Pentecostalism draws from these ancient sources in continuity with them, while also simultaneously confronting them in discontinuity."[63] It becomes apparent, therefore, that Pentecostal dreams and visions and their value for spirituality are situated at the convergence of epistemological concerns, ontological claims, religious intuitions, and Pentecostal efficacy. Anderson articulates the premise behind Pentecostal agency which is the efficacy of the Spirit in the mystical realm. This view of Spirit agency brings the discussion back to the Dreams and Visions Project and to the visioners who employ Spirit hermeneutics for discerning the usefulness of D/Vs. As will be noted in the next sections, visioners pierce the veil for hidden knowledge in the course of experiencing dreams and visions, and employ the discernment they say comes by the Holy Spirit for bringing forward what is nourishing for Pentecostal spirituality.

2   Nigerian Perspectives for Dreams and Visions Analyses

In this last section of the chapter the discussion segues into thinking of how dream and vision experiences can be understood or defined by means of the Pentecostal terms and perspectives of two scholars. These concepts will be pressed into service in this study to describe the nature of the D/V experience, how visioners interact with the experience, and how interpretations can impact the lives of the visioners.

---

61   Anderson, *Moya*, 54.
62   Ibid., 123.
63   Anderson, *Spirit-Filled World: Religious Dis/Continuity in African Pentecostalism* (New York, NY: Palgrave Macmillan, 2018), 3.

The African scholar who offers the most extensive articulation of a Pentecostal epistemology for our understanding of dreams and visions is Nigerian Nimi Wariboko. Wariboko is the Walter Muelder Professor of Social Ethics at the Boston University School of Theology, coming to academics with pastoral background (Redeemed Christian Church of God) as well as experience in Wall Street banking. He self-identifies as a theological theorist who reframes continental philosophies from a theological or religious perspective. Wariboko is clear about his epistemic as well as confessional commitments vis à vis Western philosophy. He states that his engagement with Western philosophy and political theory is conducted as one who experiences life as a Nigerian Pentecostal. His perspective "avoids the mistake" of forcing experience to conform to the "Western academic grid or analytics."[64]

This discussion engages first with Wariboko's foundational premise, the "pentecostal principle," as he describes it in the first of his four major works for Pentecostal theology.[65] The concept can serve for articulating the characteristics and effects of Spirit/spirit dynamism in the world. Then, an explanation of how Wariboko conceptualizes the assessment of hidden knowledge as "piercing the veil" of phenomenality follows. It frames the epistemological sensibilities of those who participated in the Dreams and Visions Project to the degree that "piercing the veil" can be offered as a root metaphor. The final section interacts with Nigerian scholar of African Pentecostalism, the late Ogbu Kalu. What Kalu does is to help situate the D/Vs ahead in the analyses in terms of their function as components of spiritual warfare in the "African ecosystem."[66] It will become evident that D/Vs are situated at the interface of the dreams and visions that reflect universal human experience, the African social imaginary, and the Pentecostal self, an interface which is the pneumatological imagination.

2.1 Pentecostal Principle and Emergence for Dreams and Visions Analyses

As evidenced in his volume *Pentecostal Principle: Ethical Methodology in New Spirit* (2012), Wariboko has thought deeply on how to define and express the

---

64 Nimi Wariboko, *Nigerian Pentecostalism*, (NY: University of Rochester Press, 2014), 254.
65 Among other works, the four are *The Pentecostal Principle: Ethical Methodology in New Spirit* (Grand Rapids, MI: William B. Eerdmans Publishing Co., 2012), *Nigerian Pentecostalism* (NY: University of Rochester Press, 2014), *The Split God: Pentecostalism and Critical Theory* (Albany, NY: SUNY Press, 2018), and *The Pentecostal Hypothesis: Christ Talks, They Decide* (Eugene, OR: Cascade Books, 2020).
66 Kalu, *African Pentecostalism*, 178.

creating and recreating dynamic he sees at work in the course of history, especially in terms of social issues, ethics, governance, public theology, and pentecostal spirituality. Stirred by the theology of Paul Tillich in which Tillich's Protestant principle points to the "doctrine of kairos" and "the in-breaking force coming from above or outside," Wariboko offers an alternative vision he calls the "pentecostal principle."[67] He adjusts the idea of kairos to accommodate more than an in-breaking from above. Wariboko presents the "kairotic moment" in the Spirit's outpouring of Acts 2, also known as "kairoi," the interpenetration of masculine and feminine, the old and new, the time-oriented and the spatial, the *novum* following creative disruption.[68] The event embodies the pentecostal principle, which is different than Tillich's concept in that it pertains to more than "religious or cultural form" because it "transcends them."[69] Wariboko writes, "[i]t is available in things that want to go beyond themselves to their depth, to dynamic ontological creativity, to the Spirit of creation."[70] He, therefore, universalizes the dynamic of Spirit and in another description explains, "[t]he pentecostal principle is the capacity to begin."[71] But the pentecostal principle is also more than a dynamic. It is an ontological reality, a condition of being, in which "we see that the spiritual content and the material bearers are combined or networked as the infinite restlessness of existence (life)."[72] Finally, it is more than all of these descriptors, since it is itself a pneumatological methodology for analysis of the issues of primary concern to Wariboko, matters of ethics in societal movement, change, and emergence.

This book argues that the D/V experiences and interpretations that were reported in the Dreams and Visions Project are samples of the workings of the pentecostal principle. Before explaining how that is, the significance of the research as the substance of "microtheology" should be pointed out. Wariboko's keen theological vision and conceptual exuberance deal necessarily with the abstract, but he realizes the challenge that distance from the everyday practices of Pentecostalism poses for theologians. He asserts that microtheology drawn from engagement with actualities can bring clarification or correction to prevailing theological assumptions about how Pentecostals live out every-day spirituality.[73] For that reason, the data gathered from the

---

67 Wariboko, *The Pentecostal Principle*, 50.
68 Ibid., 53.
69 Ibid., 49.
70 Ibid., 49.
71 Ibid., 1.
72 Ibid., 42.
73 Nimi Wariboko, "West African Pentecostalism: A Survey of Everyday Theology" in Vinson Synan, Amos Yong, and J. Kwabena Asamoah-Gyadu, editors, *Global Renewal Christianity,*

interviews and written surveys is important for addressing Wariboko's concern and for understanding how the pentecostal principle plays out in the every-day attentiveness to D/V experiences for pentecostal knowing.

As already noted, Wariboko describes the pentecostal principle as "the capacity to begin." The personal and social responses of some visioners to their D/V experiences illustrate what Wariboko refers to. This epistemology is manifested in the effect of D/Vs on visioners who translate and interpret the experiences for embarking on social initiatives. In those cases, D/V experiences can be looked at as evental grace-acts, what Wariboko attributes to the work of the Holy Spirit, and can be seen as resources or "novel, unexpected or unforeseeable events and developments which represent new possibilities."[74] What is key is that the new possibilities are birthed from pentecostal knowing that has taken on a new idea, passion, perspective, or vision for the future. That knowing yields personal transformation. That knowing also impacts others *beyond* the life of the visioner, producing an overflow of exuberance for societal benefit or transformation.

This social aspect is referred to by Wariboko as the "actualization process" by which the pentecostal principle impacts "human socialities" when addressing socio-political dynamics.[75] The "emergentist social world" operating by the "pentecostal principle" of the Spirit is "conscious of and open to novelty, opportunity, uncertainty, and disruption" toward sociality and pentecostal ethics.[76] This project argues that the pentecostal principle can be observed at work in the D/V experiences and interpretations which propel visioners to social engagement.

Beyond his description of the pentecostal principle, Wariboko's explanation of the dynamic of emergence is also key to explaining the effect of D/V experiences. Along with the pentecostal principle, the concept of emergence offers an appropriate term to reflect the surplus of the D/V experience and interpretive process and its qualities. Emergence is a dynamic that demonstrates the pentecostal principle as a "creative emergence" that can induce "properties and behaviors that are not explicable by the lower parts or in terms of the sum of the parts."[77] Rather, the emergence pertains to "an excess which cannot be fully incorporated or suppressed by the extant system."[78]

---

vol. 3, *Africa* (Lake Mary, FL: Charisma House, 2016) 17–18. See also *The Split God*, xx, 1–2, and Chapter 7: 155–180.
74 Wariboko, *Nigerian Pentecostalism,* 159–160. See also *The Pentecostal Principle,* 74.
75 Wariboko, *The Pentecostal Principle,* 71.
76 Ibid., 77–78.
77 Ibid., 205.
78 Ibid., 206.

Wariboko explains this creative emergence as a resource for producing citizenry that operates by an ethics that knows how "to rely on the spirit rather than on rules and predetermined ethical codes for navigating what is and what must be a world opened to surprises."[79] Therefore, Wariboko's emergence points out the creative aspect of the pentecostal principle which produces that which was not, that which is not contingent on the extant, for the purpose of springing forth new potentialities. Looking toward the analyses of dreams and visions, the dynamic of emergence will also be reflected on in the D/V experiences which inspire and motivate visioners to personal transformation and social engagement.

2.2 Piercing the Veil for Dreams and Visions Analyses

There is an aspect of the D/V experience which is marked by the claims of literal happenings in the spiritual realm, laying aside the idea of metaphorical images during the D/V experience. But whether the visioner understands the elements of D/V experience as literal happenings or metaphorical message the concept of revelation is key. These qualities are articulated in Wariboko's concept of "piercing the veil" for accessing knowledge. Before exploring piercing the veil, it is helpful to understand how Wariboko understands truth in Pentecostalism.[80] His volume, *Nigerian Pentecostalism* (2014), is the resource offering his thinking along these lines. He considers that the practices of Nigerian Pentecostal spirituality demonstrate the bridging of the cleavage Western philosophy has created between philosophy (access to truth/knowledge) and spirituality (moral subjectivation). Wariboko points out that "mainstream theology" follows a rational conceptualization of knowledge that, in the words of Michel Foucault, "allows ... access to the truth of God without the conditions of spirituality."[81]

For Pentecostal Nigerians, though, truth/knowledge and spirituality are wedded, because to have access to the truth means to have access to the Holy Spirit and to the transformation of being that leads to "technological prowess, economic development, global recognition, and respect."[82] In this way, ontological concerns are also in view so that spirituality is the means to the

---

[79] Wariboko, *The Pentecostal Principle*, 206.
[80] See also Anna Droll, "'Piercing the Veil' and African Dreams and Visions: In Quest of the Pneumatological Imagination," *Pneuma: The Journal of the Society for Pentecostal Studies* 40: 3 (2018) 345–365.
[81] Wariboko, *Nigerian Pentecostalism*, 266 and 329: Chapter 10 fn. 16.
[82] Ibid., 267.

flourishing of life and is linked to usefulness. Accessing spiritual knowledge is, therefore, an important part of attaining that flourishing.

Wariboko describes Pentecostal epistemology as that which can contradict, supplement, or complement the knowing that is bound to the phenomenal. Also, Pentecostal knowing concerns itself with ontology so that knowing pertains to the quest for the Real as it truly is, enspirited and incapable of being solely defined by what can be perceived by the senses, that is, by its representations. Pentecostal knowing is concerned with the noumenal reality of that which is perceived experientially or phenomenally. Pentecostal spirituality deals with "the struggle between epistemological finitude and fantasy, between desire and impossibility," achieving what Western philosophy deems impossible.[83] Wariboko asserts that Pentecostal knowing engages with the ontological by means of knowing (the Real) "which remains resistant to epistemological knowing."[84] In other words, the impasse to knowing is *overcome* in the Pentecostal experience, implying that the project of epistemology is itself split. Pentecostal epistemology is concerned with seeing what is the Real behind the veil (the noumenal) and therefore supersedes the split.[85] Wariboko asserts that the Pentecostal knowing thereby transforms the "epistemological coordinates of existence."[86] This spirituality contests the "conditions and limits" of "access to knowledge and truth."[87] He explains that knowing the Real entails a lifting of or "piercing" of the "veil of phenomenality" and "it is not enough to be merely saved; one must see into, hear from, and converse with beings in the spiritual realm."[88]

Lest the idea of "piercing the veil" conjure up Kantian connotations of the bifurcation of the material and immaterial or the finite and infinite, further explanation of metaphysical/ontological issues are in order. Wariboko's epistemology contradicts what is possible within the conceptualization of philosopher Immanuel Kant by mending the cleavage between the noumenal and phenomenological. Kant affirmed the noumenal as an aspect of the ontological reality of a thing, as distinguished from how it appears to the finite human senses, but deemed the noumenal unknowable and therefore inconsequential. Kant pressed this assertion into service against the notions of the

---

83 Wariboko, *Nigerian Pentecostalism*, 45.
84 Ibid.
85 Ibid. In *The Split God*, Wariboko further extends the metaphor of "splitness" in epistemology to portray the Pentecostal understanding of God.
86 Nimi Wariboko, *Nigerian Pentecostalism*, 48.
87 Ibid., 42.
88 Ibid., 42, 44–46.

transcendental realists of his day which he felt were bringing "metaphysical confusion."[89] These transcendentalists rejected the Enlightenment discounting of a more perfect store or source of knowledge found in God. Kant felt it important to counter their thinking with his own "transcendental idealism" that maintained the concept of an ambiguous and unknowable noumenality. Philosopher David West puts Kant's conclusions succinctly, "[h]uman knowledge must be understood in purely human terms rather than according to the misleading and unattainable standard of divine intuition."[90]

Wariboko concludes that "the received epistemological (Kantian) wisdom alienates the essential human spiritual capacity."[91] Rather, Wariboko asserts, Pentecostal experience proves that the noumenal and phenomenal exist in much more intimate association, one which explains the accessibility of the noumenal. To better explain, the metaphor of "piercing the veil" is accompanied by another of Wariboko's metaphors, the "twisted ribbon," which depicts how knowledge of the noumenal reality can figure into everyday human experience. An imaginary ribbon fashioned after "the Möbius Strip," twisted at the end, produces a flat surface on which an ant might walk. Wariboko ventures, "Spirituality becomes like an ant-like walk on the surface of reality whose inside (phenomenality) and outside (noumenality) are always believed to be twisted; one side becomes the other."[92] He adds, "Nigerian Pentecostals think of the body and spirit, phenomenal and noumenal knowledge, not as a dichotomy but as an intertwined whole."[93]

Wariboko fleshes out more on pentecostal epistemology in his other volume, *The Split God* (2018). There he explains the breadth of the Pentecostal project of living out a portrayal of God that reflects a fundamental usefulness and relevance of God to the material, everyday life. Indeed, the capacity to envision God as accessible in parts ("split") is at the core of Pentecostalism's unique relevance and its growth as a movement.[94] The Pentecostal God is split in the sense that Pentecostals go beyond understanding God as "a theological text" and rather employ or imagine God in ways that "fit the everyday nitty-gritty materiality of the 'here and now.'"[95] The splitting of God plays out in terms

---

89   David West, *Continental Philosophy: An Introduction* (UK: Polity Press, 2010), 23.
90   Ibid., 23. Kant refers to intuitions of a different genre, that is, those that exist *a priori* in the human mind and which function in the processing of sense perceptions and experience. See also 20.
91   Wariboko, *Nigerian Pentecostalism*, 264.
92   Ibid., 44.
93   Ibid.
94   Wariboko, *The Split God*, xvi.
95   Ibid., xvi.

of healing the noumenal/phenomenal divide (what can be known or experienced, manifested) as well as in terms of the ontological, that is, in understanding the beingness of God in ways that defy abstraction.[96] Therefore, the split God is the abstract God who is also the "concrete universality," God who is living and active. Rather than beginning from a standpoint of "repressive hermeneutic or orthodoxy," the Pentecostal begins from desire so that "God is defined through his deeds as perceived in the concrete lives of individuals or, in different terms, deed precedes essence."[97]

Situated within this Pentecostal framing of God is what Wariboko introduces as the "religious art of discernment" which can be categorized into four aspects.[98] The knowing of the Real is one of those, as mentioned in the previous section above. Other categories are termed the social, technological, and textual aspects of discernment. Wariboko explains, for example, the social as the influence of pastors or ministers who offer their discernment regarding relationship issues as "causes of problems and crises."[99] The category of the "technological" refers to reliance on discernment interacting with the usual elements of normative living in the interface of the visible and invisible, in the "coherent and smoothly functioning single world." Discernment by means of the textual pertains to the weaving of prophecies and narratives for producing the means to help one endure and for inspiring hope. Yet discernment can pertain to that which moves beyond the phenomenal to piercing the veil, and it is of a different order altogether. This access to the Real involves knowledge of ontological truth since "There is always something else, something more to a situation, and that something extra is the fount of possibility while appearing constitutively absent *without the equipment of "seeing eyes"* (italics mine)."[100] While the social, technological, and social aspects of discernment employ multi-faceted techniques for making Pentecostal assessments, discerning the Real pertains to prophetism and requires piercing the veil to see beyond into the true state. "It supplies the contexture within which dilemmas

---

96   Wariboko, *The Split God*, xviii-xix.
97   Ibid., 196, fn. 6.
98   Ibid., 46.
99   Ibid., 56.
100 Ibid., 57. This manner of knowing pertains to special knowledge. I offer an example from a report given in Enugu, Nigeria. A minister reported perceiving the hidden control being exerted through the spirit spouse as the root issue of the diminishing of strength in an athlete who came to him troubled by set-backs in his athletic performance. The interview with this participant of the study took place Aug. 30, 2017.

and challenges are related to ultimate reality."[101] Consequently, piercing the veil reveals the hidden pieces of even the split self.

Another important metaphor drawn from *Split God* is Wariboko's brief portrayal of the "pentecostal" or "spiritual warrior."[102] The pentecostal warrior employs language in prayer in the process of developing a new social identity. Wariboko sees prayer as functional in ways that are also reflected in this microtheology. Prayer surfaces in this project as an important factor having to do with the reception and reflection of D/V experiences, especially in response to warning, warning/predictive, or spiritual warfare dreams. Prayer therefore characterizes the pentecostal warrior's engagement with D/V experiences.

It is Wariboko's book, *The Pentecostal Hypothesis: Christ Talks, They Decide* (2019), which offers a Pentecostal perspective on how christological sensibilities energize the pentecostal epistemology that assesses the noumenal and phenomenal. Discourse on the tension between noumenal and phenomenal takes place in this volume as in the others, but this time from a point of departure that recognizes Jesus Christ at the core of the pentecostal rationale. This involves discerning the limits of sensory perception—"It does not make sense but it makes spirit"—and envisioning the possibilities through the Spirit of Christ.[103] According to Wariboko, this "epistemology performs itself inside christology" because "Pentecostal epistemology is captured in the narratives of christology and the processes of *Christformation*."[104] Also, "[t]he christological structures of their thought (everyday practical theology) and understanding of human life create the *habits* of their epistemology."[105] Wariboko goes on to make insightful connections between the concept of Jesus Christ as one who occupies the "middle space" (cognitive space) or the "to-come" and how that ontological Christ inspires the epistemological technique of self-identifying as "inter-people … who inhabit a hybrid space between flesh and spirit."[106] Christ, therefore, becomes the means by which the impasse of sense can be overcome by spirit. Therefore, Wariboko's thinking allows for new connotations to spring from the use of "veil" found in the epistle to the Hebrews. The body of Christ represents not only the veil, but the means of its piercing (Heb. 10:20), effecting epistemic and ontological realities. For the Pentecostal, these are part of everyday mundane spirituality.

---

101   Wariboko, *The Split God*, 57.
102   Ibid., 160–161.
103   Wariboko, *The Pentecostal Hypothesis*, 2.
104   Ibid., 12.
105   Ibid., 12.
106   Ibid., 73.

For the purposes of this study, Wariboko's concepts provide a way to understand how dreams and visions and their interpretations partake of that "hybrid space between flesh and spirit." His model for Pentecostal epistemology is also helpful for registering the gap or "middle space" which Christ is—and also represents, according to Wariboko—as the seat of the manifested will of God. The ability to inhabit, epistemologically, that gap of "middle space" is inherent to Pentecostal visioners. Conceptualized for this project, dreams and visions are experienced in that "hybrid space" of manifested will, carrying with them the weight of Pentecostal logic that equates knowing Christ (intimacy) with the capacity for spiritual knowledge.

Wariboko's episteme-Christology/Pentecostal Christology is also helpful for philosophically and theologically tracing the interpretation of D/Vs on its way to social agency ("God told me to"). As will be made evident ahead in the case studies, intimacy with Christ and revelatory knowledge are melded together and propel the Pentecostal agent. Wariboko writes, "[s]een in all this light, it-makes-spirit is an integral part of the virtue of ethics of Pentecostals or should be considered as such in any scholarly analysis of the community's social ethics."[107] Therefore, Wariboko's recent material adds to and thickens his subsequent material on social ethics. While the last chapter of *The Split God*, "Ethical Implications of a Split God," predicates Pentecostal capacity for engagement with the religious Other upon the "radical theology of alterity," the more recent material reiterates Christ at the bedrock of Pentecostal sociality.

To conclude this section on piercing the veil, it is suggested here that the concept should be appropriated as an important religious metaphor for the study of Pentecostal D/Vs. The epistemology Wariboko put forth and elaborated on conflates with the experience of certain types of D/Vs judged by visioners as revelatory of the "true state" of things. This ability to pierce the veil to the noumenal is especially driven home by the terms "seeing eyes" and "hearing ears" which Wariboko uses to refer to special perceptual abilities.[108] Additionally, Jesus figures prominently in many experiences, demonstrating the role of Christology as a legitimizing element in the experience.

Piercing the veil also has the capacity to communicate the nuances of visionary experience. Some visionaries of this study reported that they have seen beyond the visible (beyond the veil), while some also described *being in* another realm of existence experiencing literal happenings. There is, therefore, indication that these visioners understand the sleeping experience in

---

107 Wariboko, *The Pentecostal Hypothesis*, 125–126.
108 Wariboko, *Nigerian Pentecostalism*, 47.

terms that are quite elastic, so that piercing through to hidden knowledge entails the experience of transport or transmission from one realm of experience to another. Wariboko's piercing the veil is fitting as a metaphor for the broader spectrum of Pentecostal visionary experience. It can refer to accessing knowledge through D/Vs and through spiritual perception (Wariboko's discernment), but can also reflect encounter experientially with the true state of things in another realm or dimension, that is, with the literal or Real. Therefore, piercing the veil serves aptly as a root or religious metaphor for framing dream and vision experiences of different kinds in the lives of Pentecostal-Charismatic visioners. It reflects the epistemic grounding for visionary experience while also legitimizing D/Vs as carriers of hidden knowledge for Pentecostal knowing.

2.3 *Spiritual Warfare and Dreams and Visions*

Since an analysis of dreams and visions requires becoming acquainted with the elements in which D/Vs "live and move and have their being," it is helpful to explain the anatomy of an African Pentecostal approach to the problem of evil. The contributions of Ogbu Kalu are drawn from here to explain four main features of the Pentecostal approach to evil: dependence on covenant theology, the exposing of evil and things hidden, the promotion of spiritual agency, and the rehearsal of spiritual victories (testimonies). The dreams and visions of participants demonstrate a pneumatological imagination enlivened by certain presuppositions about spirit and Spirit, by a robust engagement with Scripture, and by the types of characteristics mentioned by Kalu (Figure 2).

Nigerian Ogbu U. Kalu was a highly respected academic known for writing prolifically on missions, Christianity in Africa, and global Christianity. His last post was as Henry Winters Luce Professor of World Christianity and

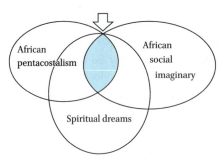

FIGURE 2   Dreams and visions of pneumatological imagination

Mission at McCormick Theological Seminary in Chicago, Illinois, in the US. He describes Pentecostalism as a paradigm shift that "unshackles theology from rationalistic/scientific ways of thinking and expands the understanding of the spiritual dimensions of reality and the operation of the invisible world."[109] As Kalu describes it, the existential problem of evil and affliction points to the "weakness of missionary theology" as much as it does to the essence of African theology. He writes, "[a]ffliction is a pivotal issue in the theology of the African primal world."[110] Kalu also emphasizes the "challenges of the eco-system" which require the propitiation of powers such as the Earth deity. In this atmosphere, spiritual practitioners serve as mediators between the community and protective spirits. At the heart of the transactions is the existential concern for upholding "moral order" and attention to ancestral covenants understood as the spiritual cure for social wrongs. Kalu offers, "[t]his is a religious worldview."[111] He adds, "[g]oing through life is like spiritual warfare, and religious ardor may appear very materialistic as people strive to preserve their material sustenance in the midst of the machinations of pervasive evil forces." "Yet," Kalu points out, "[t]he resources for responding to this fills the pages of the Scriptures."[112] In light of African religious concerns, Kalu considers the revivals of Holy Spirit vigor in Africa to be linked to "the resources of a new religiosity with an ongoing effort to solve problems in the ecosystem."[113] He also writes, "[t]he major contribution of the Pentecostal movement is how it addresses the continued reality of the forces expressed in African cultural forms."[114]

Kalu points to the African reception of the Old Testament. The concept of covenant which features so prominently in both Old and New Testaments is brought into application with fresh vigor in the African contextualization of the Bible.[115] Since covenants or agreements with unseen beings and ancestors are natural components of traditional life, it is not difficult for Africans to

---

109 Kalu, *African Pentecostalism*, 250.
110 Ibid., 140.
111 Ibid. It is also interesting to note the work of Ghanaian scholar Kwame Bediako who demonstrated the parallels between the contextualization of the gospel in African contexts and in the 2nd century of the Roman Empire. Bediako remarks, "The association of religion with the well-being of the Roman commonwealth and its validation on the grounds of ancestral custom, also meant that religious piety was the ground for social morality." See Kwame Bediako, *Theology and Identity: The Impact of Culture upon Christian Thought in the Second Century and in Modern Africa* (Eugene, OR: Wipf and Stock, 1999), 22.
112 Kalu, *African Pentecostalism*, 140.
113 Ibid., 141.
114 Ibid., 178.
115 Ibid., 174.

adopt the biblical worldview promoted in Jesus' references to Satan and Paul's principalities, powers, and rulers of darkness (Eph. 6:11). Kalu notes that worldviews intersect in other areas, as well. He writes, "African worldviews share an identical creation myth with the Genesis saga, that of an earth created by watery terrain," and importantly, "[b]oth traditional African culture and Pentecostalism affirm that "things which are seen are made of things which are not seen" (Hebrews 11:3b) and that events in the manifest world are first decided in the spirit world."[116] Kalu points out that, therefore, "life is secured through a good relationship with the supernatural."[117] Israel's covenant with God and the promise of land resonate deeply with Africans, as do the power of the Holy Spirit and of the name and blood of Jesus. The covenant made with Jesus Christ is significant since through it, "Christians have been given power to speak changes into being."[118]

It has already been noted how important hidden knowledge is to understanding the way the Real is being manifested in the temporal, mundane experience. According to Kalu, Pentecostals believe that mining spiritual knowledge (what Wariboko calls piercing the veil) for didactic purposes is essential.[119] The spiritual skills necessary to defeat evil forces is found in the power of Spirit which includes access to insight which reveals what, where, when, how, and even why. These are essential and supplied by means of spiritual perception. It will become apparent that D/Vs which supply that insight to those who can "see" are transmitters of that useful, hidden knowledge.

One of the primary features of spiritual warfare theology is the promotion of spiritual agency as part of the privilege and responsibility of the Christian. That agency is linked to the way Pentecostals "accept the power and reality in the symbols and rituals of communities and bring a "pneumatic knowing" to respond."[120] Kalu explains how Pentecostal knowing and agency is meant to secure victories over evil, not only for the individual, but for whole communities. Pentecostals offer a "reshaped sense of order" using "symbols, speech, and media to construct a new reality."[121] Tapping into the power of God's rule through Christ, Pentecostals are active agents confronting curses, witchcraft, and sorcery.[122] Examples of Pentecostals who reflect this sense of

---

116   Kalu, *African Pentecostalism*, 179.
117   Ibid.
118   Ibid., 181.
119   Ibid., 183.
120   Ibid., 185.
121   Ibid.
122   Ibid., 180–181.

responsibility, and who reported that it was derived from D/V experiences, are introduced ahead. Some reflect the concern for whole communities, as mentioned by Kalu. They reach beyond the walls of the church, sometimes alone, often taking risks or navigating the consternation of others.

Lastly, Kalu wrote about how "public testimonies about the works and victory over the wicked forces" resulted from Pentecostals addressing the problem of evil.[123] In this project, this feature of Pentecostal testimony featured prominently. Interviews contained stories of how D/Vs gave insight for victories over evil, as well as awareness of God's presence. A sense of awe was evident in the sharing of visitations from Jesus that brought comfort, or visions of the exalted Jesus that inspired wonder and deeper intimacy with God. Often, the narrator seemed to relive the experience as a precious token of God's care. Therefore, many of the narratives pertain to the genre of public testimonies that Kalu locates as springing from addressing the problem of evil. These were first shared with spouses, with family members, and with pastors and church members, long before our meeting.

3   Conclusion

Chapter 4 has situated the investigation of dreams and visions in African contexts within the discussion of epistemology and Pentecostal spirituality on African terms. It has been demonstrated that scholarship in African contexts is attentive to the need to articulate an epistemology that more authentically portrays an African epistemology, and for many, a distinctively Pentecostal one.

This chapter has also brought forth important descriptors for explaining the religious meaning found in the D/Vs of this project. The terms are drawn from the theologizing of Nimi Wariboko on the dynamics of the Spirit in the life and mind of the Pentecostal. These will be carried forward for making vivid the qualities and dynamics in the analyses ahead. "Piercing the veil" will serve as the root metaphor for framing D/V experiences as a whole. The term reflects the reception of spiritual knowledge on Pentecostal, and specifically, Christological terms and the high value of revelatory knowledge. The "pentecostal warrior" will be depicted in the way visioners engage with D/V experiences on practical levels, especially for the practice of prayer. That is because, as Kalu pointed out, spiritual victory is imperative in a worldview where

---

123   Kalu, *African Pentecostalism*, 183.

spiritual warfare is part of normative Christian living. In a milieu where one must deal with spiritual forces, D/Vs are important assets. Also, the analyses will locate the "capacity to begin" and "emergence" (of the pentecostal principle) as dynamics at work as visioners engage with D/V experiences and take on new identities as social agents.

CHAPTER 5

The Big Dreams of African Pentecostals

Visionary Impact and the Christian Life

> I saw ... the heaven open and God poured quails from heaven.
> Raymond Ajagbe, Ibadan, Nigeria[1]

∴

> Jesus came to me and informed me,
> "This lecturer has failed you but I want to show you that I'm with you."
> Elias Francis Mkata, Mwanza, Tanzania[2]

∴

> I wrote all the revelations and dreams in some diaries ... they were many.
> Rotimi Onadipe, Ibadan, Nigeria[3]

∴

Prior chapters have laid the groundwork for examining now how contemporary Pentecostal-Charismatic visioners engage with dreams and visions in African contexts. The goal is to understand how engagement with D/Vs expresses a distinctive pentecostal epistemology. The key is the "big dream," and so statements gleaned from those who wrote in the surveys and others who gave personal interviews about their memorable D/Vs will come into focus in this and

---

1 "Dreams and Visions Transcription," 3.
2 Ibid., 156.
3 A text message received in October of 2016 in reference to his 21 diaries filled with dream reports. Rotimi Onadipe was one of the case studies interviewed later in the Dream and Visions Project in 2017. He is founder/director of Onatech Centre for Research, Counseling and Control of Internet Abuse in Ibadan, Nigeria.

the next chapter. According to Kelly Bulkeley who is featured in Chapter 1, big dreams are the truest reflection of the topics and existential concerns most relevant to the visionary at the time of his or her experience. They are the most memorable and may be remembered years and decades after the experience. Big dreams are also sources of religious meaning. In this chapter, the discussion turns to how these big dream experiences—episodes of piercing the veil for accessing spiritual knowledge (about the "true state of things")—are followed up by the hermeneutical task of making spiritual sense for Pentecostal application. For visioners, it requires careful assessments of biblical and cultural factors that weigh into making meaning from experiential knowledge for living life by the Spirit.

This chapter and the next comprise a type of Luke-Acts presentation. Together, Chapters 5 and 6 describe the visionary experience made manifest in Pentecostal spirituality, including its contribution to identity formation, use of Scriptural understanding for interpretation, and ecclesial reception. Chapter 6 expands on this en-Spirited, biblically informed interpretation of D/Vs introduced here by exploring the association (and disassociation) with prayer, the broader implications for identity formation, and the impact on Pentecostal agency, that is, on missiology. Therefore, Chapter 5 and Chapter 6 are meant to be read reflexively, that is, Chapter 5 reports on issues basic to reception and the perception of Holy Spirit agency while Chapter 6 reflects ensuing missiological effects. Neither stands alone in a portrayal of the impact of D/Vs in the visioners' lives because one aspect can only be understood in light of the other. The epistemic approach described in Chapter 5 informs the meaning-making which leads to behavior, and behavior is conversely a product of the deeply embedded valuation of the D/V experience, albeit (re)shaped by the Pentecostal worldview.

This chapter is divided into two main parts. The first highlights D/V appropriation for Pentecostal-Charismatic interpretation as the process of negotiating with pre-existing indigenous cultural elements and ways of thinking. There is a discussion on universal dream categories, which includes ancestor dreams, where a break with or transformation of traditional understanding is carried out by means of a Spirit-hermeneutic. Therefore, in the first half, what the data reveals about perceptions of Holy Spirit agency in D/V reception and how those impact continuity and discontinuity is brought to the surface. In the second part, the way D/Vs are assessed with the help of Scripture—often communally and with discernment—and then transposed into nourishing and useful knowledge for Christian life is discussed.

1 Continuity and Discontinuity: Dreams and Visions and the Spirit in Africa

This section focuses on the big dreams of seminarians as reflected in their responses to the four pages of survey questions in the "Survey and Interview Guide."[4] Before proceeding, it is helpful to remember the work of Opoku Onyinah in chapter 3 for shedding light on the dynamics of D/V interpretation for the participants of this study. Onyinah explained the recontextualization of *abisa*, which is traditional divinatory consultation with seers, for Pentecostal practice. While *abisa* is a traditional practice, the stewardship of the prophetic gifts of the Spirit for revelation in the Church of Pentecost has retained *abisa* as an epistemic form but "filled it," so to speak, with fresh content derived from the Christian God. This is referred to as recontextualization in the field of religious studies and, in this case, this recontextualization results in continuing with the form of practice for Pentecostalism.

In this section, the topic of the prerogative of the Spirit, which is demonstrated by visioners in the impetus for the recontextualization of certain types of D/Vs, comes into view. It will also become evident that the process of weighing a dream or vision involves navigation of cultural and theological sensibilities that can yield, as in the case of the ancestor dream, different outcomes. This is a very different oneiric tradition than, for example, what is manifested in the dream interpretation manuals of Islamic history. As was shared in chapter 2 by John C. Lamoreaux, the dream manuals passed down through generations show that interpretations of symbols and the meaning drawn from dreams did not change through time. Traditional interpretations were retained in a type of institutionalized form. But in the Pentecostal milieu, while there are inclinations toward similar interpretations, and while D/V interpretation can be and usually is a matter of communal discourse, interpretations are not standardized. The process of D/V interpretation can yield varied results. Assessing one's dreams and visions is funded by Pentecostal culture, but it is still a very personal exercise of the Spirit. Before looking at examples of recontextualization, this next section explores the prominence of the Spirit in D/V interpretation.

1.1 *Spirit Hermeneutics and Universal Dreams*

The ancestor dream reported above is one of a type of dream experience that is reported around the world in different cultures. The categories of the flying dream, the dream of being chased, the lucid dream, along with the ancestor

---

4 See Appendix 1 and also Chapter 1 for details about data collecting.

TABLE 1   Seminarians and universal dreams

Participants	Flying	Being chased	Lucid dream	Ancestor dream
Trinity Theological Seminary, Ghana (TTS)	21.0%	63.2%	21.0%	47.4%
Pentecost Theological Seminary, Ghana (PTS)	59.52%	60.7%	11.9%	53.6%
Evangel Theological Seminary, Nigeria (ETS)	58.8%	61.8%	41.2%	67.6%

dream are represented in Table 1, in terms of participant responses.[5] In this section, the employment of Spirit hermeneutics for the interpretation of the flying dream and the lucid dream points to a Pentecostal rendering of the dream type. The en-Spirited interpretive process demonstrates the recontextualization of a traditional concept in the case of flying dreams. Additionally, the type of lucidity in some D/Vs requires an African rendering of the Western category termed the "lucid" dream. It will be evident that lucidity in the D/V experience is linked to the concept of piercing the veil brought out by Nimi Wariboko.

The dream of flying can be understood in African contexts as participation in witchcraft, a fact that was discovered in the course of interviews and through a conversation with a Ghanaian pastor as we were driving a particular stretch of road in 2014. The pastor reported that it was in that area that villagers had found the body of a witch who had succumbed to the prayers of many people when, while in flight at night, the individual hit a tree and fell dead.[6] In spite of the spiritual stigma of flying, many participants in the study showed no misgivings in sharing reports of flying, especially as they were told in a context of being chased and then rescued by being lifted up into the air by God's divine agency. These recontextualizations of the flying dream by Pentecostal-Charisamtics express the same dynamics that will be noted in the reassessment

---

5   The percentages of ancestor dreams are duplicated here from Figure 3.
6   Shared by an Assemblies of God pastor while on the road from Kumasi to Akropong in 2014.

of the meaning of an ancestor dream. In both interpretive processes, the Spirit is given the prerogative as superintendent of the dream or vision.

The prerogative of God is in view in one of the responses from a 49-year-old seminarian in Nigeria to the question, "[h]ave you ever had a dream of flying?" He replied, "[the] dream of flying is a common occurrence. It depends on what God wants to do. Witches do fly at night. People are given the ability to fly away from danger when attacked in a dream. Flying could be an escape from the enemy's camp."[7] Another seminarian, a 40-year-old man, responded, "[y]es, the Holy Spirit Himself will be flying with me in the air."[8] Another respondent wrote, "I had a dream where I met two people who wanted to arrest me. But by God's intervention, when I mentioned the name of Jesus, I found myself flying over their heads and I escaped."[9] A Ghanaian respondent wrote, "[i]t was like a force (unseen) moving me through the atmosphere to a destination. I was not afraid. I knew somehow it was the Holy Spirit."[10]

A 60-year-old Tanzanian woman recounted a refreshing journey through the air that she experienced and interpreted as a blessing from God. It occurred during a time of frustration and depression in her waking life. In the dream, an angel who came in the appearance of her good friend took her through the night hours in the air to visit different locations:

Anna:	How did you interpret it for yourself?
Interviewee:	Well, I think that when we are really depressed, God can give us relief. He can give us ... like an outing ... refreshing us!
A:	Was there special significance to the types of scenes that you saw?
I:	Well um, I didn't understand but I just thought that it was a relief from my depression and my thoughts, whatever pains ... that He's there for me.[11]

The case of the lucid dream would require much more investigation in order to understand it fully in the experience of these visioners, at least lucidity as it is defined in the West. Lucid dreaming is described in the West as awareness of dreaming during the dream experience. Researchers are advancing in

---

7   Survey #2 ETS.
8   Survey #15 ETS.
9   Survey #36 PTS.
10 Survey #39 PTS.
11 "Dreams and Visions Transcription," 143.

understanding the phenomenon.[12] The brand of lucidity located in Western dream research, though, most likely interfaces with yet does not encompass the scope of phenomena of "literal happenings" or experiencing the "true state of things" that visioners articulate concerning their D/Vs. That phenomenon is often described in this study as that which involves transport in the spiritual realm. The experience is generally described as a vision and *not as a dream*, and therefore seems to require its own categorization.

Regardless, lucidity, or awareness of self-conscious interaction with one's surroundings is characteristic of the experience, and the ability to experience it is attributed to the agency of God. The visioner is piercing the veil to see or to experience events of another, normally unseen realm yielding revelation about the realities of the noumenal (in Wariboko's philosophic terms, see Chapter 4). As Elias Francis Mkata of Tanzania shared in an interview about his experience, "I think God just wanted to show me what it is all about in heaven. He just wanted to show me, so that when I come back I can tell the people of God to prepare themselves."[13]

Vivid awareness of the travel of the soul or spirit among Pentecostal-Charismatics was evident among other visioners who reported their vision experiences. The visioners sometimes narrated visions of encounters with angels or with Jesus, himself. From Jos, Nigeria come three experiences of being transported out of the body as narrated by three different men:

> Well there was this day, which I thought was my last day. I was sleeping and suddenly I was separated from this physical body and I stood and I saw myself lying down on the bed. There was a force conveying me … But then when I was lifted up, then I saw Jesus was also coming from the north … And He was crying.[14]

The vision was reported in detail and closed with the experience of the return to his body:

---

[12] Kelly Bulkeley notes, for example, that the work of Stephen Laberge on lucid dreaming is controversial. Laberge's ground breaking experiments with dreaming at Stanford University were a milestone for dream research, but the application of the knowledge toward a philosophy of higher consciousness which points to developing lucid dreaming as a skill has been critiqued. "Some researchers have argued that actively seeking lucidity in dreams is a violation of the integrity of the dreaming process." See Bulkeley, *Wilderness of Dreams*, 59.

[13] "Dreams and Visions Transcription," 154.

[14] Ibid., 51.

> Then, He looked at me with that passionate face and I was brought back. It's like I was being thrown down and suddenly I was brought back to myself and fixed back to my physical frame.[15]

The second visioner narrated a similar experience he called a vision:

> I was kneeling down and we were singing a song. Suddenly I discovered I had left them, yeah, I found myself being guided by somebody in heaven.[16]

The third man reported:

> In a night vigil, we were holding a night vigil with? and the man of God was praying on everybody and then suddenly I saw myself … I was taken to heaven. And I was between heaven and earth. … I was suspended between heaven and earth.[17]

The purpose of offering these examples of traveling by the Spirit is to allow the visioners themselves to describe the nature of the lucidity in Pentecostal-Charismatic D/Vs that involve travel in the noumenal realm.

1.2 The Spirit and Ancestor Dreams

In the case of dreams of the dead, Pentecostal-Charismatics recontextualize the experience in accordance with their conviction regarding the prerogative of the Spirit. A clearer understanding of the interpretation of D/Vs in which the ancestor or other deceased person appears is heightened when an understanding of how ancestors and the dream life intersect. Umar Danfulani shared insights regarding dreams and visions in the traditional beliefs of his Mupun ancestry of Plateau State in Nigeria. They help to illustrate the traditional terrain in respect to D/Vs and also help to situate the responses found in the written surveys. Dreams were taken seriously in Mupun culture and the interpretation of them was carried out at a "popular level." On the other hand, those who were known for having visions were exceptional people. These seers were referred to as "good children," "beautiful children," "the seeing ones," or the *angas*, which means "the person with the long jaw."[18]

---

15   "Dream and Visions Transcription," 52.
16   Ibid., 44.
17   Ibid., 23.
18   Ibid., 36.

Certain of the respondents' survey answers point out the spiritual undertones of D/Vs among the traditionally religious. For example, a 35-year-old seminarian at PTS who is of the Bono people of the Akan, wrote: "[m]y grandparents were not Christians and therefore do not have the Holy Spirit encounter. Their beliefs in dreams and visions [were] as a result of their gods and ancestors they knew."[19] Other comments presented here come from seminarians at ETS. A 53-year-old man of the Igede people of Nigeria's Benue State wrote on the dreams of his grandparents, "[i]n fact dreams and visions were important to them that they should do or not do certain things, but as revealed to them through dreams/visions, e.g., some marriages, child naming or other family duties are carried out by dreams/visions."[20] Personal interviews also illuminate on the topic of the D/Vs of forefathers. A Tanzanian man shared about his Christian grandparents and their attitude toward dreams:

> A: How do you know dreams and visions were important to your grandparents?
> I: It [was] very important ... because in order to live, in order to do various activities, in order to know how tomorrow would be going, what they wanted to accomplish, they had to have those dreams and visions.
> A: Do you know of a dream or vision your grandparents had? Can you tell me one?
> I: They had [it about] the lands, they planted lands and got money from the crops.
> A: So who had the dream about the land?
> I: My grandfather, he shared it with my grandmother ... not in Mwanza but in Kagela, they were living there.[21]

Among the survey participants, a 31-year-old man of the Gbagyi people in Nigeria wrote, "[p]arents and grandparents in our setting appreciate dreams and visions most especially when they dream of their loved ones."[22] Yet, other informants revealed that dreams of the deceased carry a foreboding connotation in general. One Nigerian female pastor at ETS seminary explained her own perspective regarding a dream of the dead, "I see it as a negative dream with

---

19   Survey #40 PTS.
20   Survey #17 ETS.
21   "Dreams and Visions Transcriptions," 170–171.
22   Survey #16 ETS.

satanic influence which could be the spirit of death hunting."[23] A 49-year-old Igbo man attending ETS shared,

> I have had such a dream where a friend who is late [dead] came, but I resented him because I knew for sure that he was late and should not be visiting. The implication of constant visits of the dead is that the dreamer may die if the dreamer continues to welcome the dead.[24]

In the case of ancestor dreams, the experience can produce considerable anxiety for some Pentecostal-Charismatics, while for others, the prerogative of the Spirit overrides fear since God is free to choose how to relay a divine message. Figure 3 shows the frequency of ancestor dreams or dreams of the dead according to the surveys.[25] In response to the question about whether the visioner had ever dreamt of a deceased person, the Nigerian seminarians of ETS responded positively in 67.6% of the surveys, while Ghanaian seminarians of PTS and TTS responded positively in 53.5% of them, and 47.3% of them, respectively.

To help to situate ancestor dreams within the social imaginary of Africans of Ghana, Anthony Ephirim-Donkor is included here to explain the Akan understanding of ancestors in Ghanaian culture. He shares that the ancestral world is referred to as *Samanadze*, which "points to the location of the ancestral world as above and beyond."[26] Once an elder has fulfilled the requirements for entry into that spiritual community, which is carried out by fulfilling one's "purpose of being," the elder attains entry into that community upon his death.[27] From that celestial location, the ancestor is appointed to "watch over the affairs of the world."[28] Ephirim-Donkor explains, "Akan metaphysics, as we have seen, is such that events in the ancestral world have direct bearing on life in the mundane. In fact, *Samanadze* takes precedence over the mundane since it is the ideal abode of the infallible Ancestors."[29]

The West African ancestor is traditionally a hugely important figure in the community. The lineage of ancestors, for example, is inherently tied to the stool (equivalent to the throne) upon which elders sit and manage the affairs

---

23 Survey #4 ETS.
24 Survey #2 ETS.
25 Ancestor dreams are also recorded in Table 1.
26 Ephirim-Donkor, *African Spirituality*, 139.
27 Ibid., 4.
28 Ibid., 9.
29 Ibid., 141.

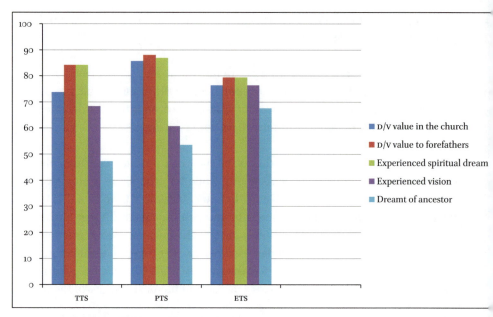

FIGURE 3   Dreams and visions value and experience percentages
TTS: Trinity Theological Seminary, Ghana, 19 survey submissions; PTS: Pentecost Theological Seminary, Ghana, 84 survey submissions; ETS: Evangel Theological Seminary, Nigeria, 34 survey submissions

of the community with the help of their spiritual forefathers. While in Ghana recently, the concept was driven home as enduring and very relevant today. Recent happenings were shared with me in regard to a Ghanaian celebrity whose husband had been called to take the stool and leadership as chief of a certain area. The woman's story was being widely circulated because she was resisting the husband's calling, since it required that he take a second wife. The public was waiting to see if the woman would flee the marriage and the situation. I asked why it was necessary for the man to take a second wife. A female Pentecostal pastor responded in a hushed tone, "[b]ecause the stool is asking for it." Consequently, until today, ancestors are the spirits understood to be in contact with those who have assumed the stool and the leadership as elder in Ghanaian culture.[30]

---

30   An observation from R. S. Rattray in the early 20th century helps to elucidate on this association. In his description of an elaborate procession of the King of Ashanti and the Golden Stool, he writes, "[i]t will be noted that this royal progress was for the express purpose of informing the ancestral ghosts of all the famous houses in Coomassie of the business on hand." See Rattray, *Religion & Art in Ashanti*, 131. Another observation from

The link between the appearance of "masquerades" in dreams and ancestors was brought out by Umar Danfulani in his interview. He explained the metaphysical world of beings as inhabiting the realm of spiritual earth in his Nigerian cosmology (Chapter 4). He also explained the significance of the masquerade as being linked traditionally to spirits since the mask is a tangible representative of the ancestor spirit. As Danfulani puts it, "[i]n traditional days you don't question a masquerade, you believe that actually it is the dead person that is inside it."[31] He also mentioned that the masquerade has taken on a fresh significance in Nigerian culture since criminals will carry out criminal acts today dressed as masquerades. They are feared by people. It would take more questioning to get at the perspective of a particular visioner in regard to the masquerade. For example, in waking life does it signify to the visioner spirits of the dead? Or does it signify violent criminals? Regardless, in the data collections, dream accounts of being chased by masquerades were not uncommon.

While the ancestor dream (and perhaps the dream of masquerades) is generally understood by Christians as taboo and as dangerous interaction with the spirit realm, some types are understood by Pentecostal-Charismatics as orchestrations of the Spirit. In order to show how individuals approached the dreams of ancestors differently, examples from the personal interviews will be interjected ahead. It provides a glimpse into the tension between continuity of traditional attitudes toward ancestor dreams/ dreams of the dead and discontinuity when it comes to the pneumatological imagination. It also demonstrates how that break is navigated in different ways. The dream of the deceased may evoke angst in some visioners, while for others, the Spirit chooses whatever image preferred to relay God's message.

The diversity of Pentecostal response points to confidence in the intervention of the Spirit and also to the powerful emotions (affect) that can accompany the D/V experience. One of the most memorable reports regarding a dream of the dead was an interview with a 29-year-old Ghanaian man. The interview afforded the opportunity to recognize the amount of anxiety that can be present when a dream of the dead is reflected on. He demonstrated a high degree of discomfort as he narrated about several recurring dreams (10 in number) in

---

Ghanaian scholar and former Prime Minister K. A. Busia reads, "[t]he Okyeame informed the ancestors whose stools were in the stool-house that a new chief, their own descendant in the matrilineal line, had been elected to take their place and govern the Division." See K. A. Busia, *The Position of the Chief in the Modern Political System of Ashanti: A Study of the Influence of Contemporary Social Changes on Ashanti Political Institutions* (New York, NY: Oxford University Press, 1951), 13.

31   "Dreams and Visions Transcription," 38.

which his deceased cousin was featured.[32] The cousin repeatedly tried to persuade him to join him in activities. The visioner shared how troubling it was to him that a dead person would keep approaching him in his dreams. According to the report, the dreams came to a stop only after the visioner spent time in fasting and prayers. On the other hand, dreams of the deceased can carry a different affective tone when the deceased is a loved one, as in the case of a Catholic widow (who self-identified as charismatic) living in a village outside of Enugu, Nigeria. Dreams of her deceased husband comforted her.

The crux of this conversation is that Pentecostal-Charismatics are able to recontextualize for a broader interpretation of the dream of the deceased. Raymond Ajagbe of Ibadan, Nigeria revealed a distinct theological framework which demonstrated the reframing of this type of dream:

> A: In the case of one man, his grandmother came to him in his dream and told him actually to go to church. What is your opinion … is it possible that God could send the figure of an ancestor to speak to someone and give them God's message?
> I: Yes, yes, I think so. You know why I said so is, you see, God will use somebody that is so dear to us, that is so close to us, somebody that we respect so much, to pass a message to us. So [God] can use maybe a father or a mother or an ancestor to speak to us, you know, because he knows that we respect those people so much.[33]

When a similar question about the ambivalence of dreams of the dead was posed to a pastor in Jos, Nigeria, he echoed the same optimism, remarking, "[b]ut for somebody to give you a message in a dream, it depends on what God wants to use to pass a message … God can use any medium to pass a message to you."[34] An interview with a pastor in Dar es Salaam, Tanzania resonated with the same confidence in God's means of speaking. In reference to a dream in which his deceased grandmother appeared and gave him information regarding his uncle's predicament, the pastor commented,

---

32   In the case of personal interviews, the oral transmission of the narratives enhanced my experience of them and their meaning—especially the emotional meaning they embodied. For example, emotional cues helped with understanding the significance of the D/V for human flourishing, as in the case of a warning D/V.
33   "Dreams and Visions Transcription," 4.
34   Ibid., 22.

I have come to realize that sometimes God uses a human picture to give someone information because God is a fearful God ... so with me, I interpreted it, He is God who used the body of my late grandmother to inform of that information.[35]

Yet, the limits of the appreciation of dreams of the deceased, especially due to the affiliation of ancestors with African traditional rituals, are evident. The Pentecostal break with ancestor worship has led, for example, according to anthropologist Katrien Pype, to suspicion of certain Spirit churches. She writes, "Born-again Christians refute these churches of the Holy Spirit precisely on the grounds of their too overt link between the Holy Spirit and the ancestors. For Pentecostals, the Holy Spirit is disconnected from ancestors ... and their rituals."[36] What Pype located was the segment of Christianity which, though Pentecostal or self-identifying as Born Again and therefore of a Spirit-oriented renewalist movement, are distinguished from more "radical" Spirit movements. Yet the break with dreams of the dead is much more ambiguous among Pentecostals. It is evident from the perspectives of the visioners of this project that the sense of the *Spirit's overriding prerogative* can inform epistemology. It can override fear of a dream of the dead, registering discontinuity, to some degree, with both traditional perspectives and the Pentecostal reframing Pype located, as in the case of Raymond Ajagbe. In those cases, the Spirit of Christ is in control and pneumatologically sound criteria for receiving spiritual knowledge through ancestor dreams are factored in.

1.3 The Agency of the Spirit and Pentecostal Visioners

The survey answers collected in Ghana at Trinity Theological Seminary (TTS), those of Pentecost Theological Seminary in Ghana (PTS), and those of Evangel Theological Seminary in Nigeria (ETS) give similar indications of the spectrum of theological stance on the agency of God in dream and vision transmission. There was indication that the Holy Spirit was often in the forefront of the minds of visioners in respect to the source of D/Vs. Personal interviews also pointed to the issue of concern regarding the source of D/Vs. One pastor from Enugu, Nigeria reported, "[w]e believe that what makes the dream divine is the source."[37]

---

35 "Dreams and Visions Transcription," 155.
36 Katrien Pype, *The Making of the Pentecostal Melodrama: Religion, Media, and Gender in Kinshasa* (New York, NY: Berghahn Books, 2012, paperback 2015), 47.
37 "The Dreams and Visions Transcription," 93.

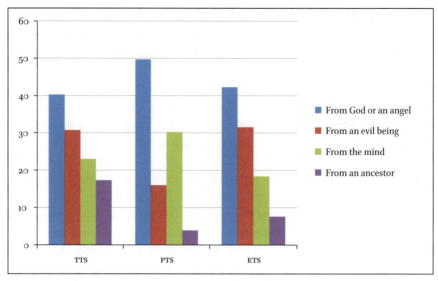

FIGURE 4   West Africa possible D/V sources percentages
TTS: Trinity Theological Seminary, Ghana; PTS: Pentecost Theological Seminary, Ghana; ETS: Evangel Theological Seminary, Nigeria
Note: Individual respondents often indicated more than one source, rather than only one.

The participants who answered the written survey were offered a selection of options to answer, "where spiritual dreams or visions come from," and "the God of the Bible" or "an angel of God" were the most frequent responses (see Figure 4).

When probed for a more specific source from among the options God, the Father, the Holy Spirit, or Jesus, answers varied and often more than one choice was made. Many respondents attributed the experiences to the agency of all three persons of the Trinity. Comparing TTS, PTS and ETS in order to gauge perspectives, it was found that participants at TTS (19 submissions) indicated the Father 16 times, Jesus 9 times, and the Holy Spirit 18 times, participants of PTS (84 submissions) indicated Father 52 times, Jesus 54 times, and the Holy Spirit 79 times, and participants from ETS (34 submissions) indicated Father 24 times, Jesus 18 times, and the Holy Spirit 26 times. There were 3 respondents who indicated *only the Holy Spirit* as the source of D/Vs among TTS respondents, 3 among ETS respondents, and 6 among PTS. One respondent each from TTS and ETS referred to the prophecy of Joel found in Acts 2:17 regarding the pouring out of the Spirit and dreams and visions in the last days:

> And it shall come to pass in the last days, says God
> That I will pour out of My Spirit on all flesh

> Your sons and your daughters shall prophesy
> Your young men shall see visions
> Your old men shall dream dreams

The concept of God as Trinity and a united agency behind D/Vs was indicated by 3 respondents at ETS and 7 respondents at PTS. Among the surveys which indicated the Holy Spirit as the sole agency, several explanations were offered to support the exclusivity of Spirit agency. One was, "[w]e are in the age of the Holy Spirit according to Joel."[38] Others responses were similar, "[w]e are operating presently under grace which is the dispensation under the Holy Spirit"[39] and from a different seminary, "[t]The Holy Spirit is more prominent in this dispensation."[40] And identifying with the Holy Spirit's agency was important to the visioners. As one participant in the survey reported, "I see myself as a Spirit filled person."[41]

While the Holy Spirit is a predominant figure in the theology of dreams and visions in West Africa, Christological underpinnings should not be overlooked. In fact, the appearance of Jesus Christ in the dream or vision was prevalent. The name of Jesus was mentioned 33 times in the D/V narratives during personal interviews and mentioned 15 times in the written surveys. Additionally, the emphasis on "born-again" as a common self-identifier among participants provides a key metaphor by which to assess the Christological support for D/Vs in West Africa.

The gospel of John records Jesus' explanation of the en-Spirited life in terms of being "born again" or "born of the Spirit" (John 3:3, 8). It is clear that the priority of Jesus' words weighs heavily for the value of Spirit agency for Christian spirituality, since one cannot enter the kingdom of God without first experiencing the new birth by means of the Spirit. Likewise, the role of the Spirit in the transmission of a dream or vision is a corollary of a solid footing in the knowledge of the Christ of the gospels. As will be seen in the reports of visions of Jesus that describe the experience as sometimes imparting a physical healing or healing effect, Jesus is very much a central figure in many D/Vs. Therefore, the pneumatological imagination at work in these visioners is inherently *Christ*ian.[42]

---

38   Survey # 11 ETS.
39   Survey #10 ETS.
40   Survey #115 PTS.
41   "Spontaneous Dream and Vision Reports from Surveys," 11.
42   Scholar of West African studies, Clifton R. Clarke, refers to the role of Christology in relation to healing in African contexts. Clarke explains that African epistemology links the

The specifics regarding Holy Spirit agency in the reception of the dream or vision were reported. One of the questions posed in the survey and personal interview was "In your opinion, how do God and the mind work together in the dream or vision experience?" A clear and in depth explanation of the pneumatological dynamics at work in Pentecostal epistemology was offered by a 44-year-old man in an interview that took place in Enugu, Nigeria. It is worth quoting here at length. It articulates Trinitarian dynamics as well as the work of the Spirit in interaction with the mind/soul, and spirit of an individual.

I: I believe dreams come from the Father, the Son, and the Holy Spirit.
A: At the same time ... or ... how do you ...?
I: Well, the Father and the Son and the Holy Spirit ... they are One Triune God with three distinct personalities. So, when the Holy Spirit is revealing I believe it is the Father revealing, when Jesus is revealing, I believe it is the Holy Spirit revealing. They work together. They are always in agreement eternally united and eternally One.
A: In your opinion, how do God and the mind work together?
I: Well, I believe that God works in our lives through the person of the Holy Spirit who indwells every individual believer. But in my own understanding, I believe the Holy Spirit dwells not in our mind but in our spirit, you know? ... I believe the indwelling Spirit joins himself to our human spirit when we get born again.
A: Then, where does the mind come into the picture?
I: Well, I believe the mind is an integral part of the soul, you know? I believe the soul simply is the mind, the will, the emotion. What we think, what we will, what we feel ... if I put it in another way: your thinker, your feeler, your willer, that's what I believe make up the soul. So the mind is the seat of thought. And this mind can be said to have two parts, the conscious and the subconscious.

---

concept of power to *healing and wholeness* and knowing Christ is experienced in terms that are tangible, embodied, and communal. Clarke shows that understanding Christ as Healer is tied to the African view of existential interrelatedness. As Clarke puts it, "[t]he appeal of Christ as Healer within an African Pentecostal context is predicated upon a worldview that healing and health are inextricably connected to social behavior, moral conduct, and spiritual forces." Therefore, Christ is the superior power who brings healing in the midst of the dilemma of collective sins and the disharmony at the root of so many social ills. This theology of healing accentuates the distinctive feature of interrelatedness that sets African epistemology apart from the Western rendering of knowledge, with its criteria of autonomy and abstraction. See Clifton R. Clarke, *Pentecostal Theology in Africa* (Eugene, OR: Pickwick Publications, 2014), 71.

A: So when a person sleeps, in the case of a spiritual dream from a Christian, then you're saying that the Spirit is not out here somewhere and coming to drop a dream in. The Spirit is already dwelling.
I: *In* the believer.
A: In the believer. So you're saying that at some point during the dream the Spirit ... of Christ imparts from within.
I: Yeah, of course. So it is with our spirit that we make direct contact with God ... Then the influence of our contact with God in the spirit impacts on the different parts of our soul, on our thinking—*especially on our thinking*—then to our will, then to our feelings.[43]

Another interview given by a 36-year-old man in Dar es Salaam, Tanzania shared a similar understanding of the priority of experiencing the Spirit of God in the human spirit and the role of the dream:

> When we go to sleep what we lose is that eyes cannot see anything, nothing you can touch. Now that spirit that remains has two influences in that realm of the spirit, influence from the power of God and the Spirit of God and the power of Satan. Because both God and Satan, they are spirits ... The spirit who dominates you is the spirit who dominates your dreams ... Many Christians do not experience the Holy Spirit the way we should experience God, because we do things for the mind, but for the spirit we don't touch. And the dreams play that important role. It can make you understand very simply. Because when you go to sleep, that dream you dream will show the status of your spirit.[44]

As indicated from this interview, the visioner believes that the Spirit enlightens through the dream experience in such a way as to inform and provide understanding about spiritual realities (the true state of things). As will be pointed out in the next chapter, visioners point to an impartation of diagnostic knowledge they say is helpful for spiritual warfare, or for the well-being of the church. Therefore, en-Spirited knowing of pneumatological imagination impacts for solving real life issues in the lives of visioners, a fact that points to a very pragmatic aspect of Pentecostal epistemology. In addition, as the excerpt from this last visioner pointed out, dreams can be the playing field for Satan

---

43 "Dreams and Visions Transcription," 104–105.
44 Ibid., 215–216.

just as much as a sacred space for God, situating the "public sphere" of D/Vs as a location of diverse influences. Hence, D/Vs can reflect spiritual warfare and the struggle between good and evil. The concern with spiritual warfare and well-being will be highlighted in the multivariate tests showing association of key variables in Chapter 6.

The way visioners associate the Holy Spirit with their D/V experiences is also demonstrated in the results of multivariate tests. For example, for East African participants of *personal interviews*, a test of the association between the mention of the Holy Spirit and the SS D/V yielded significance.[45] To be specific, in 8 out of 28 cases of non-SS D/Vs there was mention of the Holy Spirit in or around the narrative (28.5% of the time). At the same time, in 40 out of 78 cases of the SS D/V there was mention of the Holy Spirit in or around the narrative (51.2%). Therefore, the mention of the Holy Spirit is associated with a significantly higher proportion of SS D/Vs than non- SS D/Vs: $\chi^2(1) = 4.289$, $p < .05$; Fisher's exact test, $p < .05$; $\varphi = .201$.

The introduction here of the "SS D/V index score" will help to understand another method that was used for testing the association found with mentions of the Holy Spirit. Visioners were rated in terms of an SS D/V index score given to each which ranged between zero and six. A visioner with a score of two, for example, was an individual who reported a total of two spiritually significant dreams or visions (SS D/Vs). The Mann-Whitney *U* test achieved statistical significance when looking for possible association between mentions of the Holy Spirit and experience of SS D/Vs. In the case of East African visioners, SS D/V experiences were significantly tied to the mention of the Holy Spirit when the median SS D/V index total scores were examined. A significantly lower median SS D/V total score was associated with no mention of the Holy Spirit.

---

45   Apart from the "nourishing/spiritually edifying" D/V experiences drawn from the surveys, another categorization of D/V experiences called the "spiritually significant" D/Vs (SS D/Vs) was drawn from the collection of both sets of data. When a dream or vision was marked by certain characteristics, it was coded (along with demographic, gender, and other coding) according to six D/V types which comprise the SS DVs (see Appendix 2 for coding). Narrative analyses yielded these six SS DV types: (1) spiritual warfare (2) predictive (3) warning (4) warning and predictive (5) DAME (directive, affirming, motivational, or encouraging), and (6) healing (healing for self or another). While the categories for the "nourishing/spiritually edifying" D/V and the SS D/V are often the same or similar, the categories of the SS D/Vs are not taken from what visioners said about the impact of the D/V experience. The SS/DV categories are this researcher's grouping of the content of the D/V narratives according to prominent features. Again, the assessment was drawn from both surveys and personal interview transcriptions.

HS	obs	rank sum	expected
0	58	2782.5	3103
1	48	2888.5	2568

z = -2.402, Prob > |z| = 0.0163

An unexpected result found in the surveys—which, again, were for the most part representative of West rather than East African D/V experience—was a disassociation between mentions of the Holy Spirit and ss D/Vs. This is in contrast to the findings relating to the association between mention of the Holy Spirit and ss D/Vs for East Africans who took part in personal interviews (as was mentioned above). This disassociation for West Africans may signify that the ss D/V experience was not contingent upon the visioner's cognitive recognition or affirmation of the involvement of the Holy Spirit.

The following explains how that disassociation was detected. As already mentioned, the survey asked for an indication of the visioner's understanding of the origin of a spiritual dream. Participant surveys which had the option "they come from God the Holy Spirit" circled for question B were coded with hs. Surveys that featured a written mention of the Holy Spirit were coded HS, and those that featured the circling of Holy Spirit for question B *as well as offering a mention* of the Holy Spirit elsewhere were coded HSS. In the case of the Mann-Whitney U test of the association between the West African participants' reference to the Holy Spirit and the participants' ss D/V index score (again, ranging zero to six), the median score was found to be higher than expected when there was no mention of the Holy Spirit, and lower than expected when there was a mention of the Holy Spirit.

HS	obs	rank sum	expected
0	93	6761	6370.5
1	43	2555	2945.5

z = 2.001, Prob > |z| = 0.0454

If the mentions of the Holy Spirit are indications of mental engagement with the person of the Holy Spirit, the indications may be that the ss D/V experience for West African participants depicts less significance of cognitive engagement with the Spirit for these visioners. For West African Pentecostal-Charismatics, then, the person of the Holy Spirit may not have to be on your mind in order for the Spirit's benefits to come through your mind in the manifestation of dreams and visions.

In summary, the association of D/Vs with the Holy Spirit in the minds of the visioners is significant and worth noting. It reflects the valuation of the experiences and their importance and legitimacy for spirituality. Still, other sources were acknowledged. The fact that the agency of an ancestor or of an evil being is a possible source of a spiritual dream for visioners can be noted in Figure 4, as well as the understanding that some dreams simply represent the mind at work in dreams in conventional ways. Regarding conventional dreams, Umar Danfulani explained in his interview what he has learned through his role counseling at God's Divine Grace Mission. He commented on how the visioners' exploration of his or her dreams may not, in fact, reveal any foreign agencies or influences at all. Rather, dreams of the mind can "point everything back to you, yourself."[46] He said, "[s]ome you're actually dealing with yourself. In fact, some, you check, no demon, no witch whatsoever but it's just your social life, the way you handled yourself, the way you have led yourself."[47] Similarly, the understanding of dreams as mundane expressions of the mind and the psychic state of the self registered as one source of dreams.

Nevertheless, the claims of experiences of D/Vs sent by God were numerous, and the Holy Spirit was the predominant figure believed to be the agent behind their reception and the aid to their interpretation. To reinforce this is the answer given by a 29-year-old Tanzanian woman to the question, "[d]o you interpret all of your own dreams and visions by yourself?" She replied, "I highly depend on the Holy Spirit to interpret them for me."

Before moving from the topic of the sources of the spiritual D/V, the case of Opoku Onyinah should be included here since Onyinah reported knowledge derived from an angel. While some surveys from the seminarians also indicated that an angel could be a source of a dream or vision, no incident similar to that contained in Onyinah's report was offered. As was discussed in the section about the sleeping state and angelology in Chapter 3, Onyinah's associate reported to him that the angel Michael spoke through Onyinah while he was in a sleeping state. I attempted to collect the opinion of other visioners on the subject during personal interviews in which I referred to the case without mentioning Onyinah directly. I wanted to get a sense of what others

---

46   "Dreams and Visions Transcription," 38.
47   Ibid., 37.

might think about it. Responses were not uniform as is evident in the following excerpt in which I probe about the matter with a visioner in Jos, Nigeria:

A: So, do you think that it's biblical and okay if the angel, if Michael was speaking from inside?
I: It wasn't the man speaking, it was the Spirit of God speaking.
A: But the voice said, "I am Michael." Because I shared this with another Rev. and he didn't quite like it, that an angel was talking from inside of a pastor.
I: God can do anything, God can do anything.

While open to theologizing about the Spirit, my own way of knowing was tested for its limits and significantly challenged when listening to Onyinah's report. On the issue of angelology and D/V reception, the narrative impacted my theological "comfort level." As to whether visioners in African contexts would consider Onyinah's experience as orthodox, by Pentecostal standards, more research on the matter would be required to make a determination.

2 Dreams and Visions and the Christian Life

In this section, three aspects of engagement with dreams and visions for Christian life are explored which depict the epistemic exercises involved in D/V valuation and evaluation. The first is the use of Scripture and the counsel of others in the assessment of the D/V experience. In fact, a Spirit hermeneutic for D/V interpretation is in view, where the visioner (guided by the Spirit) interacts with the Word and the faith community in the process of interpretation. The second aspect of engagement involves how these interpretations effect the visioner as the divine messages are transposed for practical spirituality. It becomes evident that the experiences are spiritually nourishing in different ways and that they are interpreted as useful for personal and spiritual edification. The comments in this section on how D/V experiences impact Christian life in practical ways stop short, though, of delving into the deeper effects of the experiences. Noting the effect of the experiences on the prayer life, looking closely at how they impact Christian identity, and investigating their impact for missions is reserved for the next chapter.

The last aspect of engagement pertains to attitudes about D/V experiences, the ambivalence in the Church regarding them, and the importance of spiritual discernment for processing the D/V experience. There is a sense of caution relayed in the surveys and interviews that points to how the value of D/Vs is accompanied by reliance on discernment through the Spirit. This reliance on the Spirit for discernment allows Pentecostal-Charismatics to retain the traditional conviction that important spiritual knowledge can be accessed through a dream or vision.

2.1   Visioners and Spirit–Word–Community

The visioners of the study demonstrated that Scriptural authority is important to the process of deriving meaning from D/Vs. Therefore, Scriptures about dreams and visions hold special significance because they point to the possibilities for their own personal lives. The combination of focus on Scripture as it was introduced by teachers of the mission churches and the present day attention to the agency of the Holy Spirit characterizes this melding of the Spirit and the Word for this epistemology. Therefore, visioners find support from the Bible for gaining knowledge and insight through D/Vs perceived as experiences of the Spirit. This was true among participants in Togo. In interviews, Togolese participants shared about the influence of Western Assemblies of God missions along these lines. These missionaries taught about the spiritual value of D/Vs by pointing them out in Scripture and by sharing about their own experiences. Consequently, the visioners of the Assemblies of God in Togo expressed a high appreciation for the AG missionaries on this issue.

Engagement with D/Vs for interpretation is not only dialectic, that is, not only involving the visioner and his or her reading of Scripture. The hermeneutical process of D/V appreciation is understood as triadic, in that, not only does the visioner gain understanding through the Spirit in conversation with Scripture, but also often in conversation with others in the faith community. It is helpful to reference again the woman from Tanzania who stated "I highly depend on the Holy Spirit to interpret them for me."[48] Also, certain Scriptures have already been referenced, especially the visioners' interpretation of Numbers 12:6 and Acts 2:17, the latter containing Joel's prophecy of the pouring out of the Spirit in association with D/Vs. Yet, the voice of other trusted believers was an important key to interpretation.

Among the surveys, Scriptures were referenced 22.8% of the time, and in personal interviews the frequency of mention was 44.8%. But Scriptures are not the only elements funding narratives. The pneumatological imagination is heavily saturated with biblical metaphors, or in the case of "the true state of things," literal or quasi-metaphorical biblical icons. Elias Francis Mkata of Tanzania explained, "[w]hen it comes to interpreting dreams, God uses a

---

48   "Dream and Visions Transcription," 208.

picture, the language of picture."[49] Accordingly, images found in the narratives include the lion, the snake, the Bible, the 24 elders, the throne of God, the blood of Jesus, the hand of Jesus, angels, people in white garments, mountains that are ascended, along with the voice of God and other elements. Spirit and Word are essential elements of D/V appreciation and interpretation.

Equally important, the data revealed that the interpretation of D/Vs was often a collective process, demonstrating the Spirit–Word–Community trialectic.[50] Often the first person to hear a visioner's D/V report is a spouse or parent. As Umar Danfulani reported, "I wake up. My wife wakes up. We ask each other, "[w]hat message did you get during the night?" And we discuss our dreams."[51] As will be explained in the discussion ahead of D/V experiences in the Church, pastors are also often involved. For example, when asked if people come to him with their dreams, a pastor in Enugu, Nigeria said, "Sure! Sure! They do, and as the Lord gives me enablement I interpret dreams."[52]

In another interview, a Tanzanian woman reported that a pastor's wife dreamt that her husband had died in the hospital where he was, in fact, being treated for some illness. "So she shared it with the church members and the intercessors. All agreed to enter into prayer and by the grace of God their pastor was healed."[53]

More about pastoral influence will be included as the discussion continues, but here, it seems appropriate to add the experience of a visioner who received an interpretation from an unexpected source. It may demonstrate the importance of drawing the baseline of counselors to include an even broader segment of the community of faith in the trialectic of Spirit hermeneutics. In an unforgettable instance that took place in Nigeria, a medical doctor politely answered the questions that helped to situate him and his contribution to the study. Personal interviews were always very flexible, and at one point, the conversation leaned toward his spiritual life as the man offered a window into the reflective season he was passing through. He talked about how he had recently experienced a special season of humbling himself for a closer walk with God. The interview steered toward the last crucial questions about whether he had

---

49 "Dreams and Visions Transcription," 155.
50 This trialectic is revisited in Chapter 7 where the theology of Amos Yong is brought in. Yong explains Pentecostal theology as expressing the agency of the Spirit animating the epistemic dynamic of interaction between the Word and Community. Yong's Spirit–Word–Community trialectic frames the hermeneutical process at work in human cognition based upon foundational pneumatology. Yong, *Spirit–Word–Community*, 219–220.
51 "Dream and Visions Transcription," 33.
52 Ibid., 84.
53 Ibid., 165.

a significant dream or vision to share (big dream), and if so, how it had impacted him. He began to share about a dream that had troubled him. As he narrated it, he became visibly distressed, until he eventually began to sob. In the dream, he had disrobed out in the open, and upon awakening, it had alarmed him so much that he shared it with some trusted others. He was told that he had surely been involved in some sinful conduct in the spiritual realm at night, and that he should repent. The interpretation of the dream had followed in the characteristic manner of interpreting a dream as a literal event.

After the interview had come to a close and the recording device was turned off, a metaphoric meaning of the dream surfaced in my mind. When I offered my own sense of interpretation, sharing that the dream seemed to reiterate his humility and the stripping down of himself (of pride) before God—just as he had articulated earlier as his present life stance—the man became reflective and visibly relieved. With tears of joy he exclaimed, "Oh how I thank God that He has sent you to show me the true meaning!" As the incident illustrates, the community of faith is an important element of Spirit hermeneutics. Perhaps it speaks even beyond the matters of D/V interpretation to other considerations where the Church stands to benefit from broadening the base of counselors.

2.2   *Dreams, Visions and Practical Spirituality*

A look at the D/V themes that surfaced among the surveys gives an idea of why the visioners of the Dreams and Vision Project expressed gratitude for their experiences. The benefits that visioners said they derive from dreams and visions range from claims of inspiration for prayer to reports of having received directives as practical as blue prints for the design of church buildings and knowledge for the answers to school exams. This section explains how D/V experiences fund an epistemology that is spiritually nourishing as well as tangibly practical for meeting needs and challenges. Pentecostal epistemology is linked to a type of religious pragmatism where visioners perceive God in the interventions and solutions drawn from the D/V experience.

Seminarians of the ecumenical Trinity Theological Seminary (TTS), where Presbyterian and Methodist participants self-identified as "pentecostal" and "charismatic," valued D/Vs just as much as those of the two other Pentecostal seminaries. That fact demonstrates that the usefulness of D/Vs spills across denominational and cultural boundaries in the contexts of those who participated in the study. In fact, TTS visioners shared higher numbers of personally important D/Vs in several categories. Those categories, along with the others that surfaced, are shown in Table 2 and reflect the way the experiences provide useful knowledge for the visioners who experience them.

TABLE 2 Dream and vision themes of seminarians

Dream and vision themes	Trinity theological seminary (19 survey submissions)[a]	Pentecost theological seminary (84 survey submissions)[b]	Evangel theological seminary (34 survey submissions)[c]
Knowledge/warning	47%	25%	9.3%
Insight for church	11.7%	3.9%	4.6%
Healing/mystical	23.5%	3.9%	13.9%
Spiritual Warfare	29.4%	10.5%	13.9%
Conversion/ministry	29.4%	76%	30.2%
Nourishing/spiritually edifying[e]	88.2%	67.1%	69.7%
Angel	5.8%	1.3%	2.3%
Jesus/God	5.8%	3.9%	9.3%
Ancestor or other deceased	–[d]	2.6%	–[d]

a These written submissions yielded 17 dream accounts. These accounts and all other reports registered here in Table 2 were spontaneous contributions to the question, "[c]an you share about a dream or vision that was significant to you?" Therefore, this data does not reflect the responses to questions meant to probe on a specific topic. For example, dreams of flying ("Have you ever had a dream of flying?") were specifically solicited and are treated in Table 1. For this reason, note that seminarians of TTS here in Table 2 did not spontaneously offer a dream of an ancestor, but Table 1 shows that almost 50% of respondents shared about dreaming of the deceased *when prompted*.
b These written submissions yielded 76 dream accounts.
c These written submissions yielded 43 dream accounts.
d This reflects that there were no ancestor dreams offered among the *spontaneous contributions* from surveys of these seminarians.
e See Table 3 for details on the nourishing impact of D/Vs.

Data[54] pertaining to the "spontaneous D/V" is the contribution that is depicted in Table 2. This D/V is spontaneous in the sense that the participant did not respond to any particular prompt in the questionnaire (as was the case in questions which yielded the data in Table 1 and Figures 3 and 4). Rather, respondents were just asked to write about any significant dream or vision they had experienced. As has already been established, the purpose was to get at the big dream of religious significance. Nine categories became apparent and TTS showed the most frequency of mentions in six of them: knowledge and warning 47%, insight for church 11.7%, healing/mystical 23.5%, spiritual warfare 29.4%, nourishing/spiritually edifying 88.2%, and mention of angels 5.8%. Seminarians of PTS mentioned conversion/ministry related D/Vs more often, that is, 76% of the time, and seminarians of ETS mentioned Jesus or God within narratives most frequently, 9.3% of the time. Many D/Vs were "nourishing" ones for participants of all three groups. 88.2% of D/Vs were nourishing for seminarians of TTS, 67.1% were nourishing for those at PTS, and at ETS 69.7% were nourishing D/Vs.

The category described as "nourishing/spiritually edifying" was contructed using details drawn from a question which asked how the significant dream or vision they had reported *had actually impacted their life.* The nourishing/ spiritually edifying D/V is marked by at least one of six features: inspired faith, inspired prayer, strengthened identity and/or Christian commitment, gave guidance, gave assurance, or inspired a feeling of joy. Participants from TTS reported more incidences of a D/V strengthening identity and/ or Christian commitment, 33.3%. Respondents from PTS more frequently mentioned D/Vs which gave assurance, 17.6%. Respondents from ETS in Nigeria reported more frequently the D/Vs that inspired faith 33.3% and that gave guidance 20%. These are displayed in Table 3.

It is evident that the nourishing dream or vision is depicted by visioners as a stimulating experience for spiritual growth in Christian identity and commitment. Some participants shared about coming to initial faith in Christ through the experiences. The experience of women in particular will be addressed in Chapter 6. There are certain aspects of female experience with D/Vs that merit a look at how D/Vs provide "shoving-power" for agency requiring the navigation of impediments that arise due to gender. Here, a few examples of the practical benefits of D/V experience include the female voice. One female pastor

---

54 Some D/V narratives are counted in more than one category. For example, the dream of an attack on the pastor is categorized as a "warning dream" as well as "insight for the church."

TABLE 3   Nourishing/spiritually edifying dreams and visions

Spiritual impact of D/V	Trinity theological seminary	Pentecostal theological seminary	Evangel theological seminary
Inspired faith	26.6%[a]	21.5%[b]	33.3%[c]
Inspired prayer	20%	11.7%	20%
Strengthened identity and/or commitment	33.3%	27.4%	13.3%
Gave guidance	13.3%	19.6%	20%
Gave assurance	13.3%	17.6%	13.3%
Feeling of joy	–	1.9%	–

This data is derived from a portion of the survey which asked how the significant D/V he or she reported impacted their lives. As in Table 2, some experiences fall into more than one category.
a   Percentage out of 15 comments among these 19 submissions.
b   Percentage out of 51 comments among these 84 submissions.
c   Percentage out of 30 total comments among these 34 submissions.

from Jos, Nigeria shared about her experiences with revelations of the answers to school exams:

> I: While a student I kept asking the Holy Spirit, "Holy Spirit, the Bible says you will teach me all things." The Holy Spirit really helped me. I came first in my class every year. The Holy Spirit would show me the papers before the examination day.
>
> A: He would show you what? The questions?
>
> I: Yes, yes. In my sleep I would see it, question 1: What is the factors of this, what is this, this, this ... I'd see it. I'd write down what I saw, when I got to the examination it was exactly what I got to see there.[55]

In another case, the information offered from a Baptist pastor in Nigeria—who carefully qualified the extent of his identification with the Charismatic

---

55   "Dreams and Visions Transcription," 13.

movement—revealed how dreams were used to call him to embark on two church building projects:

> I: One day I dreamed I saw the church that I built. The Lord just gave me instruction how the church ... this is how I should get the place, how to write a letter, go from this place to this angle. That one was a rectangular form. When I finished that building I saw myself building a church again.
> A: In a dream?
> I: A second dream! The church where I saw myself coming up and down was a circle church.
> A: So when you came you saw it was circular like in the dream.
> I: No! I did the design of this church with what I saw in the dream.[56]

In some dreams, symbols and signs were pronounced in their metaphorical value and pointed to crucial issues. For example, a dream of a mango tree with unripe mangoes spoke powerfully to a woman in Enugu, Nigeria. She interpreted the warning in the dream to refrain from picking the unripe mango as a sign that she should not be hasty to become pregnant after her recent miscarriage, but rather wait until her body had sufficiently recovered from the trauma.[57]

2.3   *Attitudes in the Church toward Dreams and Visions*

The question of whether dreams and visions are valued in the ecclesiastic contexts of visioners was an important one. It revealed a degree of dissonance in attitudes toward D/Vs for Pentecostal-Charismatic epistemology and spirituality. As already mentioned in Chapter 1, one event experienced during data collection signaled the disavowal of D/Vs experience. A particular seminary campus seemed a good choice for data collection due to a conversation with a professor there a few years prior. Having heard me explain the research topic, he had shared that at least half of the applications he had seen come through included testimonies of dreams that had inspired the candidate to go to seminary. Yet, upon arriving for data collection, I experienced an unexpected glitch. The administrators explained that they preferred not to have their students

---

[56] "Dreams and Visions Transcription, 66.
[57] Ibid., 101.

take part because, "[d]reams and visions are not important to our students' Christianity." The perplexing situation does seem to imply a disconnect between the values of students and the perspective of the institutional elite.[58]

Where permission was granted, the data revealed that seminarians from all seminary locations and also the students of the Bible institute viewed the Church in their contexts as accepting of the value of D/Vs for Christianity.[59] The survey question read, "[i]f you attend a church, do you think dreams and visions are important to people at church?" Figure 3 shows that those of the Church of Pentecost at PTS in Ghana affirmed the importance of D/Vs for the Church 85.7% of the time in their survey responses. Seminarians of TTS, also in Ghana, affirmed their importance to the Church in 73.7% of the surveys, while Nigerians of ETS in Jos affirmed the importance of D/Vs for the Church in 76.4% of the surveys.

Interestingly, for all three populations, the number of positive responses regarding the value of D/Vs in the Church is fewer in comparison with the number of positive responses for the value of D/Vs in the lives of their forefathers. The incongruence resonates with the conclusions of Nelson Hayashida in regard to the Zambian context (see Chapter 3). Hayashida posited that the valuation of dreams was discouraged, to a degree, in Baptist churches.

As already noted (also in Chapter 3), the personal interview with former Chairman of the Church of Pentecost, Opoku Onyinah, revealed his high appreciation for D/Vs for the Church. For this reason, and perhaps also due to his scholarship and the published report of his own extraordinary sleep experience, it is not surprising to see in Figure 3 that the highest estimation for D/V appreciation in the churches was registered among the seminarians of the Church of Pentecost (Pentecost Theological Seminary).

The personal interviews gave several glimpses of the value of D/Vs in the churches. For example, in one interview, an associate of the lead pastor shared about a dream that had warned him that the pastor was going to face arguments in the church. The next morning in church a member began to confront the pastor angrily in front of the congregation. This associate found he had been prepared through the dream, and he quickly went to the front of the

---

58 Perhaps of significance is the fact that the senior academic officer present in our meeting was non-African. This is also shared in Chapter 1.
59 See Table 2. The survey was only administered orally in Togo in the form of a personal interview (my choice with the aim of securing a more comprehensive pool of data), but the audio of the interviews was lost and only certain notes retained. Those interviews, therefore, do not appear in the graphs. Notes that do remain from the interviews in Togo were included at the end of the document "Dream Narratives from the Audio Recordings of the Dreams and Visions Project."

church to assist the pastor.[60] Also, several excerpts from the personal interviews show the willingness of congregants to go to their pastors with questions about D/Vs and the eagerness of pastors to counsel them. There is a high valuation of D/Vs on the part of both populations. As was already noted earlier in this section, when a Nigerian pastor was asked, "[d]o people come to you as a pastor sometimes with their dream or vision?" he responded, "Sure! Sure! They do, and as the Lord gives me enablement I interpret dreams."[61]

One 24-year-old Tanzanian woman was advised by her mother to share her dream with their pastor. According to the report, "[her] pastor gave her the translation about the three stages and the fire ... that fire was not a normal fire, it was a transforming fire to help ... so that you can go to heaven."[62] A 54-year-old Nigerian woman, when asked whether people in the Assemblies of God in Nigeria feel comfortable sharing their dreams with their pastors, said, "[i]n fact when you have a dream, when you wake up ... the next person you tell is your pastor because he is a spiritual man ... and that is the best person who can give you an interpretation so you don't go astray."[63] A 26-year-old Ugandan woman interviewed in Tanzania shared that, from her perspective, the pastors of the Assemblies of God have an open attitude toward dreams.[64]

One interesting narrative describes a churchman who is a prophetic visioner and who ministered significantly to a pastor. It has the hallmarks of a case of piercing the veil for timely information that would prepare him to counsel the pastor and impact the local church for good. The case of this man of the Assemblies of God in Tanzania consists of a dream in which it was revealed to him that a pastor in another city was making the wrong choice of a marriage partner. To be specific, the dream showed that the woman the pastor was courting did not have the capacity to help the man fulfill the work he had been called to. The man, therefore, called the pastor on the phone.

After receiving the warning from the visioner, the pastor deliberated for some time, making the idea of a break off with the woman a matter of prayer. After eventually deciding to do so, he asked the visioner if he had knowledge of who he was, in fact, called to marry. The visioner prayed about the matter and received the information by revelation. He then informed the pastor of the name of the woman he believed God had chosen for the pastor. The pastor

---

60 Unfortunately, this narrative was part of the lost audio portions.
61 "Dreams and Visions Transcriptions," 84.
62 Ibid., 168.
63 Ibid., 121–122.
64 Ibid., 160.

recognized the name as that of a woman he had led to Jesus in another city, and today they are married.[65]

While many pastors welcomed the revelatory knowledge D/Vs are reported to convey, some interview responses revealed a degree of ambivalence in the churches regarding D/Vs. Others emphasized the importance of having a discerning spirit when it comes to D/V experiences. Another Assemblies of God pastor of Tanzania described a gap between the value of dreams and *teachings about their value* in the church:

Anna:	Do you think dreams are important in the Assemblies of God church … to the people?
Translator:	Dreams are very important if that kind of dream comes from God himself, yeah, we must obey and follow it. However … there are other kinds of dreams that are not from God, so he doesn't think those are important to the church … To some members of the church dreamsand visions are of importance, if they have understood about dreams.
A:	Does the pastoral staff in his church teach about dreams and visions to train the people?
T:	[He says] at present we are not yet teaching people about dreams and visions.[66]

A 60-year-old woman of the Tanzanian Assemblies of God commented:

> In church we don't talk a lot about the dreams, but when I studied the Bible is when I understood that dreams and visions are very, very key, especially [for] the born-again, Pentecostal people, because they can impact the church, help the church to grow, [and] bring things which God wants them to do.[67]

A Nigerian pastor spoke frankly about the attitude of some in respect to D/Vs. He said, "I've heard ministers of the gospel teaching against dream, condemning dream. I've heard them severally … in places on radio, on television, and then physically when I'm there."[68] In Tanzania, the issue of a false prophet

---

65 "Dreams and Visions Transcription," 158–159.
66 Ibid., 192.
67 Ibid., 143.
68 Ibid., 19.

who used D/Vs to deceive his church in Uganda and to bring them all to death by fire was brought up in an interview.[69] Therefore, the need for discernment was emphasized:

> I: The Church must be careful with dreams and visions because they are intruders coming with their own business. Yeah, there is a lot of destruction with dreams and visions if it is not well used.
> A: A lot of destruction?
> I: Yeah.
> A: Destruction, you mean the dreams and visions destroy?
> I: They can destroy! They can destroy life.[70]

A different Tanzanian pastor also emphasized discernment. He said:

> The Church should depend on the Word of God first. If dreams and visions come they should be tested by the Word of God. In 1 John 3:1 it says we should test the spirits [to see] if they come from God or the evil side. There are so many spirits operating, if you allow everyone to tell their dreams or vision you can allow chaos in the Church.[71]

In Togo, the General Superintendent of the Assemblies of God, Djakouti Mitré, shared that it is important to carefully give instruction to those who say they have had dreams revealing their enemies. The Holy Spirit brings unity and not division, and therefore there should be discernment regarding churches that may be enticing their members with manipulation through claims of dreams.[72]

It is apparent that, for the participants of the study, D/V valuation is not without its concerns, is not always straightforward and openly expressed, and nor is it found consistently encouraged throughout the Pentecostal-Charismatic churches of the participants. What has become clear, though, is that D/Vs are indeed significant to the spirituality of West African seminarians and their colleagues from neighboring African nations, along with the Tanzanian participants of this study, a revelation that offers a corrective to those who have assumed otherwise.

---

69 This incident was also brought up to me by African scholars during the conference of the Society for African Life and Thought hosted by Stellenbosch University in Sept. of 2018.
70 "Dreams and Visions Transcriptions," 176.
71 Ibid., 175.
72 "Dream Narratives from the Audio Recordings of the Dreams and Visions Project," 31. Though this audio recording was lost the notes of it were retained.

3 Conclusion

In this chapter, the contours of this epistemology have emerged to show important distinctive characteristics. Pentecostal epistemology employs basic beliefs about the accessibility of the noumenal (piercing the veil) for an epistemology that is essentially practical for Christian living. It is also a way of knowing that reshapes traditional concepts for a Pentecostal recontextualization that continues with certain aspects of traditional thought and practice for their pentecostal value. The Spirit has the prerogative to superintend such dreams, removing the traditional tension, for example, imposed upon the ancestor dream and the dream of flying. The Spirit hermeneutics used by visioners involves making sense of the D/V experience in relation to Scripture, to the counsel of others in the faith community, and to the importance of employing spiritual discernment.

While some in the churches may demonstrate ambivalence or have concerns about D/V experiences, those who value them find them spiritually and personally nourishing. In many instances, the experiences have practical value for Christian life. It becomes even clearer in Chapter 6 that pentecostal epistemology is anything but abstract. Dreams and visions carry religious meaning far beyond the pillow to the crucial concerns of pursuing the well-being of others through missiological engagement. That engagement is linked to the strong impetus evoked by D/V experiences. It will come to light that the impetus is associated with a sense of intimacy and the stirring of godly love which leads to spiritual and personal transformation and identity-shaping by means of the Spirit.

CHAPTER 6

Dreams and Visions and the Pentecostal Warrior

Prayer, Identity, and Agency

> When you have a negative dream, you stand on your feet and cancel it, cancel it, you understand. Declare that it is not going to happen.
> Nigerian CEO, Enugu[1]

∴

> It was a dream that was informing me about a disaster to happen to my family,
> but [I] did not take it seriously and so it happened.
> Ghanaian man, Pentecost Theological Seminary[2]

∴

> They were fighting with me and I was fighting with prayer.
> Tanzanian woman, Dar es Salaam[3]

∴

In Chapter 5, the metaphor of "piercing the veil" was upheld as a valid descriptor of the Pentecostal experience of acquiring knowledge through dreams and visions. That last chapter showcased data taken primarily from written surveys, information which provides a strong sense of the value of the D/V experience for Pentecostal-Charismatics. In fact, the experiences are highly valued for Christian life. The process of interpreting D/Vs is guided by a reading of Scripture that not only validates D/Vs but also promotes the Holy Spirit as the agency through whom they are received and understood. Data showed that participants of the Dreams and Visions Project also process elements of

---

[1] "Dreams and Visions Transcription," 73.
[2] "Spontaneous Dream and Vision Reports from Surveys," 10.
[3] "Dreams and Visions Transcription," 167.

traditional thinking in light of the prerogative of the Spirit when making sense of the experiences. Participants described the experiences as spiritually nourishing and showed that they applied the knowledge gained in practical ways. It was revealed that D/V experiences play a role in the process of identity formation and in strengthening Christian commitment.

This chapter adds to the framework of D/V valuation shown in Chapter 5 by exploring the profile of the "pentecostal warrior," the individual who moves beyond passive reception of D/Vs to Pentecostal agency. The discussion here deals more in depth with the corollaries pertaining to spiritual impact on the identity of the visioner, the link to missiological impulse, and the connection between D/Vs and prayer. The collection of personal interviews features prominently, and the D/V narratives therein help to enlighten in regard to how visioners interpret the experiences and then move toward agency. Of particular interest to this author are the cases involving agency and women.

Agency is the hallmark of the "pentecostal warrior," the Pentecostal agent described by Nimi Wariboko as an individual who uses prayer creatively in spiritual warfare and in the fashioning of new identity. Nimi Wariboko describes the profile of the pentecostal warrior, first of all, as one collaborating with the Holy Spirit. He writes,

> Holy Ghost is not just the name of the Third Person of the Trinity; it is a cliché that articulates the dominant worldview and ideology of West African Pentecostalism ... The invisible Holy Spirit represents and performs the supernatural power of God.[4]

This Spirit emphasis is also noted among these visioners who refer to the Spirit as being at work through the D/V experience. Therefore, dreams and visions also enhanced the sense of interaction and intimacy with God, and as the case studies up ahead demonstrate, affectivity and godly love are part and parcel of that sense of intimacy.

The pentecostal warrior demonstrates the link between D/V experiences and the practice of prayer in general, and also to spiritual warfare. For example, prayers were common before the D/V experience, demonstrating an association of the experience with divine response. Prayers also often followed the D/V experience. In terms of style and efficacy, Wariboko explains how the pentecostal prayer of the warrior combines theological language and everyday oral culture as performative speech. He writes, "[t]his ability to assess

---

4 Wariboko, *The Split God*, 161.

vernacular culture of the spiritual warrior opens up the deep structure of his prayer. At once he is calling on supreme power and exuding power, imaginatively re-creating himself through performative speech ... thus forging a new social identity."[5] In this chapter, the forging of identity is aligned with the practice of prayer as visioners pray in regard to what has been revealed in the D/V experience. Often, the pentecostal warrior prays and declares "cancellation" of certain D/Vs in an act of spiritual warfare. Identity formation is also linked to how D/Vs impact for transformation into agents, particularly of the type that venture into social engagement. In this respect, the impact of D/V experiences is linked to Wariboko's "pentecostal principle" and to the resulting phenomenon of "emergence" (Chapter 4). As Wariboko describes it, the pentecostal principle is operating when visioners demonstrate the "capacity to begin" and the "creative emergence" into new possibilities, qualities found in the pentecostal social agent.[6]

This chapter brings Wariboko's epistemology to life, moving beyond piercing the veil for access of hidden knowledge to the spiritual, psychological, and missiological impact of spiritual knowledge. The material is divided into two parts. In the first part, the association between D/Vs and the prayer life of the visioner is brought out. In the second part, the D/V experience and its association to the capacity to begin and emergence into the social agent is examined. The potency of D/V experience for affecting women and their will to act is significant, in light of the challenges they face. Also, the way D/Vs have affective impact and stir the emotions for godly love, and the way the interpretations of D/Vs are transposed as fuel for a Church compelled to mission will also be discussed.

1   Dreams and Visions and the Pentecostal Pray-er

One of the most significant findings of this project is how frequently prayer is associated with the reception of dreams and visions. These associations drive home the importance of the practice of prayer to the process of receiving, interpreting, and applying the knowledge ascertained through D/Vs. Since

---

5   Wariboko, *The Split God*, 161.
6   Wariboko, *The Pentecostal Principle*, 50, 53, 205. Additionally, portions of my Chapter 6 are also found in Anna Droll, "Pentecostal Principle and the Dreams and Visions of African Visioners" presented at "The Philosophy of Nimi Wariboko" Conference, Nov. 21, 2020, a virtual conference, and published in *Public Righteousness: The Performative Ethics of Human Flourishing*, ed. Abimbola Adelakun (Eugene, OR: Pickwick Publications, 2023), 101-119.

prayer is also linked to intimacy with God, it follows that dreams and visions play a key role in the development of that intimacy.

One example of the emphasis on prayer is found in the testimony of a 30-year-old Tanzanian woman who attends an Assemblies of God church in Dar es Salaam. During her interview, she spoke of prayer multiple times in connection with her dreams:

> A: How do you explain that? Why do you think you're having so many dreams for other people?
> I: It happens that when I pray about somebody, I can get a dream about him or her. It happens when I pray for my parents, or when I pray for my pastors ... I dreamt about my grandmother. I dreamt that her leg was in pain ... Prayer is very important, prayer. Maybe it's not only prayer, He may want you to talk to that person, counsel that person.[7]

Other respondents emphasized prayer, as well. For example, in answer to how his vision had impacted him, a Ghanaian seminarian from Trinity Theological Seminary responded, "[i]t made me long [for] more visions and made sure I pray for all such supernatural encounters."[8] Other Ghanaian men also responded with references to prayer. From the Pentecost Theological Seminary there were several who mentioned prayer. For example, "I repent and pray for or against,"[9] "[It impacted me] to keep on interceding for our fellow believers,"[10] "It inform[ed] me to pray concerning the work over there,"[11] and "Most of the dreams and visions I had inform me how to strategize my spiritual life in prayer."[12] Nigerian men of the Evangel Theological Seminary of Jos, Nigeria reported similarly. For example, one 54-year-old Nigerian seminarian reported: "I then saw someone who appeared in white cloth, he told me I should rather pray for him, to forgive the responsible for the attack I had. He used cotton wool and scissors to clean the pains from my head to my legs. I then woke up and discovered the pains were gone. It taught me that God would rather want me to pray for the salvation of my enemies."[13]

---

7   "Dreams and Visions Transcription," 190.
8   "Spontaneous Dream and Vision Reports from Surveys," 4. Words are sometimes added—or replace others, as in differing verb tenses—in brackets for a smoother reading of the text.
9   Ibid., 5.
10 Ibid., 7.
11 Ibid., 7.
12 Ibid., 11.
13 Ibid., 20.

This association between prayer and dreams and visions, as well as other associations, are examined here first using multivariate computations for analysis. Following are the significant associations that were found when examining the coded content of the personal interviews along with the report of prayer.[14]

According to the personal interviews, praying after a SS DV was associated with the occurrence of three types of D/Vs: the warning D/V, the warning/predictive D/V and the spiritual warfare D/V.[15] For East Africans, praying after was more common following the warning D/V, $\chi^2(1) = 5.679$, $p < .05$; Fisher's exact test, $p = 0.068$; $\varphi = .231$. There was also significant association between praying after and the warning/predictive D/V, $\chi^2(1) = 14.618$, $p = 0$; Fisher's exact test, $p < .01$; $\varphi = .371$. Therefore, for East Africans, 24.9% of the incidences of prayer-response offered after a dream were in response to a warning D/V or a warning/predictive D/V (that is about 1 in 4 instances).

For West Africans, praying after was also more common following a warning/predictive D/V. To be specific, when the West African visionary responded to a D/V with prayer, 30% of the time it was to a warning/predictive D/V, $\chi^2(1) = 14.204$, $p = 0$; Fisher's exact test, $p < .01$; $\varphi = .346$. Also, with respect to West Africans, the results found that 30% of prayer-responses occurred in association with the experience of spiritual warfare D/Vs, $\chi^2(1) = 4.082$, $p < .05$; Fisher's exact test, $p .078$; $\varphi = .185$.

Visioners were also rated in terms of the SS D/V index score (ranging between zero and six, see explanation of this score in Chapter 5). A Mann-Whitney U test was conducted examining whether there was a significant median difference in this measure on the basis of praying after. For East African visioners, the median SS D/V score was significantly higher in cases where the visioner prayed after the dream. There was, therefore, a significant association between the SS D/V and prayer after, so that it is reasonable to say that a visioner who experienced more SS D/Vs also prayed after more frequently.

---

14   American statistician David Kremelberg assisted in the project by conducting tests with the data using the STATA/MP13.0 multiprocessor. Tests included Pearson chi² along with Fisher's exact test. These registered measurements such as Pearson's r, phi-coefficient, and rank sum for ascertaining medians in the data sets. These functions signaled significance or insignificance when questions were asked about associations among certain elements of data.

15   The SS D/Vs are distinct from the "nourishing/spiritually edifying" D/Vs, though the categories can overlap. The nourishing dreams are classified according to how the visioners themselves reported that the dreams impacted them (which I coin "spiritually nourishing/edifying"). The SS ("spiritually significant") D/Vs are dream categories ascertained by looking at the data as a whole and noting which types of dream narratives surfaced.

PA	obs	rank sum	expected
0	78	3872.5	4173
1	28	1798.5	1498

z = -2.542, Prob > |z| = 0.0110

1.1 Dreams and Visions and the Pentecostal Warrior

It has been established that the experiences of warning, predictive and spiritual warfare D/Vs are linked to the prayer life. These types of D/Vs are prevalent enough in dream narratives to warrant looking at samples of them. That is because the frequent appearance of D/Vs that deal with evil protagonists or enemies, or which otherwise indicate a mindset concerned with victory over evil or temptation (for the visioner or another person) is a notable feature within the data collections.

The discovery of the recurring theme of victory over evil in the D/Vs reported reflects an observation made by Nigerian scholar Ogbu Kalu. He wrote, "[g]oing through life is like spiritual warfare" for Africans used to dealing with the "machinations" of unseen agents at work in human affairs.[16] Echoing Kalu's conviction, demonology and awareness of witchcraft featured as part of the social imaginary of visioners. D/Vs were noted as products of a biblical worldview which understands spiritual conflict as the existential reality for Christians. The experiences were associated with the voice of God, with the deciphering of coded knowledge, and with revelation regarding spiritual realities, all of which played a part in achieving spiritual victory. For the visioners, D/Vs are divine messages of a diagnostic nature and are deemed crucial for spiritual warfare.

It has already been established that the data points to the importance of the practice of prayer to the reception and interpretation of D/Vs in the lives of visioners. It is apparent from the dream narratives that prayer is an integral part of processing the D/V experience, and especially so when the D/Vs are interpreted as indications that evil is afoot. Sometimes spiritual warfare D/Vs were narrated with much heaviness of heart, especially when it involved information that was interpreted as revelation about a loved one. Some dreams featured snakes or a fierce lion which were interpreted metaphorically as evil

---

16   Kalu, *African Pentecostalism*, 140.

agency. In other instances, the will of the enemy was revealed and upon awakening visioners employed a Pentecostal technique of spiritual warfare called "dream cancellation" used along with prayer. This technique was mentioned in both West and East Africa.

The first incidence of hearing about dream cancellation was not during data collection, but some time before while sharing about a dream with a Nigerian colleague at Fuller Theological Seminary in California. As we discussed my research topic and the question of whether D/Vs can be significant in Christian spirituality, I shared about a recent disturbing dream I had had a few days prior. In it I found I had cancer in my body. He urged us to immediately declare a cancellation of the dream in the name of Jesus Christ, which he led with bold and resolute faith. It became evident later during data collection in African contexts that the technique of dream cancellation is a common practice. It was mentioned once in a written survey and several more times during interviews in Nigeria and Tanzania.

A 59-year-old woman from Enugu, Nigerian shared of how church members may, together, cancel a dream narrated by a member, if that dream "is not good."[17] She also shared about cancelling dreams in which a deceased person appears. She commented, "[i]f they show themselves in the dream, when I wake up, I cancel all their dreams, I say, '[l]et every imagination they are putting on my dream, let it be destroyed in the name of Jesus.'"[18] Another participant from the same city, this time a 33-year-old man, shared his view of how the devil can sow into the dream life, and how he, himself, responds to those negative dreams. His comments also demonstrate the importance of Scripture for understanding D/V experiences:

I: The battleground is the mind, right? And if that is true, it means the devil will use whatever channel to lay hold of your mind. The Scripture says that the enemy sowed tares. When your mind is busy, the devil may not get much access but then when your mind is less busy, you discover at such a point it is so easy for the enemy to come and have an effect on your mind. That's how it works, if care is not taken right, you start saying things you should not be—
A: You say care, what kind of care?

---

17 "Dreams and Visions Transcription," 68.
18 Ibid., 70.

I: Like when you have a negative dream. You stand on your feet and cancel it, cancel it, you understand. Declare that it is not going to happen.[19]

A Nigerian woman studying at Evangel Theological Seminary wrote in her survey, "I have discovered that most of the revelations I receive usually come through dreams ... I have learned to depend on God ... I will cancel the negative and then decree the positive come to pass."[20] One Nigerian villager, in fact the only Roman Catholic participant[21] (who also self-identified as charismatic), shared her response to "bad" dreams through the translator:

A: What does she do, does she do something after she sees a bad one?
T: She said that once she sees a bad dream, a negative one, she gets up from the bed and she goes into prayers and cancels it, believing God [that] it will not manifest in the physical.[22]

A different Nigerian woman shared similarly in a personal interview, "I'm still thinking about the dream but at some point I cancelled it, I prayed against it because I didn't like it."[23] More Scriptural support for the practice of dream cancellation was shared by a Nigerian man, reiterating that these en-Spirited visioners are engaging with Scripture in the process of drawing spiritual meaning from D/Vs:

One thing I want to say is that dreams are given ... to warn you of a coming event. When you ... have faith you may cancel it. Or if it is a good one receive it, accept it, call it into being. The one you don't like, cancel it, and once you cancel it according to Matthew 16:19, Whatever you unlock is unlocked, whatever you lock is locked, not in heaven where God dwells but the zone where the demons [dwell].[24]

A final example was narrated by a 28-year-old Tanzanian woman who responded to a violent dream by cancelling it:

---

19 "Dreams and Visions Transcription," 73.
20 "Spontaneous Dream and Vision Reports from Surveys," 20.
21 She is also mentioned in the section "The Spirit and Ancestor Dreams" up ahead.
22 "Dreams and Visions Transcription," 95.
23 Ibid., 99.
24 Ibid., 131.

> I had a dream that I helped some people [having] a difficult life. But me and my family, we came together to help those people. But later on those people we helped, they stabbed to death some of my relatives ... I didn't understand that dream much, but I told my mother, and my mother told me, "[l]et's pray." We cancelled all the bad things that were to happen to our family and all that.[25]

Many D/Vs were explained as messages of divine knowledge that encouraged the visioner to pray, were later referred to in precarious situations, or helped to guide him or her in the course of making a difficult decision. The case of a man in Ibadan, Nigeria who had a dream in which he saw enemies "kicking" against his upcoming marriage is a prime example. He narrated:

> I had no money and I was praying to God for God to give me money for this marriage and God revealed to me in my dreams, that look, don't pray for money, but pray against enemies. Now the way He revealed that dream to me was that I saw some group of people, like a community, kicking against what I wanted to do, kicking against the marriage ... I began to pray. The day of the wedding [in waking life] when the pastor asked the father—the person who [stood in] as the father of my wife—when the pastor asked him to bring the bride to the altar, the man hesitated. He didn't want to bring the bride! Everybody was turning and looking ... So the man manifested the evil plan of the community. But thank God for the Holy Spirit that [drew] him up to come up![26]

In another case, a Nigerian man reported a dream that kept recurring which he interpreted as a possible indication that his wife was involved in witchcraft. The issue was deeply disturbing to him. There was another report of a witchcraft dream linked to a wife that was narrated in a different interview in East Africa. The Tanzanian man shared that he had dreams after prayers and fasting for answers regarding his marital tensions. He interpreted the dreams as revelations about demonic oppression afflicting his wife. This example is also important for demonstrating the role of the man's pastor:

> There was time when I was sleeping, then I was sleeping with my wife, then it came in my dream that where my wife was sleeping was a very big

---

25   "Dreams and Visions Transcription," 166.
26   Ibid., 3.

snake, very big snake. In fact, it shocked me so much that I found myself jumping out of bed. Then when I went to church while the pastor was sharing, just sharing normal talk, the pastor said—it was a men's fellowship—"Well, there are people here who think they are staying with wives but they're staying with snakes." Then I realized my wife didn't have a good spirit.[27]

In this case, the man's pastor also offered spiritual care when the man went to him for personal counseling afterward. The pastor later said to him, "I have prayed and God says that that problem, He will finish it."[28] When in the interview, the man was probed regarding his understanding of spiritual warfare, he explained:

> As far as the spiritual concern there is no confrontation between people. It is confrontation between God and the devil, right and wrong, holy and dark. Now human beings are just agents, servants of whichever side somebody may take ... there are two areas of influence. If we are Pentecostals we need to lean on Him to get support. For example, we as Pentecostals, God is using dreams to tell us what to do. Therefore, I take dreams as a medium of communication but it's not an end in itself.[29]

In an interview with a 46-year-old man in Enugu, Nigeria, the idea of satanic attacks coming through D/Vs surfaced:

> I: There's this form of visitation, what we usually call satanic attacks you receive after binding and loosing, in dreams at time you see people trying to pursue you, people trying to arrest you, and so on and so forth, even trying to handcuff you. We know that this is because of the warfare, the prayers you've been going through, those forces of darkness are coming back. I have had a very serious encounter in that area that actually changed my life. I saw a woman come out of a window—not in a dream, now, there are several apartment blocks around the church. So I saw a woman come out of a window, inside the house, but she opened the window blind and she blew something like white powder towards us. I complained to the pastor, "I saw somebody come to that window and blow something." So I got close to the house and

---

27 "Dreams and Visions Transcription," 184.
28 Ibid., 185.
29 Ibid., 185–186.

> I said, "[w]hatever it is, I bind you in the name of Jesus, I destroy you!" You know, all those things, I said them and I prayed and prayed and prayed and prayed and I thought the whole thing was over. But then when I went to lie down, the moment I lay down, I saw a dream, and I saw people dressed like occult people dressed in a certain form, with a ... native wrapper. They were coming towards me with something ... and then some word of God began to come into my spirit and I began to declare, "It shall not stand, it shall not come to pass." I was saying ... "I bind you in the name of Jesus, by the blood of Jesus!" The minute I said that they would run away, but that wasn't the end.
>
> A: You mean, you would dream it again?
>
> I: Yes, it happened and happened. But one day, about three months from that point, one day I lay down, and they again began to suppress me, you know. But God opened my eyes, I saw ... surprising! Oh my God, sister, I saw Jesus on the cross! And the blood gushing out from his body ... and then those people never came again.[30]

An important feature of the spiritual warfare D/V is the way it is interpreted as diagnostic. Visioners consider them to be insightful for revealing the impediments that can be blocking the Christian life from flourishing. In order to understand how D/Vs can reveal realities that point to spiritual obstructions, it is important first to understand how some visioners see the capacity of the human spirit. For them, the spirit is capable of activity in the spiritual realm while the body is sleeping or in the resting state. This was already mentioned in Chapter 3. There, the British anthropologist R. S. Rattray and Ghanaian scholar Anthony Ephirim-Donkor were cited in respect to the activity of the Sunsum (*sunsum*) or human spirit of the individual.

The enduring Akan understanding of spirit travel in Ghana was also shared by visioners in Nigeria and by a visioner in Tanzania. Their interviews enlightened regarding how they diagnose through D/Vs what they believe to be a connection to a "spirit spouse." This condition was defined as a malady in which the human spirit trafficked sexually with other spirits, and it was their conviction that it could be treated by means of Pentecostal prayer and deliverance.

One story shared in Nigeria dealt with an athlete who claimed to have sexual relations in his dream life which affected his athletic performance. The 44-year-old pastor who was interviewed shared that his contact with the members of the football club began through an invitation to give a short weekly Bible

---

30   "Dreams and Visions Transcription," 81–82.

message to the athletes. The player was later referred to him for counseling. Upon hearing the player narrate a series of dreams, the pastor encouraged him to put his faith in Jesus Christ, saying that the situation was serious and could not be resolved without dependence on prayer and the Holy Spirit. After this meeting and conversion to Christ, the player later shared about his healing. The pastor narrated, "[t]hat day it was like a wonderful reunion. He was so happy. I was asking him, '[w]hat has been happening since then?' He said, '[t]he dream has stopped.'"[31]

Another Nigerian, a 75-year-old pastor who offers private counseling in his parachurch ministry, also leads men and women through deliverance from a spirit spouse. Clients who come to him are first required to fill out a registration form which also inquires about their dreams. The pastor uses the dream accounts as reference points for diagnosis of spiritual issues and to pinpoint "spiritual traits," such as habitual fearfulness which he stated can open a person to satanic oppression. When asked how he was led to this type of ministry, he shared about his prayer ministry in the church and how he felt led to offer this specialized prayer counseling and deliverance because of the needs he saw. He replied, "I'm an evangelist. I had a burden for souls."[32] He also said, "[s]ome of these people would fall, but the problem is this, when they fall they are not delivered … many people—in the church, even!—have trouble with the spirit spouse … some people [who come here] even wear chains, spiritually."[33]

In Tanzania, a 36-year-old pastor explained his understanding of the usefulness of D/Vs:

> God uses that to communicate, but it's not the basis of our faith, we don't just rely on dreams and visions, we rely on the word of God. If you want victory over spiritual warfare, you need to understand dreams and visions … how would you know that you are at the center of spiritual warfare, say, if a spirit was following you? God would let you know. He can use dreams and visions. He can use other ways, but most of the time He will show you in a dream or vision.[34]

When this pastor was asked about the situation of the spirit spouse, he responded:

---

31 "Dreams and Visions Transcription," 108.
32 Ibid., 134.
33 Ibid., 134.
34 Ibid., 217–218.

> I: First of all ... a woman of that kind, I know she needs deliverance because already she is in sexual affairs with what we call [the] marine spirit or spiritual husband. That is a spirit who will appear to her. Sometimes she will have affairs with that man.
> A: With a spirit?
> I: She's in a dream, but it's sometimes not a dream ... it's a spirit.[35]

One last example comes from another interview which indicated the usefulness of D/Vs for deliverance ministry. The interview took place in Jos, Nigeria where an evangelist shared of a dream that prepared him for deliverance ministry to a village "occultist." He also shared of revelatory visions that came to him during the act of deliverance and healing for a man who was believed to have been made crippled by evil spirits:

> I: Some two sisters came to me and said, "[b]rother, we have a deliverance prayer for somebody in a village." So when I slept I told God before I slept, I said, "God, I don't know about this deliverance case, but I want you to reveal it to me." And I slept, and God showed me the person we were going to deliver ... he was crippled ... he had entered into occultism and he didn't follow with their rules and they punished him and made him a cripple. So he was sitting. In the dream God showed him to me seated with a cup on his head. And arrows were coming out from the cup. So I got up and I drew him. I got up and drew it the way God revealed it to me in the night. I drew it on a piece of paper. So the following day the sisters came and they took me to the village. Immediately, when we arrived some yards to his house, I saw him seated as I drew last night.
> A: You mean he had something on his head?
> I: Yeah, the cup actually, you would not see the arrows, because those were the spiritual powers. So when we went and met him we greeted him and we said ... the sisters introduced me to him [and] that we have come to pray for you. So we said, "[l]et us ... you should remove your cup for us to pray." He resisted. He said, no, he would not remove his cup and we should leave him in his condition and we should go back. ... So we just started praying and revelations kept coming. Different people were coming, we were seeing different people coming on

---

35 "Dreams and Visions Transcription," 218–219.

horses, this one would come with a spear. I would say, "[b]ehold, there is somebody coming with a spear, this is how he is dressed," then the man we were praying for said, "[i]t is so and so," he named the person, nine of them. And after the last one he was delivered. He got up, he jumped up and he removed the cup and I told him, "[g]o and burn it, hallelujah!" And he jumped on his feet and started walking.[36]

The Pentecostal preoccupation with the potential for evil and the way that D/Vs fuel faith for attaining victory over evil agency is evident. This section has shown that there is a high incidence of prayer as a practice after a warning D/V, a warning/predictive D/V, or a spiritual warfare D/V. On the other hand, ahead the discussion turns to a type of D/V experience associated with prayerlessness. It seems that the experience impacted in a way that did not evoke the usual need for protection, answers, and strategies associated with spiritual warfare. Instead, this type of D/V experience inspired confidence and exuberance. These were the DAME dreams and visions.

1.2 The DAME Dream or Vision and Pentecostal Agency

One observation made is that prayerlessness is associated with the DAME D/V. As noted above, the category of the DAME D/V experience was created after an assessment of dream narratives and their unique features. It is one of the types of the "spiritually significant" D/V experiences (SS D/Vs).[37] The DAME experience (directive, affirming, motivating, or encouraging) was associated with other variables with significance when multivariate testing was applied. First, it was linked more frequently with the vision experience rather than with the dream experience in both West and East Africans:

Dreams and visions (east)
- prtesti 106 .4783 .6000
- $Pr(|Z| > |z|) = 0.0105$

Dreams and visions (west)
- prtesti 119 .3529 .6111
- $Pr(|Z| > |z|) = 0.0000$

For East Africans the difference in proportions test achieved statistical significance with this result indicating a significantly higher proportion of visions

---

36   "Dreams and Visions Transcription," 46.
37   See also Chapter 5 for information on the SS/DV categories.

(.6000) as compared to dreams (.4783). For West Africans this result also indicated a significantly higher proportion of visions (.6111) as compared to dreams (.3529). These findings make sense when noting the type of lucidity that visions seem to be characterized by. The details of visions were narrated with specific details that were clear to the visioner and this clarity understandably contributed to their effect as directive, affirming, and so forth.

Secondly, the DAME D/V was associated among West Africans with prayerlessness after the experience, rather than with prayer. The testing for association between DAME D/Vs and prayer after D/V experience in the case of West Africans who gave personal interviews resulted as follows: $\chi^2(1)$ = 4.175, $p < .05$; Fisher's exact test, p = 0.048; φ = .187. Pertaining to the 48 cases in which the visioner had a DAME D/V, in 47 of those cases the respondent did not mention responding in prayer after the experience. The one case in which the visioner did pray was a case of the DAME *dream,* and as explained above, dreams were sometimes not as clear in all details as visions were or offered metaphorical images.

The visioner who prayed after the DAME dream was a Nigerian woman and the DAME classification was given to the experience because its interpretation motivated her to begin a ministry in the church. She had dreamt that people were lined up to be attended to by her, and some of the people were holding her legs. The people holding her legs puzzled her, but upon awakening and after prayer, she concluded that God was calling her to a ministry and that the people represented people in the waking life who were in need of her. As in the experience of the other types of D/Vs that elicited prayer, her DAME dream had left her in a state of inquiry.[38]

In an effort to explain the phenomenon of prayerlessness as the general response to the DAME D/V, it helps to consider that the experience more often answered existential questions, or offered an affirmation or directive in the message relayed. In those cases, at least as portrayed and even relived in the retelling of the dream or vision, a sense of wonder and exuberance accompanied the experience, and a sense of assurance rather than a sense of urgency for prayer. The association between visions, the DAME experience, and prayerlessness again points to the lucidity of the experience. It makes sense that prayer for more clarity or guidance might *not* follow the DAME experiences simply for that reason. For example, visions were characterized by the lack of symbolism and were often narrated as the literal, real life happenings previously discussed, happenings taking place in the realm of spirit. As Umar Danfulani

---

[38] "Dream Narratives from the Audio Recordings of the Dream and Visions Project," 3.

might say, they were experiences in the realm of the "spiritual earth" where the physical realm and the spiritual realm dovetail.[39]

The potency of the DAME D/V is featured in the next sections. The impression at the time of listening to the interviews is that the revelation received in these experiences leaves one with no questions to ask, and no need for further insights for strategy. The message is clear and definitive and the sensible response in the mind of the visioner is action. That action demonstrates personal transformation and emergence according to the pentecostal principle.

2 Dreams and Visions and Pentecostal Agency

When the visioner is assessing a dream or vision as the reception of spiritual knowledge, the experience has a dynamic effect on thinking and on decision making toward agency. The belief that the source of the experience is found in God, and more specifically the person of the Spirit, funds the high value of D/Vs in the life of the visioner. Feelings and emotions (affectivity) play a part in the force of impact, especially the deep assurance that God has spoken and that a response is necessary. These are the components of pentecostal agency and this section argues that this agency reflects Nimi Wariboko's "pentecostal principle."

Wariboko explains the dynamic of Spirit for stirring the "capacity to begin" and the emergence of "novel properties" as the "pentecostal principle."[40] Emergence is a dynamic that demonstrates the pentecostal principle as a "creative emergence" that can induce "properties and behaviors that are not explicable by the lower parts or in terms of the sum of the parts."[41] Therefore, the power to initiate and the surplus of energies evoked by the D/V experience provides a sample of the working of the pentecostal principle. That dynamic is brought out of the abstract and into the tangible in the case of the majority of D/V narratives, but especially for the women introduced here and in the case of the men featured later in the chapter. In the case of women, though, living by the Spirit and the pentecostal principle can be a challenge. For them it can be difficult to navigate a course of action for implementing the knowledge gleaned from D/Vs.

Again, affectivity is key to the dynamism of the pentecostal principle. Dream and vision experiences impacted not just how the visioner felt about God,

---

39 "Dreams and Visions Transcription," 33.
40 Wariboko, *The Pentecostal Principle*, 1, 76.
41 Ibid., 205.

but how the visioner felt about himself or herself. D/V experiences impacted a shift in identity. The impact of the testimonies on the visioners in just the act of re-telling the narratives was notable. Many of the narratives evoked a visible sense of "lift" in the visioner as he or she spoke, and in many cases it was clear by the words of the visioner that it was connected to the idea of being cared for by God. To be the recipient of the Spirit's attention through the D/V experience made significant impact on the visioner. On many occasions, the visioner shared how the experience made them feel, but it was the way in which they spoke about God in the course of the narrative that was demonstrative of deep emotion. This section offers a window into the emergence of pentecostal agents. It describes the way D/V experiences stir emotions and consequently shape identities, catapult individuals into ministries, and inspire ideas for effective public service.

2.1   The Agency of Visionary Women

While human agency is born of a complex negotiation of conflicting voices, for women, the pressure of that complexity can be heightened by the "subversive" nature of a D/V message in respect to cultural norms.[42] Nevertheless, the emotive D/Vs that surfaced in narratives stirred feelings that evoked strength for demonstrating courage, love, and compassion. The energies of creative emergence demonstrated in these women point to Wariboko's pentecostal principle. The behaviors and initiatives that D/Vs evoke are the hallmark of dynamism Wariboko describes as "properties and behaviors that are not explicable by the lower parts or in terms of the sum of the parts."[43] In this first example of the impact of a D/V for women's issues, the D/V interpretation which was the conclusion of a 29-year-old Tanzanian woman competed with a certain man's influence on her in waking life. It led her to make a difficult relationship decision. She said:

---

[42] British sociologist Margaret Archer explains how individuals manage their experience of moving toward agency. The information sheds some insight on the possibility of situations for female African visioners. For example, Archer references how the structures of social stratification have an effect on human agency. "Because of the pre-existence of those structures which shape the situations in which we find ourselves, they impinge upon us without our compliance, consent or complicity." About the role of emotions Archer writes, "[e]motions are morally significant, because without their shoving-power we would get little done, but they are not always morally good or right and therefore the notion of 'moral emotions' should be resisted." The elements of both social stratification and affectivity are important factors in the case of women's agency. See Margaret Archer, *Being Human: The Problem of Agency* (UK: Cambridge University Press, 2000), 232, 262.

[43] Wariboko, *The Pentecostal Principle*, 205.

I: I was in a relationship and I was praying so God could tell me if I was in a right relationship or not. So, God gave me this dream that ... we went to a high building. I and that person, but when we got to the top of the building, the building started to shrink like it was about to break. So, I could hear this voice tell me—because I was thinking, "[w]hy does this building want to break?" So I heard a voice telling me, "[y]ou know what, it had a weak foundation, that's why it wants to break." After that dream I broke up with him. I said, "Ok, He is speaking to me. This relationship is not taking me anywhere."
A: So you acted on your dream?
I: Yes, I did.[44]

In another incident reported by a different unmarried Tanzanian woman, the dream in which her fiancé was trying to persuade her to have premarital sex was taken seriously. She responded in prayer, took her concern about the dream to her female pastor, and decided to discontinue the relationship after the incident of temptation actually transpired. She understood the dream as a warning from God.[45] The implications of these D/V effects lead to the question of how D/Vs might even awaken a perspective for the visioner that she consciously or subconsciously denies in waking life.

Two women in particular exemplified unusual resolve when processing their D/V experiences. Both of them have had long histories of ministry to troubled and vulnerable youth or women in need. The first is a woman from Aba in Abia State, Nigeria, and the other is the woman from Dar es Salaam, Tanzania mentioned in Chapter 1. Other female exemplars of agency were found in Togo. Their cases will also help to bring awareness regarding the difficulty women encounter when weighing the messages they interpret from D/V experiences against other factors.

The story of the woman from Aba is multi-layered since she felt compelled to act against both the religious norm and the norm for women. For her, the emphasis on God's love for others was significant to the processing of her experiences (godly love will also be discussed in the next section). In her situation, first an audible instruction came during prayer and then a dream followed some time later giving confirmation. She reported that while praying "God told me to stop teaching the Sunday school ... that there are people outside that

---

44 "Dreams and Visions Transcription," 209.
45 Ibid., 189.

nobody goes to. ... The voice I heard said, 'Can't someone care for these ones ... They are precious to me. I love them.'"[46]

Thereafter, she began an outreach to the Agbaro boys, homeless and sometimes dangerous youth who lived in the motor parks across her city. She began the work alone and shared how the decision to do so was not an easy one to make. "I was thinking, 'How can a woman enter into the midst of these boys that are hard,' you know, they are stubborn. But he told me, 'I will be with you.'"[47] She reported that she later had a dream that encouraged and confirmed God's will. In it she was shown a mansion under construction, and in the dream God spoke to her that the mansion would one day be her heavenly reward for her hard work on earth. At that point in the interview, I became curious regarding the strength of perceived impediments in her case.

One of the questions I sometimes posed during interviews was in respect to the perceived strength of an obstacle to a specified course of action prescribed by a dream or vision: On a scale of 1 to 10, how would you rate the strength of that obstacle? In her case, she rated the obstacle of *being a woman* as a "10 ... because of culture."[48] In time, her efforts among the youth eventually resulted in life change for many of the young men. Most of the transformation of the youth involved reconciliation with family members, and some incidents involved the youth being led to employment opportunities.

The same clarity of call came to the woman of Dar es Salaam, Tanzania. She first became a contact through my visit to her youth outreach during a short stay in Tanzania unrelated to research. She had organized instructors to teach various skills such as sewing and craft making in a program for street youth in an outdoor venue. At that time, it was stunning to hear her begin the story of the founding of her outreach with the phrase, "I had a dream" and I returned the same year to interview her personally. Her case involves two major perceived impediments to social work: a disinterested spouse and the lack of resourcing. Yet, she reported that she had a dream in which she saw the whole of Tanzania as in a map and in the dream a voice informed her that she must go to the youth of the whole nation to reach them for God. She narrated two more dreams. "Many girls were running to my house and then I just opened the door and they came and filled my house."[49] In the other dream, she reported

---

46   "Dreams and Visions Transcription," 124.
47   Ibid.
48   Ibid., 126.
49   Ibid., 144.

"seeing children crying, needing help, needing me and I called them and they heard and they smiled."[50]

When a recruiter from PACT Tanzania, an organization which meets the needs of vulnerable children, contacted her offering a position in their ministry, she was willing to accept it. She said, "I accepted the offer because of the dream."[51] Eventually, she founded her own NGO called the International Youth Development Program. At a later time, dreams came again and gave her emotional strength and encouragement. She had one particular dream on three different occasions. It was a dream of going to a certain pastor for assistance with her work, and after the third, similar dream she decided to contact him.[52]

Similar stories of women acting on their dreams were reported in Lomé, Togo. In one instance, a woman with a good paying position at the prison experienced a dream in which she was called to leave the job in order to go to Bible College, which she did. Another woman had a similar dream in which she was also called to Bible College, but in her case enrollment required a discussion with her husband regarding closing down her clothing boutique, a move he did not support. However, she did decide to enroll in the college. An account of the same type was also narrated in Jos, Nigeria. In that case, the woman also experienced a call to go to Bible College by means of dreams. Yet, the fact that her husband was not inclined toward biblical education presented some tension. As she recounted it:

I: The man I got married to was not interested in being a pastor. Then I said, "God, if you are actually calling me now speak to my husband." The day my husband would tell me, "[m]y wife, come, God has spoken to me that he wants me to be a pastor and go to Bible school," it would be a confirmation. Then he woke one day. He said, "I think God wants me to go to Bible school."

A: Would it have been too extraordinary for you to move forward even if your husband wasn't interested in ministry?

I: Traditionally, in Nigeria, a woman must get permission from the husband to do anything. And if God does not reveal to your husband it is difficult. So he went to Bible school before me. Today we are both pastors.[53]

---

50 "Dreams and Visions Transcription," 144.
51 Ibid.
52 Ibid., 144–145.
53 Ibid., 10.

In a different account given by a 61-year-old woman, her vision experience came at a time when she was responding to male pressure to close down her church in Enugu, Nigeria. She reported:

> Then I now invited some Assemblies of God pastors ... and called them and asked them to pray. Then the man said, "[a] woman does not run a church." So they said I should close down the church. So when I wanted to close down the church, God! I saw the big hand of Jesus, very rough, very big! So now I carried the white plastic chairs, I carried one off, lifted off two, lifted three ... so when I wanted to carry one I saw a very big hand [and a voice] saying "Stop!"[54]

Yet the pressure to close down was strong. She added:

> Then I gave the women off to one man of God, and now they are excelling. I transferred my members to him. My daughter in South Africa now called me and said, "Mom, why are you listening to carnal people. Why aren't you doing the ministry that God gave you?" [Later] I went by invitation to Lagos for a program, and when the servant of God was ministering the power came on. The man now said, "[y]ou are suffering ... because you have neglected what God has called you for." So, all these are the challenges I'm having.[55]

The impact of others' dreams can also be motivational for female visioners, as was the case for a Nigerian woman who was procrastinating with starting a ministry in the church. She had a visioner approach her with a dream about women with heavy loads on their heads:

> I had a lady in my church who wanted me to start. She told me, "Mommy, start this thing. Call all ... there are so many girls out there that need help." So I wouldn't start. I kept on in procrastination. One day she came to me and she said she was sleeping and she saw some young ladies with heavy loads on their head and with some hanging on their neck and they were going, they were moving and a lady came and said, "[p]eople are dancing

---

54   "Dreams and Visions Transcription," 77–78.
55   Ibid., 78.

and you are carrying heavy loads. Why are you carrying heavy loads all around?"[56]

A similar report of how the dream of another impacted for inspiring agency came from a 30-year-old Tanzanian woman:

> I: I dreamt I had a very good shop, business … and it was full of different things inside and there were many customers saying, "[c]an you give me this, this, this"
> A: When you had that dream was it a surprise?
> I: It was a surprise … I have a friend, we were praying together and she told me, "I have dreamt of you having a wonderful shop full of mirrors and good clothes." Before that dream, I hadn't any shop.
> A: But before those dreams, was it in your heart to open a shop?
> I: Yes! It was in my heart and I was praying.[57]

The examples above are some of the scenarios depicting Pentecostal-Charismatic women negotiating the interpretations of their dreams and visions or those of others. They give indications of what is required for women to act when encountering conflicting ideals, along with a look at the efficacy of D/V experience for stirring up resolve and for building female identity along a certain course of personal and spiritual development.

2.2 Visionary Love and Ministerial Agency

A 48-year-old Nigerian pastor and academic of the Assemblies of God closed his vision narrative with the words, "I love Jesus so much."[58] He reported an extraordinary audition in which his life's timeline and ministerial positions were revealed. He shared his sentiments about God:

> It has made me to see God personally, to see God as more personal to me. Some of the times I break down and I weep and I ask God, what have you seen in me? You know … sometimes the way He does things. He does it in such a way and it's so sweet, you know … He carries me.[59]

---

56 "Dream Narratives from the Audio Recordings of the Dreams and Visions Project," 3. This is the same woman who had her own dream of people needing her and clinging to her legs, which was mentioned in the previous section.
57 Ibid., 188–189.
58 "Dreams and Visions Transcription," 21.
59 Ibid., 31.

In many narratives, the expression of love for God surfaced along with expressions of love for others because of God. That love, coupled with the assurance of knowing God's specific will received through direct encounter, produced the shoving power for agency. Visionary experiences, and the interpretations of them for personal agency, exemplify a knowing attributed to the Spirit and in tune with the deep needs of others. For a 54-year-old Nigerian man, God's love for all people was emphasized through his dream. His case was mentioned earlier in this chapter. He wrote in his survey, "[i]t taught me that God would rather want me to pray for the salvation of my enemies over their destruction."[60]

In other interviews, references to the tears of Jesus pointed out how the emotive Jesus evoked a strong sense of endearment in the minds and hearts of the visioners. In one case, according to the vision of a 19-year-old Ghanaian man, Jesus Christ was seated on the throne crying. When he became concerned as to why Jesus was crying, an angel next to him explained that he was crying for all the Christians who had backslidden. In the interview, the man said, "[t]he vision made me serve Jesus more. I knew about Him before, but now I knew for myself that He is real!"[61]

One of the visioners in Jos who reported an encounter with Jesus Christ in heaven narrated, "[t]hen He tapped me on my back and said, "[g]o back and finish your work." And then I discovered that I was kneeling down ... and I started crying because I didn't want to come back."[62] Another visioner in Jos described a vision in which he was transported out of body for an encounter with Jesus "coming from the north." He narrated:

> I could feel His heart ... I was sharing His pains, His burden. And suddenly when I was looking at His eyes there were two things I saw ... I saw passion and judgment. There was nothing on the left eye, no tears, just the right eye. And while I was looking at the tears that [were] coming then it's like there was this force that came, electricity, it moves to every joint in my body. My joints were dismantled. Every joint in my body was dismantled by the power of that current.[63]

A 37-year-old woman of Enugu, Nigeria narrated an emotion-packed sighting of Jesus after her third miscarriage:

---

60 "Dreams and Visions Transcription," 20.
61 "Dream Narratives from the Audio Recordings of the Dreams and Visions Project," 31.
62 "Dreams and Visions Transcription," 44.
63 Ibid., 52.

> Everyone would be asleep in the night, I would wake up and I would start crying. I would cry and I would be asking God, "[w]hy, why am I going through all this? Why am I losing my children? What is happening to me? Give me an answer, Lord." I would pray ... I would just talk ... my eyes are open but I would be sobbing, crying, shaking. Then it happened one night when I was just sitting by the bed like this, crying and weeping, I saw [that] someone stood by the door like this ... God came and stood by that door. The minute I saw Him ... with my eyes open ... the minute I saw Him, I started smiling, I was weeping before, but now I'm happy ... He comforted me really ... after that vision I didn't sob again.[64]

During interviews, the visioners were visibly reliving the emotions of their dreams and visions, and the potency of that emotion drew me in, as well. One particular interview with a female academic and pastor's wife in Nigeria was especially moving. She shared about various D/V occurrences, including dreams in which the answers to exams were revealed the night before (also mentioned in Chapter 5). She wept during a portion of her interview as she narrated her struggle to pursue higher education on very limited resources, "God raised people to assist me." I also wept as she shared of the pastor who received an audition in which he heard God tell him to assist her with resources, reportedly calling her by name and saying, "[g]o look for My daughter."[65]

The emotions of joy and wonder were manifested as well as feelings of love and endearment. In a survey, a 28-year-old Ghanaian man wrote about his dream, "[i]t gave me joy in the dream." In another instance, a 61-year-old Tanzanian pastor shared exuberantly of a dream which directed him to a choice parcel of land:

> I had a dream of a certain place which is very productive, fertile, and with the name of [?]. I went to check on the map ... and I found that name, though it is not exactly the same, but related. I went there physically ... and I was astonished to find that it was a place with water and irrigation and it was good for farming. I founded my project there! But I got it from a dream! A very good area for farming, readily available, [with] different crops growing, and I started my projects. But I got it from a dream![66]

---

64   "Dreams and Visions Transcription," 101.
65   Ibid., 12.
66   Ibid., 186.

The sense of wonder was also expressed in an interview with one of the male visioners from Jos, Nigeria:

> Before I got married to my wife I was on my knees in the afternoon praying and suddenly an angel appeared to me … I was on my knees. And he was holding a baby boy. He said, "[t]ake." I said, "[n]o." He said, "[i]t's your son, take." I said, "I'm not married!" Then he threw the child … I caught the child, but then I discovered it was a vision. I was still on my knees in the same position and the angel wasn't there anymore. Ahhh! I said, "what is this?"[67]

It is apparent that these experiences have promoted strong affections and spiritual transformation, or in other words, an emergence toward deepened intimacy with God. In fact, the observation is that the strong sense that he or she is known and cared for by God accounts for the epistemic vitality that visioners exhibit. Additionally, when I shared that some Christians in the West do not experience D/Vs, visioners expressed their surprise that it is possible for Christians to have no dreams or visions. For them, such a state of the visionless Church is to be pitied, as is clear from what the pastor of a thriving ministry in Jos commented, "[s]ome of them from my denomination condemn dream[s]. And I always felt very sorry for them. I am a product of dream[s]."[68]

One recent study contributes to understanding the affections and their link to Pentecostal-Charismatic love for God and others. The Flame of Love Project was made possible by a grant from the John Templeton Foundation and researchers included several social scientists including Margaret Poloma, Matthew Lee, and Donald E. Miller along with ethicist Stephen Post and theologians Amos Yong and Mark J. Cartledge. Valuable insights from the project are shared in the volume *The Heart of Religion: Spiritual Empowerment, Benevolence, and the Experience of God's Love* (2013). Set within the American context and substantiated by interviews with over one hundred Christian men and women, research findings showed a distinct correlation between Pentecostalism, experiences of divine love, and selfless benevolence or expressions of godly love.

The experiential aspect of spirituality and the generative aspect of the affections in terms of the sharing of godly love interface with results of this Dreams and Visions Project. According to the researchers of the Flame of Love Project,

---

67 "Dreams and Visions Transcription," 56–57.
68 Ibid., 20.

those who self-identified as Pentecostal or charismatic (pentecostal) scored higher on the "Divine Love scale" and concomitantly higher on community outreach. At the core of the impulse toward social engagement was the relationship between spirituality and benevolence. And within that core, findings showed that experiences of being loved by God, or divine love and a sense of call have a direct connection with community benevolence. While the experience of God's love was not a prerequisite for acts of benevolence, the link was apparent. "Our survey finding suggests that a personal and experiential knowledge of God's love is indeed an important factor that has been too long overlooked."[69]

The findings of the Dream and Visions Project enhance what can be known from the Flame of Love Project by pointing out the crucial influence of dreams and visions in the lives of African Pentecostal-Charismatics who develop deep love for God and others. The quest for understanding the pneumatological imagination and D/Vs has come upon the impulses of love, perceived, received and shared with others, as a corollary of the investigation on spiritual knowledge. The goal of the dreams and visions research was to be able to describe the nature of a pentecostal epistemology that values D/V experiences as part of Christian spirituality and as sources of spiritual knowledge. An aim was to understand the dynamics involved in how the experiences led to translation into spiritual knowledge and, at times, into action. But a key generative dynamic that surfaced was the experience of deep affection and love, of awe, and the resultant sense of intimacy with God, as noted in the interviews and surveys cited above. These affective elements show an intersection with the findings of the Flame of Love Project, and are also made evident in the following section.

2.3   *The Visionary Church and Missionary Agency*

Whether characterized by love, anguish, joy, or wonder, D/V experiences are remarkable for the emotions they evoke and for the resolve toward action those emotions can produce. The D/V narratives have left the strong impression that the pneumatological imagination represents the locus of Pentecostal affections and passion. Dreams and visions fuel the Spirit-compelled Church. This section explores more case studies which reflect emergence toward social engagement, cases in which visioners begin to see themselves as agents in the public sphere. As in the case of women featured earlier in this chapter,

---

69   Matthew T. Lee, Margaret Poloma, and Stephen G. Post, *The Heart of Religion: Spiritual Empowerment, Benevolence, and the Experience of God's Love* (New York, NY: Oxford University Press, 2013), 29.

the pentecostal principle and the dynamic of emergence are reflected in the capacity to begin and the development of new identities as missional agents.

One example of identity formation toward the en-Spirited agent is depicted in the 31-year-old Ghanaian man who wrote that the dreams he received influenced him to see himself as a Spirit-filled person.[70] The concept of identity shaping was also emphasized in the narrative given by an evangelist in Jos, Nigeria who shared how dreams and visions have inspired confidence regarding what he can do for God:

> A: How have your dream life and your visionary life changed the way you see yourself?
>
> I: I was a timid person. I don't speak in the congregation. I'm always shy. I'm a reserved person, even in school, nobody knows me. I'm not educated, I'm not trained, but my vision and dream [have] transformed me into a man of confidence. I've [stood] before thousands of people, 15,000 people and ministered to them in stadiums, in auditoriums at home and abroad ... My vision and dream have given me confidence in God. It has given me confidence, it has given me hope, it has given me courage ... I don't serve God with doubt.[71]

Cases which show the agency of women in ministry in the churches and also in the public sphere were highlighted in the section above discussing D/Vs and Pentecostal-Charismatic women. Here, men who are also exemplars of the compelled visionary Church are introduced. An example of the impact of a vision to produce the shoving power for acting against socially accepted behavior, in this case, in the eyes of local church leadership, comes from Nigeria. Pastor Ayo of Livingstar Church and Ayooluwa Kukoyi Missions in Ibadan, Nigeria shared about the vision he received from God in which the mandate given was to bring relief to village children who had no recourse to education. He began the work of building relationships with the families and then transported village children to the city to attend schools. He also cared for their nurture in the word of God. He remarked that the call to such work ran against the grain of what pastors in his region regarded as acceptable, since it was considered mixing "social work" with pastoral ministry.

Pastor Kukoyi felt that others regarded him as a politician rather than a "man of God," and that type of stigma was a challenge to him. Pastor Kukoyi

---

70 "Spontaneous Dream and Vision Reports from Surveys," 11.
71 "Dreams and Visions Transcription," 26.

exemplifies that element of social emergence so often connected to the D/V experience. His story also reflects the strength of the vision experience to impact his personal understanding of his spirituality. Like the woman of Tanzania and the Sunday School-teacher-turned- evangelist of Aba Motor Park, Nigeria, Pastor Kukoyi, depicts the "Progressive Pentecostal" as described in a recent ethnography of socially active Pentecostals.[72]

The report from Pastor Magesté Merope of Lomé, Togo is intriguing because of how his experience brought about an awareness of a marginalized group he had never considered. Up until the time of the vision, he had not given much thought to the plight of drug addicts in his community, nor had he considered their needs. As he reported the incident, Magesté had a vision of a piece of paper floating down from heaven. In the vision, he picked up the paper and read the words on it: "Jesus for drug addicts." He had no understanding of how to go about ministering to the addicted of his community, but at the suggestion of the overseers of his denomination, he traveled to Brazil to receive training from ministry leaders there.[73]

Another example of emergence in the Church is evidenced in the narrative of Sam Akaakaa, founder of the House of Recab orphanage in Jos, Nigeria. He shared of a dream he had in which he said God directed him to read Jeremiah chapter 35 and then to establish a home for orphans modeled after the principled lives of the Recabites of the Bible. Sometime after receiving a few orphans into the home, he and his wife were contacted by a friend who was a teacher in the northern region. "Can you take some more orphans?" He later came to find out that his friend was referring to about 200 children that had fled the area of the Boko Haram attacks on foot. Sam and his wife brought them all to their residence and now oversee a staff of several workers who provide educational and other services at their campus.[74]

The report from a Ghanaian man who converted from Islam to Christianity because of a vision is important because of how the experience evoked a dramatic change of identity, and also for how it redirected him back to his rural village. The decision to go back to live in the village was not an easy one to

---

72   Miller and Yamamori, *Global Pentecostalism*, 2–3. See also Chapter 1 fn. 8.
73   This information was shared with me while attending a Global Teen Challenge Africa conference with Merope in Accra, Ghana in 2015.
74   "Dreams and Visions Transcription," 57. In a response to the critique that the rationality of Spirit hermeneutics and D/Vs should not overlook scholarship on the detrimental effects of large orphanages, I affirm the helpfulness of blending rationalities. See Anna Droll, "The Spirit and the Poor in West Africa and Tanzania: A Pentecostal Response to David J. Bosch's 'Mission in the Wake of the Enlightenment,'" *Missiology: An International Review* 48:2 (2020) 181–191.

make. The village is generally understood as the place one customarily leaves behind in search of work and the activities and comforts of urban life. But in the vision, two people dressed in white healed him of his sickness and then directed him to go back to his village to preach about Jesus Christ. Thankful for his healing and having surrendered to the call to service there, he returned to teach at the village school and to develop relationships with the children and their families in hope of also sharing the gospel of Jesus.[75]

The founder of Onatech Centre for Research, Counseling and Control of Internet Abuse, Rotimi Onadipe, described a prolific history of dreams and visions which he had recorded in twenty-one notebooks he brought to our interview in Ibadan, Nigeria. As in the case of other Pentecostal activists, Onadipe took the initiative to reach out to the marginalized of his community, yet his story is notable for its focus on the obscure subculture of internet fraudsters. Onadipe stated that in his D/V experiences he saw himself ministering to the youth involved in internet scamming. Onadipe eventually decided to research the activities of fraudsters, managing to spend long periods of time with them and observing their lifestyle and their means of acquiring their skills in computer technology. His research took him outside of Nigeria to other West African countries, as well. Today, Onadipe's Centre serves people willing to be counseled and rehabilitated out of internet fraud and provides ministry to their parents, as well. Onadipe's work has gained the attention of local and international media.

There is one last notable example pointing to the impact of the compelled Church for social engagement, an impact made in a more private way and expressed in just a few sentences. It came from a male seminarian who filled out a written survey in Ghana and who had practiced medicine before entering the seminary. The experience was described as a dream and as "my conversion story":

> [I] was on the way to perform an abortion and saw a group of children looking at me. When [I was] about to beat them, a person came behind them. His awesomeness and stern[ness] attracted me. He beckoned me and I followed Him. That figure, or the personality, turned [out] to be Jesus of the Bible, and that [is] my conversion story.[76]

---

75   "Dream Narratives from the Audio Recordings of the Dreams and Visions Project," 31.
76   "Spontaneous Dream and Vision Reports from Surveys," 3.

3   Conclusion

In this chapter, the dynamic of the pentecostal principle at work in the reception and interpretation of D/Vs in the lives of Pentecostal-Charismatic visioners was the focus. It was shown that visioners processed what they understood to be insights of spiritual knowledge and responded to them through the practice of prayer and sometimes dream cancellation, distinctive practices reflecting Nimi Wariboko's profile of the pentecostal warrior. The D/V narratives pointed to a pentecostal epistemology which wielded strong impact on the identity of visioners. Pentecostal knowing resulted in missional impulses which demonstrated compassion for the marginalized and shunned populations such as the nefarious Agbaro boys of Aba and the fraudsters of Ibadan. The data revealed that the journey to a transformed identity and missional agency was also linked to the affective impact of the D/V experience. The feelings one has about oneself and about God and which lead to deeper spiritual and religious commitments are evoked by the D/V experience. That affectivity reinforces what scholars in the West have been discussing about the nature of Pentecostal spirituality in their own contexts. There is, therefore, an implication that affectivity is a transcultural characteristic of Pentecostalism, one which the visioners of this project bring into particular and vivid display. This point and other implications of the study will be touched on in the next chapter.

As made evident in Chapter 5, the extent to which D/Vs and their interpretations carry such significance in Pentecostal spirituality is due to their biblical moorings in the minds of visioners. Accordingly, Spirit-emphasis saturates the pneumatological imagination and enlivens the Pentecostal-Charismatic with a posture of optimism for the potential of a dream or vision experience. Visioners perceive the Spirit as able to divulge hidden knowledge and superintend such experiences, while also giving discretionary wisdom for the interpretive process. That discretion allows for transforming the experience for Pentecostal significance. In that case, the ancestor dream may lose its foreboding connotations for the Christian, and be received as the Spirit at work, while the night flight of traditional witchdemonology is rendered a refreshing excursion gifted by God. Therefore, Chapters 5 and 6 have offered a window into some of the distinctive characteristics of a pentecostal epistemology funded by the dream or vision experience and have highlighted their significance for Pentecostal life and spirituality.

In Chapter 7, the discussion turns to the significant "take-aways" from this study for African Pentecostal theology. It also explores the usefulness of the data for engaging in conversations being had in non-African contexts regarding the nature of Pentecostal or charismatic epistemology.

CHAPTER 7

African Dreams and Visions for Pentecostal Epistemologies

> God, if it's You, give me another dream.
> Tanzanian pastor, Dar es Salaam[1]

∴

> God is still in the business of speaking to people.
> WILLIAM A. DYRNESS[2]

∴

This study has shown that the dream or vision has held special significance in African traditional religions as well as in Near East religions, and that D/Vs remain of enduring value today in the lives of certain Pentecostal-Charismatics. Here, Chapter 7 explores the implications of the study for Pentecostal-Charismatic theology in Africa. The idea that D/V experiences and their interpretations show an intersection of epistemology with an implicit theology of dreams and visions is pressed into. Then, the contributions of the study for engaging the contemporary discussion on Pentecostal or charismatic epistemologies which is taking place outside of African contexts is explored. It will be demonstrated that rather than presenting entirely novel epistemic values, this pentecostal epistemology affirms the intuitions about Pentecostal knowing being voiced in the West, while also providing samples of the actualities in African contexts. In the West, the so-called remedies of modernity and Westernization have not succeeded in completely turning away from the life of the interior. The result is that there are threads of transcultural affinity that can be traced in the way Pentecostal-Charismatics expect the Spirit to speak, how willing they are to assess spiritual knowledge on more elastic terms, and how

---

[1] "Dreams and Visions Transcription," 217.
[2] William A. Dyrness, *Insider Jesus: Theological Reflections on New Christian Movements* (Downers Grove, Illinois: IVP Academic), 80.

important experience is to them in the development of relational knowing. The D/Vs of African Pentecostal-Charismatics are important interlocutors on these topics.

1 African Dreams for African Pentecostal Theology

One of the achievements of this research is the verification of the value of D/V experiences in contemporary Pentecostal-Charismatic spirituality in some African contexts. It, therefore, bridges the reality of epistemic orientation with Pentecostal experience. Before venturing to offer intuitions about what the study means for Pentecostal-Charismatic theology in those contexts, it is best to bring in an interlocutor here who can refocus the discussion on the African epistemic milieu that D/Vs appear in.

Caribbean-born British theologian Clifton R. Clarke studied under Allan Anderson at the University of Birmingham in the UK. He is helpful to consult in this chapter because of the understanding of Ghanaian modes of thought he has gleaned from research among the Akan peoples of AIC churches and his knowledge of African epistemology in general. He explains epistemology in that context in his investigation of the formation of Christian thought and theology.

One of the issues that Clarke drives home in regard to African epistemology is the fact that understanding African thought is a matter of engaging with sources of thought expressed in various cultural modes. Clarke has argued that the story of epistemology for Africa is tied to the eddies of Egyptian thought in existence far earlier than the thinking of pre-modern and modern Europeans. That thought culture relied upon symbolic imagery, carried by various vehicles of expression, for communicating reality about truth and spirituality. Therefore, Clarke posits that one should be prepared to cull "epistemic sources found in African culture as an alternative to cerebral and rationalistic premises," for example, modes of expression such as myths, songs, dance, symbols such as Adinkra symbols, and proverbs.[3]

---

3 Clarke, *Pentecostalism*, loc. 767, and 1042. Additionally, a reference to the awakening of non-Africans to the value of myths and oral tradition is noted in Nigerian Isidore Okpewho's comment: "Daniel McCall weighs the place of oral historical narratives within the scheme of historical knowledge and is convinced that they are as valuable as written accounts in terms of providing the raw materials out of which historical judgment can be formed." See Isidore Okpewho, *Myth in Africa* (UK: Cambridge University Press, 1983), 116.

In this way, one can locate the trajectory leading from traditional, theistic epistemology and the recognition of the Supreme God to African Christianity. Unfortunately, Western assumptions led to what Clarke calls the "suffocation of other sources of knowledge, particularly those of traditional societies."[4] Clarke locates the neglect of interest in understanding African thought embedded in normative cultural forms as having negatively impacted the transmission of Christianity. He writes, "[i]t was the lack of insight to effectively tap into this realm that made Christianity epistemically marginal."[5]

Certain symbols reflect a language of African thought that enrich one's understanding of traditional concepts. Clarke makes reference to the *Adinkra* symbols used by the Ashanti of Ghana, pointing to their meaning as laden with references to God. An example is the *Adinkra* symbol that relays *Gye Nyame*, "Except God," which Clarke explains is an indication of God's independence and self-sufficiency as Supreme God in the Ghanaian mindset.[6] Another *Adinkra* icon that expresses an attribute of God is the *Hye Anhye* which translates "Unburnable One," and which Clarke points out is uncannily reminiscent of the Exodus account of the burning bush.[7] The fact of being "unburnable" points to God's ontological nature as indestructible. Clarke notes how that nature is understood among Pentecostal preachers to be transmitted through the Holy Spirit to those who serve God so that they are able to survive evil attacks in spiritual warfare.[8]

Clarke also explains the importance of drawing from myths for an understanding of the concepts which populate the African mindset. His example is the myth in which a woman pounding grain with a long pestle inadvertently knocks it against the sky so as to annoy God with the disturbance. She then goes farther so as to unwittingly hit him in the eye and cause his withdrawal and distancing from the earth and from humans. The old woman attempts to bridge the gap between earth and the sky by stacking wooden mortars, but it crashes down and kills her with her children and other observers. Clarke points to this myth as an indication of the underlying sense of being distanced from God due to evil deeds.[9] A theological lens, therefore, notes the

---

4   Clarke, *Pentecostalism*, loc. 729.
5   Ibid., 729.
6   Ibid., loc. 976.
7   Ibid., 996.
8   Ibid., loc., 1006.
9   A female reading yields additional insights. Mercy Amba Oduyoye notes the use of myths to portray women in denigrating ways. For example, in regard to other West African tales, Oduyoye comments, "[t]here is a tendency in folktalk to use women to illustrate negative traits … The telling of the story is used by society to warn everyone of the potential

preparation for understanding the need for reconciliation embedded at the "subliminal level" of African thought life.[10] Clarke traces traditional religious beliefs to the African Pentecostal born again experience, noting that the "cosmic outlook" and biblical worldview are in agreement and that the milieu for "deploying the power of the Holy Spirit into the cosmological realm" has also enabled Pentecostal beliefs to flourish.[11]

Clarke also describes the dynamics of orality in African cultures as carrying the "epistemic symbolism of words."[12] That symbolism is far from static, but imbued with power for moving between the realms of the physical and the immaterial, thereby "transcending verbalism" with an impact that reaches multiple dimensions.[13] Clarke again traces the implications for contextualization of Pentecostalism. He notes the Pentecostal emphasis on the Word of God as *Rhema*, that is, as utterance, in contrast to the emphasis on the Scripture as written expression. Clarke makes reference to Jesus' indications of the intrinsic link between thoughts and words, as described in Jesus' exhortation regarding culpability connected to thinking adulterous thoughts (Matt. 5:28). Thoughts and words both translate into powerful agents in a world of the seen and unseen beings. Clarke concludes that due to epistemic intuitions regarding orality, African Pentecostals also take seriously Jesus' instruction that his own words are "spirit and life" and, therefore, emphasize preaching as the most robust transmission of Christian faith.[14]

The enduring value of D/Vs should be introduced here in the discussion of the importance of symbols and the significance of orality for the transmission of religious thought. It does not seem difficult to trace these values through to the Spirit hermeneutics employed in D/V interpretation and the theologizing necessary to transpose D/Vs for spiritual nourishment. These processes

---

misuse of woman power." Mercy Amba Oduyoye, *Daughters of Anowa: African Women & Patriarchy* (Maryknoll, NY: Orbis Books, 1995), 33–34.

10   Clarke, *Pentecostalism*, loc. 888.
11   Ibid., 826.
12   Ibid., 900.
13   Ibid., 900.
14   Clarke also challenges the Western penchant for "glorification of cognitive knowledge" and mental constructs in a book chapter devoted to proposing that Pentecostals aim for a "dialogue of life" for Christian-Muslim relations. There he adds a fresh dimension to communication through words. The "dialogue of life" would involve "mutual exposure" and contact in "the spirit of *ubuntu*." See Clifton Clarke, "Nigerian Pentecostalism and Islam: Toward a Pentecostalized Vision of Interreligious Coexistence Through Ubuntu Philosophy" in *Global Renewal Christianity: Spirit-Empowered Movements Past, Present, and Future*, vol. 3, Vinson Synan, Amos Yong, and J. Kwabena Asamoah-Gyadu, editors (Lake Mary, FL: Charisma House, 2016), 357, 359.

are especially highlighted in Chapter 5. The assessment of symbols through a Christian lens and the function of dream narration as a personal and communal practice are basic to making Pentecostal sense of D/Vs. At the same time, the project of articulating theology is more implicit and expressed through praxis rather than an exercise of another type. In this study, except for the case of Opoku Onyinah of Ghana, who articulated his thoughts on dreams in his published writings as well as during an interview (see Chapter 3), the production of a theology of dreams and visions is reflected as an oral exercise enacted in the impromptu responses to personal interview questions, as well as the product of thinking through the questions in the written survey.

In light of Clarke's contributions, and echoing the sensibilities expressed by prior scholars of African studies, the conclusion is that D/V appreciation for Pentecostal-Charismatics is characterized by a traditional cosmic worldview and the value of symbols and oral transmission. The importance of this study is found in how it makes explicit that a theology of dreams and visions is in operation within that epistemic milieu, if not specifically and comprehensively documented as such. In response to some academics of West Africa, the study contradicts the assumption that dreams are not important to Christians in West African (and Tanzanian) contexts. There is an existing theology, however implicit, which leads to D/Vs valuation and which draws from embedded modes of biblical and traditional thought. These support the value of D/Vs for production of a distinctive pentecostal epistemology. It points to the embracing of a way of knowing that is energized by the robust reception of D/V experiences in Pentecostal-Charismatic spirituality.

2 African Dreams for Western Pentecostal Epistemologies

It was noted in the analyses of D/V narratives that the hallmarks of the pentecostal principle and of emergence—elements of a Nigerian Pentecostal epistemology—are manifested in the visionary lives of those who participated in the study. In this section, certain prominent features of the D/V valuation of visioners and their dynamic impact on pentecostal spirituality are used as interlocutors for conversation with non-African scholars. The first theme addressed looks at the potency of the D/V narrative as also mirrored in Jean-Daniel Plüss' scholarship on the dynamism of the pentecostal narrative. Plüss examined the narratives of primarily European visioners and noted their evocative qualities. While Plüss offers a theological and philosophical examination of vision narratives, resesarch from the anthropological sector done in the USA is featured alongside that of Plüss because of its intersection on the point of visions. Tanya Luhrmann explored the experience of hearing the voice of God among charismatics of Vineyard churches in the USA, and in doing so located D/V narratives that bring insight about the pentecostal epistemology of her research participants. Both researchers contribute to shedding light on the contours of transcultural Pentecostal-Charismatic epistemology in ways that seem to converge at the horizon of this project.

The next three subsections follow suit in bringing out some epistemic features marking Pentecostal spirituality across cultures. The elements of relational knowing and of Pentecostal affectivity described in the experiences of this study are highlighted as complementary to the theologies of Pentecostals Cheryl-Bridges Johns and Steven J. Land. Similarly, the issue of embodiment in the Pentecostal experience of D/Vs is offered as reflective of the charismatic philosophy of James K. A. Smith. Finally, the interactive process of D/V interpretation demonstrated in D/V valuation and interpretation is held up to the light of Amos Yong's trialectic in Spirit hermeneutics. It is argued that the theological dynamics Yong proposes can be located in the praxis of the visioners of this project. Therefore, the section ahead proceeds in a series of correlations in order to drive home the observation, "this is that."

2.1 Religious Language and Hearing God's Voice

In 1988, Pentecostal Jean-Daniel Plüss published a dissertation written for the Catholic University of Leuven in Flanders, Belgium, *Therapeutic and Prophetic Narratives in Worship*. In it he reports about how visions and their narratives were upheld for their value to spirituality among the European Pentecostals he studied. Plüss explored the experiences for their impact as special religious language, and made observations regarding the effects they evoked.

In regard to functionality, he found that visions "relate a christian imperative (from an inter-subjective point of view) to any given situation," and they yield a "surplus value" which is "recognizable in the action that results."[15] The vision narratives function therapeutically for the Church, and also specifically for navigating the socialization brought on by secularism. And because their benefit moves beyond the privacy of individualism, Plüss suggests that the reports of religious experiences be described as vision-narratives that "belong in the public forum of interpretation and in the congregation of praise."[16] As that which promotes worship, Plüss mentions the "doxological movement" that flows from vision interpretations that point to "God's faithfulness and

---

15   Plüss, *Therapeutic and Prophetic Narratives in Worship*, 209.
16   Ibid., 158.

love," and again, in regard to impetus, he writes on the discernible value of visions assessed by their effects on initiating "Christian action in view of the other and the self."[17]

Plüss describes a distinctive epistemology congruent with the experience of visioners in this study. He also gives insight on the collaboration between the agency of the Spirit and human mental activity and therefore draws attention to the pentecostal epistemology funding vision narrations. For example, Plüss notes that "human mental activity is always involved in the production of spiritual insight" and "the hermeneutic activity of visions" so that "one can speak of a contextualization between mundane and spiritual knowledge."[18] The result of that knowledge generation is what Plüss locates at the heart of vision narratives. That narratives derived of that "insight" are described as having "therapeutic function" (nourishing/edifying), and also as having an impact on socialization and on initiating Christian action resonates with what this project defines as "identity-shaping" and "compelling." One example of the therapeutic function of a narrative from among reports in the Dreams and Visions Project is the report of a vision of Jesus that a woman experienced after she had suffered a series of miscarriages. She divulged, "[a]fter that vision, I didn't sob again, I knew that God is interested in my case. I knew that soon it would be over."[19] The experience was nourishing to her, but it is not difficult to imagine its therapeutic impact on others, as this author also experienced firsthand.

Plüss also refers to visions that result in promoting "the realization of the humanum."[20] The value of religious visions as "truly therapeutic" is manifested when they "initiate christian action in view of the other and the self," as mentioned above. D/Vs that compelled the visioner to Christian action have already been highlighted in Chapter 6, but similar types of compelling D/Vs will be noted briefly here, as well. One which impacted for personal growth was shared by a 31-year- old man in Tanzania:

I: I was sleeping then I was dreaming that I was wearing my graduation gown. So I used to work on it so I could graduate one day.
A: Where do you think that dream came from?
I: I think it was from God, yeah.[21]

---

17   Plüss, *Therapeutic and Prophetic Narratives in Worship*, 226, 209. 250–251.
18   Ibid., 251.
19   "Dreams and Visions Transcription," 101. She is also mentioned in Chapter 5.
20   Plüss, *Therapeutic and Prophetic Narratives in Worship*, 209.
21   Ibid., 171.

In another case, the use of narratives for congregational edification was brought out by a 57-year-old woman also from Tanzania. She first shared about a vivid audition she experienced in which she said God's voice woke her at night while sleeping to alert her regarding an intruder planning to enter her home. She then shared of how narrating the incident has nourished the faith of others:

> A: Do you think dreams and visions are important to women's ministry?
> I: I think they are very important.
> A: Why do you say that?
> I: They create awareness.
> A: How do you know? Do they tell you they are having dreams?
> I: Yes we had some programs for witnessing in our meetings. If she had [a] special dream which she thinks that she can share with us, she can ask for a time to share and it can be encouraging, if it's an encouraging dream—it can encourage the whole congregation.
> A: But you actually did that in your group?
> I: Yeah, I've been using this [testimony of the audition experience] to encourage girls.[22]

Such a testimony of rescue from danger reported to the congregation would no doubt result in what Plüss describes as the "doxological movement," demonstrating the emotive power of narratives to express sacred moments of wonder and gratitude toward God. In summary, congruent, fundamental aspects of pentecostal epistemology are on display when data from this project is held up to the light of Plüss' research on pentecostal visions.

The audition, that is, the hearing of a voice during a dream or vision episode, was often reported in the D/V narratives of this project. This is demonstrated in another excerpt of the interview with the woman who had perceived a call to care for youth in Tanzania:

> I: I knew it was God and I said, "[w]hat do you want me to do?" And then, I started hearing a voice telling me that "I want all the young people in Tanzania to be saved." Ha!
> A: You heard a voice?
> I: Yeah!
> A: A man's voice?
> I: It was like a man's voice.[23]

---

22 "Dreams and Visions Transcription," 204.
23 "Dreams and Visions Transcription," 144.

In respect to the experience of an audition, anthropologist Tanya Luhrmann found that those of the Vineyard churches she researched in the USA place a high value on learning to hear God's voice. Neither Pentecostal nor charismatic herself, Luhrmann's research within charismatic contexts has been widely acclaimed from various camps such as the *New York Times Book Review* and the *San Francisco Chronicle* as well as Harvard University and the Anthropology Department of UC San Diego. One of the important features she explains about Vineyardian epistemology is that these Christians train their attention and learn hermeneutical skills for hearing God's voice. The skill that Luhrmann located at the heart of the spiritual practices was the ability to "suspend disbelief, to create an epistemological space that is safe and resilient."[24] In fact, she found that the role of the leaders of Vineyard churches she experienced was to teach congregants regarding the nature of God as being the God who can be felt and known.[25] Therefore, "[t]he congregants practice having minds that are not private but open to the experience of an external God" and "They report vivid imaginative encounters with God."[26]

Luhrmann points out that the approach of *learning* to hear God's voice, and the assertion that He is always speaking, implies that those who cannot hear may only need to cultivate sensitivity and awareness. For these charismatics, a person's skill and style of seeking to experience God does not constrict God's supernatural ability to make himself known. Luhrmann describes the experiences of two women that portray the way congregants can learn to hear God's voice. The woman named Sarah shared how she understands prayer as a bidirectional link between the prayed for and the pray-er forged by the Holy Spirit. Luhrmann comments, "[s]he had learned to pay attention to her mind with the expectation that God would communicate images and impressions and she had begun to identify some of the mental events as instances of hearing God."[27] It is apparent that this type of God-communication depicts an epistemological posture of expectation and openness.

Luhrmann's account of Elaine's experiences describes D/Vs as important aspects of God-communication. While seeking the will of God for her life,

---

24 Tanya M. Luhrmann, *When God Talks Back: Understanding the American Evangelical Relationship with God* (New York, NY: Random House, 2012), 316.
25 Ibid., 131.
26 Ibid., 132.
27 Ibid., 134.

Elaine had a dream of an African safari and of a certain missions booklet. In waking life, soon after, a visiting female missionary showed her the same booklet at church and the pieces of the voice of God seemed to come together. Confirmation of the idea of missions in Africa came from another congregant sometime after. That woman had had a vision of Elaine being mentored by another woman who fit the description of the missionary visitor. These incidents were relayed to Luhrmann as the elements of Elaine's journey that included "direct experience of the Holy Spirit" and learning to listen to and act on the voice of God.[28]

This insight into the practices of American charismatics brings out an important point of affinity between Vineyardians and the visioners of the Dreams and Visions Project. Hearing the voice of God and its importance for Christian spirituality is found in both contexts. In fact, in the course of sharing about my research topic with others in the US, many Americans have eagerly shared their own D/Vs with me. I have heard narratives from American scholars (either their own or an experience of another), seminary colleagues, female pastors, and first time acquaintances.[29] Apparently, the US is home to a population of Pentecostal-Charismatic visioners experiencing their own big dreams.

2.2 Relational Knowing and Orthopathy

The visioners and their narratives demonstrate the interplay of knowledge reception and relationship development with God when their D/V experiences are framed as spiritual encounters. That intimacy was often relayed in the way they spoke fondly and trustingly of God. For example, a 29-year-old Ghanaian seminarian wrote of the effect of a dream on his life, "[f]rom that day, I believed that God really wants to use me for something purposefully."[30]

This relational dynamic is at the core of the Pentecostal epistemology that Pentecostal Cheryl Bridges Johns explains in her theology. She is the Robert E. Fisher Chair of Spiritual Renewal at Pentecostal Theological Seminary in the US. She argues for a turn away from the rationalism of evangelical epistemology in the pursuit of understanding Pentecostal education and formation. She makes a theological case for the inherent link between knowing and

---

28 Luhrmann, *When God Talks Back*, 275–278, citation 278.
29 At an informal dinner for the conference attendees of the Society of Pentecostal Studies held in San Dimas, CA in 2016, a student shared a dream in which he saw a casino machine and pulled the lever. The machine produced a jackpot in which the word "Claremont" came up three times. In his waking life he had been debating where to earn a graduate degree. When I asked where he decided to apply, he responded, "Claremont University."
30 "Spontaneous Dream and Vision Reports from Surveys," 2.

relationship, grounding learning and formation in the experience of God. The concept of knowing as the product of relationality offers the assist needed for conceptualizing epistemology according to biblical faith, and Johns brings that piece convincingly to the forefront in *Pentecostal Formation: A Pedagogy among the Oppressed* (1998).

In her volume, Johns interacts with the philosophy of education put forth by Brazilian Paulo Freire, appreciating, critiquing, and augmenting his theory. She resonates with his concerns but places her focus on a biblical epistemology of encounter which she sees at the core of transformation. That epistemology includes a knowing that is not marked by a distant, "objective" stance characteristic of the Greek idea of knowing, but one that reflects the covenant theologies of Old and New Testaments which demonstrate submission and obedience as the evidence of knowing intimately. Knowing is experiential and relational and measured by the response of the knower. Johns offers that "the nature and goals of biblical knowledge are best seen in the Hebrew word *yada*; to know is to encounter."[31]

Johns' *yada* epistemology also resolves the problem of praxis by answering: what is the impetus promoting and shaping praxis? That problem was located by another of Johns' interlocutors, practical theologian Daniel Schipani, who impacted Johns in terms of thinking about the way knowing through encounter develops into praxis. Currently on faculty at McCormick Theological Seminary in the US, Schipani had a concern for grounding liberation theology in an "epistemology of obedience." He warned that there is the possibility that praxis can become "making the truth through historical *praxis* rather than practicing the truth which is ultimately being revealed to us."[32] Schipani's comment highlights the lacuna that detachment from revelation presents. Addressing that conceptual gap, Johns asserts that Pentecostal spirituality involves encounter and interrelationality, openness to revelation, and deep emotional attachment to God. So, for Johns, an assessment of praxis of the Pentecostal type requires an awareness and appreciation of the deeper dispositions in order to explain the true heart of Pentecostal spirituality.

Johns also suggests that the comingling of knower and known in Pentecostal epistemology, which is the essence of *yada,* is situated in the biblical framing of the kingdom Jesus proclaimed.[33] She writes, "[t]he praxis that would flow

---

31 Cheryl Bridges Johns, *Pentecostal Formation: A Pedagogy among the Oppressed* (Eugene, OR: Wipf and Stock, 2010), 40 (previously published UK: Sheffield Academic Press, 1993).
32 Ibid., 40. Citation from Schipani, *Religious Education Encounters Liberation Theology*, 1988.
33 Concordantly, on pentecostal knowing James K. A. Smith writes, "[t]he way we know is more like a dance than a deduction." See James K. A. Smith, *Thinking in Tongues: Pentecostal*

out of such encounter would generate a fresh vision of the kingdom of God, a vision that incorporates an ethic that is consistent with an epistemology which joins knowing and loving."[34] Therefore, Johns touches on the type of impetus that has already been noted as a prominent feature of the D/Vs experience and its interpretation. Knowing, loving, and an ethic of caring demonstrated in social engagement is a distinctive of the pentecostal epistemology generating the big dreams of the visioners of this project.

The role of the affections in Pentecostal spirituality, noted especially in the analyses of Chapter 6, but also in Johns' comments above, is also emphasized in the theology of Steven J. Land. He is one of the earliest American scholars to venture beyond historical or exegetical work to theologize about Pentecostal spirituality.[35] In his volume *Pentecostal Spirituality: A Passion for the Kingdom* (1993), Land represents the reflective integration of the thoughts of the second generation of American Pentecostal theologians who came before him. His book is hailed as a benchmark work for making explicit the self-awareness of the Pentecostal regarding a distinctive epistemology. He highlights prayer and recognition of the Spirit in his work and writes, "[t]o do theology is not to make experience the norm, but it is to recognize the epistemological priority of the Holy Spirit in prayerful receptivity."[36]

Land's theology offers a distinctive articulation of the role of the affections. He writes, "[a]ffections are abiding dispositions which dispose the person toward God and the neighbor in ways appropriate to their source and goal in God."[37] Land shows how Pentecostal spirituality is an integration of orthodoxy, orthopathy, and orthopraxy, where orthopathy involves the affections and a sense of the love of God. He refers to theologian Theodore Runyon's use of "orthopathy" as derived from Runyon's study of John Wesley and 18th century Methodism. Runyon points out that the affective element expressed in the theologies of Wesley and Jonathan Edwards indicates a way of knowing

---

    Contributions to Christian Philosophy (Grand Rapids, MI: William B. Eerdmans Publishing Co., 2010), 82.

34   Johns, *Pentecostal Formation*, 40.

35   There was a spurt of theological thought generated from the early Pentecostals as reported by Douglas Jacobsen. See *Thinking in the Spirit: Theologies of the Early Pentecostal Movement* (Bloomington, IN: Indiana University Press, 2003) and Douglas Jacobsen, ed., *A Reader in Pentecostal Theology: Voices from the First Generation* (Bloomington, IN: Indiana University Press, 2006). James K. A. Smith and Amos Yong both began to publish in 1997 after Land.

36   Steven J. Land, *Pentecostal Spirituality: A Passion for the Kingdom* (New York, NY: Sheffield Academic Press, 1993), 38.

37   Ibid., 136.

God that involves feelings that focus energy and give passion. Runyon asserts that orthopathy is "religious experience as an event of knowing between the Divine Source and human participant."[38] He describes four factors pertaining to orthopathy:

1. "The divine source of experience who makes impressions on the spiritual senses of the human being."[39] This first factor links orthopathy to the confessional, religious convictions and self-understanding of the visionary. It also affirms that spiritual/bodily perceptions are facts undergirding the experience and funding it with substance for meaning-making.
2. "The *telos* of experience: the intention of the source, the purpose and goal for the human being."[40] In regard to discerning the purpose in a religious experience, the process of interpretation— which is referred to in this project as Spirit hermeneutics—involves conclusions on the part of the visionary about divine intentions.
3. "The transformation brought about through experience."[41] This third factor of orthopathy noted by Runyon deals with religious experiences of a therapeutic quality. It was also noted by Plüss to be linked to visions and their narratives which promote the theme of finding "wholeness."[42] Transformation was also featured in the quality of emergence exhibited by the visioners of this project.
4. "The feelings that accompany experience."[43] It is argued here that the D/Vs of many of the visioners of this project are marked by the feelings and emotions Runyon locates as part of the essence of orthopathy.[44] For the visioners, these experiential D/Vs register as encounters with God and are accompanied by emotion, emotions that Land's Pentecostal theology links to deeper dispositions of affection toward God and toward others.

Each of the four aspects of Runyon's concept of orthopathy, that state of being associated with feelings and dispositions linked to the religious experience of divine knowing, has its counterpart in the narratives of the Dreams and Visions Project. Runyon's assertion that religious experience involves impressions received by the "spiritual senses" leaves the definition of such impressions open to interpretation. Yet there is a definitive description visioners shared of

---

38   Land, *Pentecostal Spirituality*, 43.
39   Ibid., 43.
40   Ibid., 43.
41   Ibid., 43.
42   Plüss, *Therapeutic and Prophetic Narratives in Worship*, 162.
43   Land, *Pentecostal Spirituality*, 43.
44   Ibid.

the experiences *making spiritual sense*, and often because of what is sensed, whether in disposition or in bodily sensation. A Nigerian pastor shared, "[a]t times I will feel my body very weak and immediately, before I know it, I see some vision."[45] Similarly, the sensation of light was shared by a visioner in Jos. He said, "He was going up and I wanted to grab his leg and suddenly He diffused into light. And that was the light that I saw, that pierced through every cell of my being ... When I woke up I could still see the light all over my room."[46]

In respect to Runyon's next two points, discerning the *telos* of divine intention is a process that often goes hand in hand with the phenomena of personal transformation and "therapeutic" benefit. For example the narrative of a 40-year-old Tanzanian business woman offers this example:

> A: Tell me, how did it make you feel? Did it change the way you see yourself?
> I: Yes! The voice of God changed me from where I was. You know, He showed me that the first thing is to love people ... what God has done to me is to make me to un-love money.[47]

A 52-year-old Nigerian pastor also shared of life change, "I'm not educated. I'm not trained. But my vision and dream has transformed me into a man of confidence."[48] In a similar blending of the effects of religious experience, therapeutic benefits can also be tied to feelings and dispositions, such as in the case of a Tanzanian man who shared, "I just continued serving the Lord because I had peace in my heart that now…I'll go to school … so I went to the university."[49] In the case of a 59-year-old Nigerian woman in Enugu, joy was part of her story:

> My sister, she got sickness and that sickness took her to the hospital … 7 months in that place. I'm on the bed, and in the night I saw her in my dream … she is rejoicing! Rejoicing with me-o! Dancing, singing! So after three months … I went to her house and at the house we danced and danced and danced![50]

---

45 "Dreams and Visions Transcription," 61.
46 Ibid., 48.
47 Ibid., 221.
48 Ibid., 26.
49 Ibid., 217.
50 Ibid., 69.

2.3 Embodied Knowing

To add to the physical experiences of weakness of body and the sensation of seeing light, the sense of warmth was reported by a Tanzanian woman. In her case, she dreamt of being in a place where there was fire. Her translator shared, "[t]here were Christians who were enjoying things and who were not pleasing God at all. And there was a place of fire ... so she woke up and she felt very warm."[51] The woman came away with an interpretation of the dream, concluding that she had been given divine warning regarding the erring ones, and the sensations accompanying the dream played a part in extracting that knowledge. Embodied knowing reflects an epistemology that does not privilege abtract knowledge, but rather a holistic engagement with that which can be known, sometimes with senses of perception that are themselves undefinable. The discussion turns now to include the voice of an American charismatic philosopher who challenges a Western rationality that leaves no room for knowing of this type.

James K. A. Smith is unique among Western interlocutors because he is the first charismatic philosopher to seriously engage the deficiencies of Western epistemology. Smith holds the Gary & Henrietta Byker Chair in Applied Reformed Theology and Worldview at Calvin College in the US and has written several volumes explicating Pentecostal themes. Smith is convinced that Pentecostals should not accept "off-the-shelf" theological assumptions uncritically. "My goal is to sketch how we might articulate a uniquely Pentecostal philosophy, and what that Pentecostal philosophy has to offer broader conversations."[52] Along these lines, Smith uses the term "countermodernity" to describe the way that pentecostal knowing demonstrates bold contradictions to the "idolatrous reliance on reason" imposed by Enlightenment epistemology.[53] Harmonious with the epistemic stance of African visioners, Smith offers a conceptualization of a rationality of the Spirit, one that envisions God's self-disclosure as both possible and perceivable. He, therefore, argues against rationalist assumptions that render pentecostal knowing untenable.

Smith also claims that embodied knowing has been problematic for the West until today. He notes that "devaluation of embodiment as a source of

---

51 Dreams and Visions Transcription, 168.
52 K. A. Smith, *Thinking in Tongues: Pentecostal Contributions to Christian Philosophy* (Grand Rapids, MI: William B. Eerdmans Publishing Co., 2010), xiv-xv.
53 Ibid., 53. Smith borrows the term "idolatrous reliance on reason" from Andrew Rice, "Mission from Africa," *New York Times Magazine* April 12 (2009) 158. Note also that "pentecostal" without capitalization is used here as Smith uses it, to denote the Spirit-emphasis of the spirituality with no denominational implications.

deception and distress" marks the Euro-Western attraction to the abstract, and to the "cultural privileging of what is *cognitive*."[54] In his discussion of a pentecostal worldview, Smith offers that pentecostal epistemology holds to "a nondualistic affirmation of embodiment and materiality."[55] It understands the incarnation and resurrection of Christ, along with Jesus' concern for healing others as depicted in the gospels, as indications of the goodness of bodies and materiality. The value of bodies and holistic appreciation of the material contradicts the Manichean association of the body with evil, and this valuation is evident also in other trends of Christian thought, since, as Smith points out, attention to embodiment is also found in the attitudes and concerns at the heart of Catholic social engagement as well as liberation theology.

Smith suggests that prosperity teachings also represent the same type of values rooted in the sense that God "cares about our bellies and bodies" and that, accordingly, the prosperity teaching employs a holism and even demonstrates a "worldliness" in pentecostal theology.[56] The point is that, in this sense, pentecostal intuitions which override the dualism polarizing the body and Christian spirituality are made manifest in the occupation with healing and the holistic well-being of persons. Holism, embodiment, and attention to materialism are, therefore, distinctions of the pentecostal worldview, according to Smith.[57]

Once again, D/V experiences and their valuation reflect these pentecostal intuitions coming from a Western interlocutor. They are also the subject of much study for others in the West who explore their inherent link to bodily functions. The act of dreaming itself accentuates the embodied nature of cognition. Dreams are scientifically assessed as sensory experiences and have been investigated for their attendant biological manifestations, especially during REM (rapid eye movement) sleep. Scientific research concludes that they involve strong emotions (due to sustained functioning of the amygdala) and the activating and deactivating of certain neurological functions such as

---

54 Smith, *Thinking in Tongues*, 54.
55 Ibid., 41.
56 Ibid., 43.
57 From the sector of pedagogical and feminist philosophy, Barbara J. Thayer-Bacon offers engaging scholarship which interfaces with Johns' concerns for defining epistemology as relational and with Smith's locating of the estrangement of the bodily. She makes similar observations about the duality of the bodily and the intellectual. In her assessment of the epistemological cleavage, it was set in place long before Descartes and the Enlightenment, since there was a severing of the mind and body in Platonic thought. Thayer-Bacon locates it in Plato's theory of knowledge that argues that the body was the cause of human forgetfulness of knowledge. See Barbara J. Thayer-Bacon, *Relational "(e)pistemologies"* (New York, NY: Peter Lang Publishing, 2003), 26.

higher level visual cortex (for processing imagery) and that which induces the paralysis that accompanies the REM state.

The scholarly discussion regarding activation within these processes in the brain suggests there is a growing understanding of just how complex these functions are.[58] Neuroscientist Warren S. Brown explains the issue of embodiment and cognition this way, "[t]o say we are *embodied* is to move away from the Cartesian idea of a disembodied soul as the source of our religiousness and spirituality and toward the idea of humankind as nested in God's physical creation. We were created by God as beings inescapably implicated with the physical and biological world. What is more, a lot of recent research and theory suggests that we are truly em-bodied and not just em-brained."[59]

The D/Vs of this project draw attention to this embodied aspect of knowing in Pentecostal-Charismatic epistemology. Along with its other hallmarks, embodiment marks pentecostal knowing as distinctive. This way of knowing is also valued as that which gives insight to the true state of things with wisdom from "behind the veil." Knowledge from D/V experiences, and the often attendant experience of audition, is understood as spiritual knowledge from God which is meant to promote the well-being of visioners and others. Additionally, it is a relational knowing which fosters prayer and intimacy with the Spirit and which expresses the divine *telos* of mission. In concert with Smith's concern for upholding divine value for the material, it is not difficult to see how the D/V experience, embedded as it is in physicality, contributes to Smith's "countermodernity" critique against the "idolatrous reliance on reason." Yet, dreams have not been ignored by the sciences but have been been validated as important specimans of human experience. Therefore, ironically, they have found value in the academic arena of the Western rationality Smith finds suspect, although perhaps for different reasons than the Pentecostal-Charismatics have put forth.

2.4 *Knowing in the Trialectic of Spirit–Word–Community*

In an interview in Tanzania, a 60-year-old Assemblies of God pastor emphasized how careful the visioner must be in his or her efforts to interpret a dream or vision. He said:

---

58 Erin J. Wamsley and John S. Antrobus, "Dream Production: A Neural Network Attractor, Dual Rhythm Regional Cortical Activation, Homeostatic Model" in *The New Science of Dreaming*, Volume 1, Deirdre Barrett and Patrick McNamara, eds. (Westport, CT: Praeger Publishers, 2007), 174–177.

59 Warren S. Brown, "The Brain, Religion, and Baseball: Revisted," *Fuller* 5 (2016) 47.

If dreams and visions come they should be tested by the word of God. In 1 John 4:1 it says we should test the spirits [to see] if they come from God or the evil side. There are so many spirits operating. If you allow everyone to tell their dream or vision you can allow chaos in the church.[60]

Also, according to a 59-year-old woman of a Pentecostal church in Enugu, Nigeria, dreams of a negative nature are reported by members to the pastor:

The Holy Spirit of God, when He comes to me, my own mind will know that it is from God because of what He shows me in the Bible ... what is in line with God. If any of our members dream, if that dream is not good, he will come to the church. He will tell pastor or she will tell pastor ... So we join together and pray and cancel the dream and the dream will not come out.[61]

The Spirit hermeneutic described above also portrays the concepts Pentecostal theologian Amos Yong describes in his volume *Spirit–Word–Community: Theological Hermeneutics in Trinitarian Perspective* (2002). In his work, Yong explains the process of theological interpretation in terms of a Trinitarian theology which puts due emphasis on pneumatology, or the agency of Spirit. The dynamics portrayed above in the interview excerpts—that of Scriptural referencing and communal interpretation by the Spirit—reflect Yong's theological framework conceptualized to include dreams and visions, as shown modeled in Figure 5.

Amos Yong is Professor of Theology and Mission at Fuller Theological Seminary in Pasadena, California. He has had a verdant academic career as a scholar and educator who has produced an array of published works. He has written on a host of topics and has been noted for developing Pentecostal thought for the theology of religions, interfaith dialogue, and missiology. Yong's ecumenical posture and ability to apply theological intuitions across disciplines have proven both theologically and philosophically fruitful.

Yong explains the substance of his volume thus, "[m]y central thesis is that theological hermeneutics—the activity of reading or interpreting things related to the divine—is a continuous interplay of Spirit, Word, and Community."[62] For Yong, a pneumatological-trinitarian epistemology (way of

---

60   "Dreams and Visions Transcription," 175.
61   Ibid., 68.
62   Amos Yong, *Spirit–Word–Community: Theological Hermeneutics in Trinitarian Perspective* (Eugene, OR: Wipf and Stock, 2002), 14.

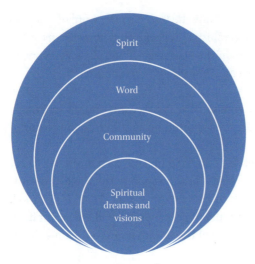

FIGURE 5   Dreams, visions and Spirit–Word–Community

knowing by the Spirit) goes hand in hand with a trinitarian ontology for producing a "comprehensive theological hermeneutics and methodology."[63] In essence, an interpretive grid and approach for evaluating human contact with God and the world must be grounded in the Spirit as the agency guiding how one thinks (rationality) as well as how one knows (epistemology). And that divine experience is not tepid. Yong writes, "[a]s irruption, the Spirit breaks forth from within our lives, from inside, as it were, to transform us, our ways of living, understanding, anticipating."[64]

Yong envisions the role of the Spirit of Christ, who is rationality, from within a construct of the Spirit's creative scope understood as "foundational pneumatology." Drawing from biblical tradition, he notes that the Spirit is "the fundamental notion of intelligibility itself" as well as "the mediator or communicator of rationality."[65] Yong also relates the dynamic of Spirit to knowledge thus, "[r]ationality or intelligibility … can be seen as the correlation between the forms of things and the structures of the mind: this issues forth in knowledge."[66] Yet more specifically, the process of human receptivity, knowledge acquisition, and agency are tied to semiotic theory (the appraisal of signs),

63   Yong, *Spirit–Word–Community*, 19.
64   Ibid., 224.
65   Ibid., 35.
66   Ibid., 16.

concepts pertaining to perception for knowing which Yong borrows from C.S. Peirce and which he envisions as reflective of the processes of pneumatological imagination within Spirit-generated hermeneutics.[67]

Yong also touches on the subjectivity of interpretation, first of all pointing out, "[a]ll interpretation is motivated by practical concerns."[68] Yet, subjectivity is the condition for interpretation and not an impediment since the Spirit and the Community guide epistemic processes. For the Christian, interpretation is the function of reading Scripture in faith, but also the function of employing "discernment of the divine presence."[69] Yong writes, "[t]heological knowledge emerges from these particular matrices as the Spirit manifests herself through interpretive actions by such selves-in-communities on datum that are continuously shifting and evolving."[70]

The exercise of interpreting and making meaning of spiritual dreams and visions brings the abstract dynamics of Yong's theology into the realm of praxis. The quest for interpretations of D/V experiences is, in fact, a seeking out that reflects practical concerns. The D/V narratives have shown that semiotic appraisal within the interpretive process functions in dialogue with the biblical witness (with its particular signs) and with the expectation of the Spirit as guide. Importantly, the weighing of D/V datum is a communal activity for the visioner situated in the Pentecostal-Charismatic church. After all, the often dominant narrative of spiritual warfare that informs the social imaginary requires that the hermeneutics guiding D/V valuation be superintended by none other than the Spirit who is Lord.

3   Conclusion

This chapter has showcased how the theological musings of Pentecostal-Charismatics in Western contexts resonate with the actualities in theology and praxis in African Pentecostal-Charismatic contexts in regard to knowing God experientially. What comes into view is a transcultural concern for the articulation of a rationality of the Spirit for those who claim to live by the Spirit. This study has added to the conversations in the West by highlighting a rationality of the Spirit that includes the reception of dreams and visions. It is suggested here that the Spirit hermeneutics at work when visioners of this project reflect

---

67   Yong, *Spirit–Word–Community*, 151–164.
68   Ibid., 237.
69   Ibid., 243.
70   Ibid., 243–244.

on their experiences mirrors the Spirit–Word–Community paradigm set forth by Amos Yong.

Yet, the participants of the study have also voiced concern about the limits of subjectivity when it comes to interpretation. In the case studies of this project, it is apparent that discernment regarding D/V interpretation is a matter of ecclesiastic concern. Pastors are held in high esteem as those who can interpret them circumspectly using biblical wisdom. As already mentioned, some D/V narratives can be judged as divisive and manipulative strategies, as Rev. Djakouti Mitré of the Assemblies of God in Togo shared.[71] As General Superintendent of the denomination, he has been called upon to mediate in difficult situations, not only in his own country, but also in other places of West Africa. The implication is that perhaps some instances have dealt with claims of receiving special insight through visionary experiences. It was explained in the story shared by Opoku Onyinah of Ghana that his sleep experience was kept in confidence between himself and his closest ministerial connections in order that it not give rise to suspicions that he was touting self-promoting ambitions.[72] Yet, among themselves a conclusion was made regarding the significance of the experience and Onyinah himself derived personal encouragement from it.

The issue of spiritual knowledge, D/V interpretations, and discernment places the discussion of dreams and visions into crucial conversation with how the problem of discernment affects issues of accountability in and outside the Church. For example, what of the allegations of witchcraft that can stem from visionary experiences? Might visions of this type be impacting the trend in Ghana toward the ostracization of women, compelling them to seek refuge in camps?[73] And what of the abuses that could be spawned from claims of visions used to manipulate those caught off guard, especially the impoverished? The horrific situation in Kanungu, Uganda where hundreds died at the hands of the leaders of the Movement for the Restoration of the Ten Commandments of God is one such case of control, though it is not clear whether D/V narratives were involved.[74] According to the research presented here in this study, D/Vs were taken to pastors for their counsel and weighed also among the family members. Yet, is there room for what Opoku Onyinah refers to as "corporate

---

71 See Chapter 5.
72 See Chapter 3.
73 See Karen Palmer, *Spellbound: Inside West Africa's Witchcamps* (New York, NY: Free Press), 2010.
74 Patience Atuhaire (2020, March) "Uganda's Kanungu cult massacre that killed 700 followers" BBC News, https://www.bbc.com/news/world-africa-51821411, accessed Dec. 5, 2020.

discerning" of the prophetic in the Church even beyond the local body?[75] Are Pentecostal-Charismatics, especially of the independent congregations, willing to live transparently in accountability to a broader base of ecclesiastic council in order to prevent the abuse of the prophetic office? In the case of witchcraft allegations, humanitarians have located a social issue dealing with the production of Pentecostal films that have story lines developed from D/V experiences and their narratives.[76] To what extent, if at all, does the sovereignty understood as gifted by divine mandate upon the Christian Church require acquiesence to the discernment of those outside of her?[77] These questions are part of the project of understanding the big dreams of African Pentecostal-Charismatics and the spiritual knowledge derived from them in respect to the broader issues of ethics and civil disobedience.[78]

---

75   See Chapter 4.
76   See Roxane Richter, Thomas Flowers, and Elias K. Bongmba, *Witchcraft as a Social Diagnosis: Traditional Ghanaian Beliefs and Global Health* (Lanham, MD: Lexington Books, 2017). I want to appreciate Dr. Bongmba here for guiding me through my PhD tutorial on African religions. In their book, the authors express concern with the Pentecostal belief in the power of the Holy Spirit as an antidote for countering the power of witchcraft. They write, "[l]umping all those beliefs into demon possession has led to excesses in the Christian community ... religious leaders have themselves engaged in abusive behavior in the name of exorcism ... This idea of demonization takes on increased significance where there has been 'Pentecostalization'" (pp. 13–14). See also Anna Droll "Dreams, Visions, and the Pentecostal Melodrama: A Commentary on the Interface between Cinematography and Pentecostal Epistemology," *PentecoStudies*, 21:1(2022) 51–72, in particular pp. 51–53.
77   Ruth Marshall's concerns regarding the problems associated with "Born-Again" sovereignty in the Nigerian mileu are of interest to me and worth more indepth study. See Ruth Marshall, *Political Spiritualities: The Pentecostal Revolution in Nigeria* (Chicago, IL: University of Chicago Press, 2009), 61–62, 168–71, 173. She voiced concerns again regarding Pentecostal sovereignty at the "Philosophy of Nimi Wariboko Conference" (virtual) hosted by the University of Texas at Austin and Boston University, Nov. 21, 2020.
78   Similar dynamics of epistemic tension can be seen in the recent dispute regarding opening or closing churches during the Covid-19 pandemic in the US. An epistemology that generated an "I heard from God" logic served as justification for some Pentecostal and other church leaders in their decisions to maintain open churches against state mandates.

CHAPTER 8

Conclusion

Dreams, Visions, and the Missiological Spirit

This conclusion reflects on what the study of Pentecostal dreams and visions, their interpretations, and their effects might imply about the missiological Spirit. Before proceeding, a brief summary of the ground covered is in order. In Chapter 1 it was proposed that Pentecostal-Charismatics demonstrate a distinctive epistemology when it comes to interpreting dreams and visions for Christian spirituality. The term "piercing the veil" was mentioned to explain the reception of a D/V according to the Pentecostal understanding of Nigerian Nimi Wariboko. There was also an explanation of how research of the big dreams of visioners can be approached using renewal methodologies. In particular, dialectics in the Spirit offers concepts which validate pneumatology and experience in the study of what research participants say about Spirit mediation. Chapter 2 explored the significance of D/V experience in Near East religions in a brief historical survey of attitudes and practices among Jewish, Christian, and Islamic adherents. The fact that D/V valuation has had universal acceptance among the religions was established. In Chapter 3, the discussion turned to the valuation of D/V experience in African cultures, that is, among those of traditional African religions, among people of the AICs, among Zambian Baptists, and also among those of the contemporary Church of Pentecost in Ghana. Chapter 4 brought in African scholarship on the issue of epistemology, including the critique of Western epistemic impositions, and ventured into an exploration of ontological aspects within African cosmology. Chapter 4 also contained a shift toward looking intently at the Holy Spirit and Nimi Wariboko's concepts for framing Spirit dynamics in the Nigerian Pentecostal milieu. In Chapter 5, the high valuation of D/V experiences among populations of Pentecostal-Charismatics of Ghana, Togo, Nigeria, and Tanzania were examined. Quantitative and qualitative data demonstrated the benefits of D/V experiences as spiritually nourishing and also revealed how Spirit hermeneutics is employed for parsing the experiences for Pentecostal spirituality. Chapter 5 settled the issue regarding whether Christians value the D/V experience, and explored the interpretive process as represented by interactions among the triadic Spirit–Word–Community. In Chapter 6, the links between D/V experiences and prayer, identity formation, Christian commitment, and missions were made evident. The impetus generated by D/V experiences and

CONCLUSION   201

their interpretations resulted in agency of a spiritual type. The implications of experiences for visioners were potent and enduring, and resulted in courses of action that were particularly missional. In Chapter 7, the study brought its findings to bear upon conversations outside of African contexts which have brushed with broad strokes the contours of a Pentecostal epistemology. Data from the Dreams and Visions Project has served to help fill in those contours.

In light of the above, what can be said about the missiological Spirit in terms of pentecostal knowing? What can be surmised about the mission of the Spirit, in terms of both *telos* and methodology, when one steps back from examining the visionary lives of Pentecostal-Charismatics in African contexts? There are a few ideas that surface in regard to pentecostal epistemology, one in regard to the Spirit's scope of mission demonstrated in the project of pentecostal knowing through D/Vs, and the other regarding what may be the very crux of Pentecostal spirituality, the divine penchant for embodiment. Therefore, the first observation is 1) there is a need for a Pentecostal redefinition of missiology and 2) there is a need to broaden the emphasis of embodiment and empowerment, usually reserved for baptism in the Spirit and speaking in tongues, to include the phenomenon of D/V reception and its effects.

A conclusion that surfaces from researching the D/V narratives and their effects is that they may be read as portraying the desire of the Spirit as the desire for the interior of the man or woman, that is, for the mind and heart of the visioner. This expands, considerably, the concept of mission and the salvific work of the Spirit so that it rests first on the personal, spiritual formation of the visionary before venturing to include evangelism and church planting. Put another way, it requires attention to the furnace where the "heat" and energy for service is generated. It also requires a reframing of soteriology whereby conversional moments of knowing replace the Idea that salvation is static. This mission of the Spirit means that it is not only evangelism the Spirit seeks, but the evangelist. It is not just church planting that the Spirit desires, but the church planter him or herself. There seems to be a thematic quest portrayed in D/V narratives, the quest for allegiance, trust, intimacy, partnership, and love that the Spirit is on in the wilderness of the territory of the human heart and mind. Wooing that allegiance and love involves the revealing of Christ and of the messages that are equated with caring in the revelation of intimate knowledge. That the relational Triune God seeks worshippers and desires to be made known through the work of the Spirit is the theological conclusion if the assertion of Spirit agency voiced by visioners is to be taken seriously.

Suggesting that divine purpose mandates the mission for relationship as the mission of the Spirit helps us also to recognize and reconcile many other things. For example, the deeper purposes being resolved in the supposed "failed" mission comes into view. In fact, this perspective of the missional Spirit enlightens us to the value of unexpected delays, distressing betrayals, and painful chastening when the focus of the Spirit's attention is understood to include, even, perhaps most importantly, the heart and mind of the missionary. Where trust, patience, and obedience to God is being wrought, the Spirit's mission is flourishing. A mission agency "may go under" but many mission organizers may be being saved in the process as the Spirit continues in relentless pursuit of the heart, using the very sense of failure or incompetency as a touchstone for spiritual formation.

This realization that the *missio Spiritus* involves the spiritual formation of the whole interior, of both mind *and* heart, also frames the comments of Nelson O. Hayashida for fresh relevance. In Chapter 3, the work of Hayashida among Zambian Baptist visioners was highlighted. His research brought him to the conclusion that Christians needed to develop a theology of dreaming and to offer pastoral care to visioners. The dreams of those he interviewed were often distressing, but some Christians felt that leadership was disinterested and unwilling to be engaged. Yet, pastoral counseling would have helped to guide the visioners, Hayashida asserted.[1] Herein is an indication of the importance of the pastoral counselor to spiritual formation. In fact, the pastoral counselor is also the missionary counselor when the *telos* of the Spirit comes into full view. It is required, therefore, that missiology be re-envisioned to include the pneumatological imagination as the site of the continuous and personal, salvific work that is the *missio Spiritus*.

This perspective features the Spirit superintending *the experience* of the saving knowledge of God, a knowledge understood perceptually, bodily, and emotionally. The concept of knowing is stretched beyond what Western epistemology understands as normative. It requires the re-envisioning of salvation, not only as non-static, but as embodied and affective, that is, as holistic. Salvation is not understood as simply isolated moments of epistemic assent involving the will and intellect in the production of faith.[2] This soteriology postulates a spectrum of interconnectedness possible in the salvation event/

---

[1] Hayashida, *Dreams in the African Church*, 279.
[2] In regard to embodiment in spirituality, Yong presents a theology of love from a pentecostal perspective in *Spirit of Love: A Trinitarian Grace* (Waco, TX: Baylor University Press, 2012). He deals with embodied experience of the Spirit in the interconnectedness between mind and body in the examination of the virtue of love. He does so in conversation with interlocutors from the sectors of sociology, biology, and neuroscience who have researched the phenomenon of altruism. He writes, "All this is to say that we are only at the beginning stages of understanding love in relationship to our brain and embodied minds." See loc. 884.

process, one that understands knowing by intellect as operating *in trialectic* with the Spirit and experiences in the course of human be-ing.

These suggestions for expanding our understanding of the *missio Spiritus* seem to complement the theological and missiological concerns of William A. Dyrness expressed in his volume *Insider Jesus: Theological Reflections on the New Christian Movements* (2016). He explains that the phenomena of insider movements that reflect Christian spiritual formation occurring and developing within the spaces of indigenous cultural and religious contexts should stir up fresh theological reflections. The "indigenous impulse" necessarily disrupts Western notions of contextualization and inculturation, challenging the epistemic site on which Western Enlightenment epistemology and Western theology have traditionally framed notions of mission from inflated assumptions about Western agency.[3] Additionally, Western notions of salvation have absorbed Enlightenment assumptions and framed salvation as disconnected from geography, indigenous cultural realities, and religious life.[4] Dyrness brings the compelling argument that we do well to come to terms with the efficacy of indigenous hermeneutical method and to learn from what emergent movements can teach about the process of conversion to Christ. The assumption that "God has actually arrived in the luggage of the missionary" stands now corrected by more current implications: "God was present and working in that culture long before missionaries arrived, and the indigenous values and even the religions of these people pay important tribute to his Presence."[5]

The Pentecostal missionary Karl Härgestam reported an encounter in Ethiopia that portrays exactly what Dyrness is getting at with the appeal to re-evaluate constrictive Western assumptions. Härgestam landed near the Omo River by helicopter and was greeted by the tribal chief and his linguist who immediately asked about Jesus Christ. Amazed by the question, Härgestam asked how the chief had come upon the name of Jesus Christ and the chief explained that he had dreamed of a shining man and of messengers who would come within 5 days from the sky to tell about the man. In the dream the man's name was revealed to the chief as "Jesus Christ."[6]

---

3 Dyrness, *Insider Jesus*, 4. See also Willie James Jennings, *Christian Imagination: Theology and the Origins of Race* (New Haven, CT: Yale University Press, 2010), 81–82.
4 Dyrness, *Insider Jesus*, 10–12.
5 Ibid., 21.
6 This account of my interview with Karl Härgestam in 2018 is also shared in Anna Droll, "Dreams and Visions as Welcoming Spaces for Interfaith Dialogue" in *Journal of Pentecostal Theology* 28:1 (2019) 153.

Returning to Dyrness, the acknowledgment of the possibility of God's self-disclosure apart from human agency does not minimize the need for deeper discussion about ecclesiology and syncretism (or better, synthesis, as the case may be) but rather suggests re-examination and critique of *Western* concepts, including its own syncretistic tendencies.[7] Dyrness' material is important to this examination of D/Vs in African Pentecostal-Charismatic spirituality for the way it provides a theological context for appraising D/Vs and their function as evidence of the "insider Jesus." His conclusions strike a similar chord. This book argues that the realities require a theological revisioning of the scope of salvation and the purposes and methods of the missiological Spirit in light of pentecostal epistemology.

The second observation in regard to the mission of the Spirit that surfaces simply reiterates the Pentecostal emphasis of embodiment, as is expressed in the valuation of empowerment for witness and speaking in tongues. The conclusion is that the experience of D/Vs are significant manifestations of Pentecostal embodiment for Pentecostal epistemology and are important to the discussion of empowerment. The methodology of embodiment in the D/V experience can be interpreted as an expression of the willingness of the Divine to take up humanity, a testimony to God's desire to touch bodies in the course of renewing spirits. There is a sense of the incarnational at work when the Spirit broods in such a way so as to birth epistemic intuitions equal to Yong's "irruption" or Wariboko's "emergence." As in the case of Jesus "compelled by the Spirit" to go to the desert (Mark 1:12), the Spirit is portrayed as moving on the mind of the visioner with a similar compelling effect which produces bodily agency. Significantly, embodiment is present in the effects as well as the inception of Spirit agency as seen in the reports of how these participants moved from an enhanced sense of identity to promoting the flourishing and bodily well-being of others (missiology). While the visioner becomes one who is determined to reach and impact others with godly love, the concern is often accompanied by holistic intentions. Therefore, the marks of embodiment are evident throughout, indicating that the phenomena of dreams and visions found to enliven the pneumatological imagination should accompany other distinctives of a Pentecostal self-understanding. At least, these are the indications according to the sub-Saharan horizon of the pneumatological imagination.

---

7 Dyrness, *Insider Jesus*, 124, 125.

A last closing thought is the suggestion that there is surely much yet to discover regarding what Pentecostal-Charismatic visioners in other contexts have to say about the impact of the missiological Spirit through dreams and visions. To that end, may this work cast light toward more distant horizons in the exploration of the pneumatological imagination.

APPENDIX 1

Written Survey and Interview Guide

1   Written Survey

My name is Anna and I am a researcher from Fuller Theological Seminary in California, USA. Thank you for helping me with my research about dreams and visions. This time together will be done in two parts. Part 1 is this written part. You may write in the answers or you may say them and I will write them. Part 2 is the interview.

Your name:
Email or phone contact information:
May I contact you if it will help my research to ask you another question?

Questions about Who You Are

Were you born in Africa?
Do you presently live in Africa?
If yes, where in Africa do you live?
Have you ever spent periods of time living outside of Africa? For how long?
Are you male or female?
What is your age?
What ethnic tribe are you and your parents from?

Questions about Spirituality

Do you consider yourself a spiritual person?
If yes, can you describe for me what you mean by "spiritual"?
Is there a name for the type of spirituality that informs and guides your life?
Do you belong to a certain religious group?
Do you have encounters with a god?
Do you have encounters with a supreme God?
Do you have encounters with a spirit?
If yes, is the spirit you have encountered a supreme Spirit?
Have you heard of the term "Pentecostal"?
If yes, do you consider yourself a "Pentecostal" person?
Have you heard of the term "Charismatic"?
If yes, do you consider yourself a "Charismatic" person?

Questions about Dreams and Visions

I will be describing dreams as *visions received while asleep*. As for visions received while awake, I am calling these visions "closed visions" when they are received with eyes closed. Visions received while awake with eyes open I am calling "open visions."

A. In your opinion, where do spiritual dreams come from? (Circle the answer, you may circle more than one):
   1. the influence of an ancestor
   2. the influence of the God of the Bible
   3. the influence of my mind
   4. the influence of a witch
   5. the influence of a local god
   6. the influence of Satan or a demon
   7. the influence of the God of the Bible who may use an ancestor, my mind, a witch, a local god, or Satan or a demon to impart a dream or vision
   8. something else, which I explain here:

B. If you answered "God of the Bible," which of the following best explains the exact origin of a spiritual dream, in your opinion? (You may circle more than one):
   1. they come from God the Father
   2. they come from an angel of God
   3. they come from God the Holy Spirit
   4. they come from Jesus

Can you explain this choice further?

In your opinion, how does God and the mind work together in the dream or vision experience?

If you attend a church, do you think dreams and visions are important to people at church?

Do you think that dreams and visions are important to your parents?

To your grandparents? Please explain.

Have you ever had a dream of flying? If yes, please describe it.

Have you ever had a dream of being chased? If yes, please describe it.

Have you ever had a dream in which you knew in the dream that you were dreaming? If yes, please describe it.

Have you ever had a dream in which you were visited by a person who is no longer with us on the earth? If yes, please describe it.

Have you ever had a dream that you consider to be spiritual and important to your life?

Have you ever had an "open" or "closed" vision (a vision while awake) that you consider to be spiritual and important to your life?

Can you share about a dream or vision that was significant to you? (in 10 sentences or less, you may also use the back of this paper to write)

2   Interview Guide

Anna: "I'm going to read you some questions after I turn on the recorder. Please relax and know that you may take your time to answer. There is no hurry. Let's enjoy this time of discussion. Whenever you would like to pause or take a break, just let me know and I will turn the recorder off."

Do you experience dreams and visions often? How often?

In your opinion, what caused the dream or vision experience?

Have you been able to interpret the dream or have you needed the assistance of someone else to interpret it?

If you are a Pentecostal-Charismatic, did you experience spiritual dreams and visions before your faith in Jesus Christ?

If yes, how would you describe your spirituality at that time? Were dreams and visions important to you then? Are your dreams important to you now?

In your opinion, were those dreams similar to those you have experienced as a Pentecostal-Charismatic? How so? If they were different, how so?

Can you describe a dream or vision you experienced most recently that has been important to your life?

- Are there significant events that happened in your life before you had the experience that you believe are linked to the dream or vision?
- Do you consider this dream or vision to be a spiritual dream? If no, what type of dream do you think it was?
- What meaning has this dream or vision had for your life?

Did the dream or vision have an effect that moved you to take an action? What action? In your opinion, was there an obstacle in your way to taking the action? For example, something in your own mind, or in your life or environment or situation that would make it difficult for you to act on the dream or vision? Please explain.

Please give that obstacle a rating of between "1" and "10," where "1" means it only caused a mild resistance to your decision to act, and "10" meaning that the obstacle was very, very difficult to push through in order to act.

Is there another dream or vision you would like to share with me?

APPENDIX 2

Coding for Surveys and Personal Interviews

Category	Code
Dream Vision	DV
Auditory element (audition)	A
Dream experienced by specified other	OD
Vision experienced by specified other	OV
Subject identifies it as spiritual warfare	SW
Subject prays before	PB
Subject prays after	PA
Healing in the narrative	H
Circled HS (answer 3) on question B	hs
Written mention of Holy Spirit[a]	HS
Circled and written mention of Holy Spirit[b]	HSS
Prompted content[c]	PC
Considered predictive[d]	PRe
Considered warning	W
Considered warning and predictive	WPRe
Considered directive, affirming, motivational and/or encouraging	DAME
Mentions word of God/Scripture reference	SCR

a This indicates that the subject wrote the words Holy Spirit or Spirit (capitalized) in an answer in the survey.
b Means the subject did both (wrote of the Holy Spirit within a survey response and also circled Holy Spirit as source of D/V in survey question B).
c Prompted content links content (e.g., spiritual warfare or dreaming of the dead) with a prompt question. Answers to questions about whether parents or grandparents valued dreams are also in this category. Unless thus indicated, other narratives offer the subjects' self-generated narrations to a prompt for a significant dream or vision experience.
d "Considered" means considered by the subject, as indicated by the context surrounding the dream narrative.

APPENDIX 2: CODING FOR SURVEYS AND PERSONAL INTERVIEWS

Demographic	Code
Burkina Faso	BF
Congo	C
Ghanaian	G
Kenyan	K
Liberia	LI
Nigerian	N
Sierra Leone	SL
Tanzanian	T
Togolese	TO
Ugandan	U
Man	M
Woman	W
Age	Age
Clergy[e]	CL
Clergy of the Assemblies of God	CLAG
Clergy, Baptist	CLBap
Church of Pentecost	CoP
Translator	Tr

[e] Clergy is a man or woman with pastoral oversight in a congregational or para-church ministry.

Institution	Code
Trinity Theological Seminary	TTS
Pentecost Theological Seminary	PTS
Evangel Theological Seminary	ETS

Glossary

Auditions Experiences of hearing an audible voice while receiving an open or closed vision or in a dream.

Born-again Self-identification of Christians who distinguish themselves from nominal adherents of mainline denominations. Born-again is the most frequent self-identifier used by those I contacted.

Charismatic Used as synonymous with "pentecostal" denoting Holy Spirit emphasis.

Christian One with a faith commitment to Jesus Christ as the salvific personality of the Trinity.

Classic Pentecostalism Refers to the proponents of the earliest waves of Holy Spirit revival in Africa. They include the Church of Pentecost, Christ Apostolic Church, and the Assemblies of God in Ghana of West Africa. They are institutionalized bodies distinct from other churches marked by Holy Spirit emphasis (Spirit-churches, or pentecostal) as well as Western mission churches (Anglican, Methodist or Presbyterian) which have become Charismatic in practice.

Dreams and visions Dreams are visions received while asleep *or* experiences of the spirit while outside the sleeping body. The term "sleep experiences" seems a better all-inclusive term for dreams. A closed vision is what may be experienced while dozing or in a trance-like state. An open vision is what may be experienced while awake with eyes open.

Pentecostal Used to refer to Christian persons who recognize the Holy Spirit as the operant, immediate presence of God interacting experientially in their daily lives. The delineation between Pentecostal and Charismatic in the African context is not as distinct as in the West due to differing characteristics of historical Spirit movements in each respective region. Therefore, the term "Pentecostal-Charismatic" might be interchangeably used for "pentecostal" and suggest the same idea: a Holy Spirit orientation for living with little to no implications regarding denomination.

Pentecostalism Used to refer to the theory and practice of Classic Pentecostals (the earliest institutionalized Pentecostal churches) as well as pentecostals and charismatics across denominational lines in Africa.

Visioner Use in the same sense that one would use the term "visionary." It represents the subject who has experienced the dream or vision.

Bibliography

Abraham, W. E. 1962. *The Mind of Africa*. London, UK: Weidenfeld and Nicolson.

Acolatse, Esther E. 2018. *Powers, Principalities, and the Spirit: Biblical Realism in Africa and the West*. Grand Rapids, MI: William B. Eerdmans Publishing Co.

Adogame, Afe. 2011. *Who is Afraid of the Holy Ghost? Pentecostalism and Globalization in Africa and Beyond*. Trenton, NJ: Africa World Press.

Afnan, Soheil M. 1958. *Avicenna: His Life and Works*. London, UK: G. Allen and Unwin.

Agana, Wilfred Asampambila. 2016. *"Succeed Here and in Eternity": The Prosperity Gospel in Ghana*. Bern, Switzerland: Peter Lang.

Ahmadi, Nozhat. 2013. "The Role of Dreams in the Political Affairs of the Safavid Dynasty." *Journal of Shi'a Islamic Studies*. VI: 2: 177–198.

al-Akili, Muhammad M. 1992. *Ibn Seerin's Dictionary of Dreams According to Islamic Inner Traditions*. Philadelphia, PA: Pearl Publishing House.

al-Bukhari, Muhammad b. Ismail. *Sahih al-Bukhari in the English Language*.

al-Haj, Muslim ibn. *Sahih Muslim*.

Alexander, Estrelda Y. 2011. *Black Fire: One Hundred Years of African American Pentecostalism*. Downers Grove, IL: InterVarsity Press.

Alexander, Paul. 2009. *Signs and Wonders: Why Pentecostalism is the World's Fastest-Growing Faith*. San Francisco, CA: Jossey-Bass.

Allen, Diogenes and Eric O. Springsted. 2007. *Philosophy for Understanding Theology*. Louisville, KY: Westminster John Knox Press.

Anderson, Allan H. 1991. *Moya: the Holy Spirit in an African Context*. Pretoria, South Africa: University of Pretoria.

Anderson, Allan H. 2001. *African Reformation: African Initiated Christianity in the 20th Century*. Trenton, NJ: Africa World Press.

Anderson, Allan H. 2014. *An Introduction to Pentecostalism: Global Charismatic Christianity*, 2nd. ed. UK: Cambridge University Press.

Anderson, Allan H. 2014. "The Pentecostal Gospel, Religion, and Culture in African Perspective." In *Pentecostal Theology in Africa*, Clifton R. Clarke, editor. Eugene, OR: Pickwick Publications.

Anderson, Allan H. 2018. *Spirit-Filled World: Religious Dis/Continuity in African Pentecostalism*. New York, NY: Palgrave Macmillan.

Anderson, Allan H., Michael Bergunder, André Droogers, and Cornelis Van Der Laan, editors. 2010. *Studying Global Pentecostalism: Theories and Methods*. London, UK: University of California Press.

Appiah, Kwame Anthony. 1992. *In My Father's House: African in the Philosophy of Culture*. New York: Oxford University Press.

Archer, Margaret. 2000. *Being Human: The Problem of Agency*. UK: Cambridge University Press.

Asamoah-Gyadu, J. Kwabena. 2013. *Contemporary Pentecostal Christianity: Interpretations from an African Context*. Eugene, OR: Wipf and Stock.

Asamoah-Gyadu, J. Kwabena. 2015. *Sighs and Signs of the Spirit: Ghanaian Perspectives on Pentecostalism and Renewal in Africa*. Eugene, OR: Wipf and Stock.

Asamoah-Gyadu, J. Kwabena. 2017. *The Holy Spirit Our Comforter: An Exercise in Homiletic Pneumatology*. Accra, Ghana: Step Publishers.

Atuhaire, Patience. (2020, March) "Uganda's Kanungu cult massacre that killed 700 followers" BBC News, https://www.bbc.com/news/world-africa-51821411.

Ayoub, Mahmoud M. *Islam: Faith and History*. 2004. London, UK: Oneworld Publications.

Bangura, Abdul Karim. 2015. *Toyin Falola and African Epistemologies*. New York, NY: Palgrave Macmillan.

Barrett, Deirdre and Patrick McNamara. 2007. *The New Science of Dreaming: Biological Aspects,* vol. 1. Westport, Connecticut: Praeger Publishers.

Barrett, Deirdre and Patrick McNamara. 2007. *The New Science of Dreaming: Cultural and Theoretical Perspectives*, vol. 3. Westport, Connecticut: Praeger Publishers.

Bashir, Shahzad. 2003. *Messianic Hopes and Mystical Visions: The Nurbakhshiya Between Medieval and Modern Islam*. Columbia, South Carolina: University of South Carolina.

Baum, Robert. 1999. *Shrines of the Slave Trade: Diola Religion and Society in Precolonial Senegambia.* New York: Oxford University Press.

Baum, Robert. 2016. *West African Women of God: Aliensitoué and the Diola Prophetic Tradition*. Bloomington: Indiana University Press.

Bediako, Kwame. 1999. *Theology and Identity: The Impact of Culture upon Christian Thought in the Second Century and in Modern Africa*. Eugene, OR: Wipf and Stock.

Bediako, Kwame. 2004. *Jesus and the Gospel in Africa*. Maryknoll, NY: Orbis Books.

Boahen, Adu. 1975. *Ghana: Evolution and Change in the Nineteenth and Twentieth Centuries.* London, UK: Longman Group Ltd.

Bowdich, T. Edward. 2015. *Mission from Cape Coast Castle to Ashantee with a Descriptive Account of that Kingdom*. London, UK: Griffith and Garran.

Brown, Warren S. 2016. "The Brain, Religion, and Baseball: Revisited." *Fuller* 5. Pasadena, CA.

Browning, Don. 1983. *Religious Ethics and Pastoral Care*. Philadelphia, PA: Fortress Press.

Bulkeley, Kelly. 1994. *The Wilderness of Dreams: Exploring the Religious Meanings of Dreams in Modern Western Culure*. Albany, NY: State University of New York Press.

Bulkeley, Kelly. 1995. *Spiritual Dreaming: a Cross-cultural and Historical Journey*. Mahwah, NJ: Paulist Press.

Bulkeley, Kelly. 2000. *Transforming Dreams: Learning Spiritual Lessons from the Dreams You Never Forget.* New York: NY: John Wiley and Sons, Inc.

Bulkeley, Kelly. 2008. *Dreaming in the World's Religions: a Comparative History.* NY: New York University Press.

Bulkeley, Kelly. 2016. *Big Dreams: The Science of Dreaming and the Origins of Religion.* New York: Oxford University Press.

Bulkeley, Kelly and Kate Adams, and Patricia M. Davis, editors. 2009. *Dreaming in Christianity and Islam: Culture, Conflict, and Creativity.* Piscataway, NJ: Rutgers University Press.

Burgess, Richard. 2008. *Nigeria's Christian Revolution: The Civil War Revival and Its Pentecostal Progeny (1967–2006).* Eugene, OR: Wipf and Stock.

Busia, K. A. 1951. *The Position of the Chief in the Modern Political System of Ashanti.* London: Oxford University Press.

Cappucci, John. 2015. "Selecting a Spiritual Authority: The Maraji'al-Taqlid among First- and Second-Wave Iraqi Shi'a Muslims in Dearborn Michigan." *Journal of Shi'a Islamic Studies,* VIII: 1: 5–17.

Cartledge, Mark J. 2012. *Practical Theology: Charismatic and Empirical Perspectives* Eugene, OR: Wipf and Stock.

Cartledge, Mark J. 2015. *The Mediation of the Spirit: Interventions in Practical Theology.* Grand Rapids, MI: William B. Eerdmans Publishing Co.

Cartledge, Mark J. 2017. "Can Theology Be 'Practical'? Part II: a Reflection on Renewal Methodology and the Practice of Research." *Journal of Contemporary Ministry* 3: 20–36.

Chinkwita, Mary. 1993. *The Usefulness of Dreams: An African Perspective.* London, UK: Janus Publishing Company.

Clarke, Clifton R. 2011. *African Christology: Jesus in Post-Missionary African Christianity.* Eugene, OR: Pickwick Publications.

Clarke, Clifton R. 2014. *Pentecostal Theology in Africa.* Eugene, OR: Pickwick Publications.

Clarke, Clifton R. 2016. "Nigerian Pentecostalism and Islam: Toward a Pentecostalized Vision of Interreligious Coexistence Through *Ubuntu* Philosophy," *Global Renewal Christianity: Spirit-Empowered Movements, Past, Present, and Future, Volume 3: Africa,* editors Vinson Synan, Amos Yong and J. Kwabena Asamoah_Gyadu, Lake Mary, FL: Charisma House. 338–361.

Clarke, Clifton R. 2018. *Pentecostalism: Insights from Africa and the African Diaspora.* Eugene, OR: Cascade Books.

Corten, André and Ruth Marshall-Fratani, editors. 2001. *Between Babel and Pentecost: Transnational Pentecostalism in Africa and Latin America.* Bloomington: Indiana University Press.

Cox, Harvey. 1995. *Fire from Heaven: The Rise of Pentecostal Spirituality and the Reshaping of Religion in the Twenty-first Century.* Cambridge, MA: Da Capo Press.

Crenshaw, James L. 2010. *Old Testament Wisdom: An Introduction.* Louisville, KY: Westminster John Knox Press.

Daneel, M. L. 1974. *Old and New in Southern Shona Independent.* The Hague, Netherlands: Mouton.

Daldianus, Artemidorus (translator Robert J. White). 1975. *Oneirocritica: Interpretation of Dreams: Noyes Classical Studies.*

Danquah, J. B. 1968. *The Akan Doctrine of God.* London, UK: Frank Cass.

Darley, Alan P. "The Epistemological Hope: Aquinas versus Other Receptions of Pseudo-Dionysius on the Beatific Vision." *HeyJ* LIX (2018) 663–688.

Daswani, Girish. 2015. *Looking Back, Moving Forward: Transformation and Ethical Practice in the Ghanaian Church of Pentecost.* Toronto: University of Toronto Press.

Dayton, Donald W. 1987. *Theological Roots of Pentecostalism.* Grand Rapids, MI: Baker Academic.

Deconick, April, editor. 2006. *Paradise Now: Essays on Early Jewish and Christian Mysticism.* Atlanta, GA: Society of Biblical Literature.

Dilley, Roy. M. 1992. "Dreams, Inspiration and Craftwork Among Tukolor Weavers" in M. C. Jędrej and Rosalind Shaw, eds., *Dreaming, Religion & Society in Africa, 74.* Leiden: Brill.

Dixon, Patrick. 1994. *Signs of Revival.* UK: Kingsway Publications.

Domhoff, G. William. 1996. *Finding Meaning in Dreams: a Quantitative Approach.* New York, NY: Plenum Press.

Dosset, Rena. 2014. "The Historical Influence of Classical Islam on Western Humanistic Education." *International Journal of Social Science and Humanity,* 4:2, 88–91.

Droogers, André. 2001. "Globalisation and Pentecostal Success." In André Corten and Ruth Marshall-Fratani, *Between Babel and Pentecost: Transnational Pentecostalism in Africa and Latin America,* 41–61. Bloomington, IN: Indiana University Press.

Dyrness, William A. 2016. *Insider Jesus: Theological Reflections on New Christian Movements.* Downers Grove, Illinois: IVP Academic.

Edgar, Iain R. 2011. *The Dream in Islam: From Qur'anic Tradition to Jihadist Inspiration.* New York, NY: Bergham Books.

Engelke, Matthew. 2007. *A Problem of Presence: Beyond Scripture in an African Church.* Berkeley CA: University of California Press.

Ephirim-Donkor, Anthony. 1997. *African Spirituality: On Becoming Ancestors.* Trenton, NJ: Africa World Press.

Ephirim-Donkor, Anthony. 2010. *African Religion Defined: a Systematic Study of Ancestor Worship among the Akan.* University Press of America.

Ephirim-Donkor, Anthony. 2015. *The Making of An African King: Patrilineal and Matrilineal Struggle among the Awutu (Effutu) of Ghana*. Lanham, MD: University Press of America.

Ephirim-Donkor, Anthony. 2016. *African Personality and Spirituality: The Role of Abosom and Human Essence*. Lanham, MD: Lexington Books.

Falola, Toyin. 2007. "The *Amistad*'s Legacy: Reflections on the Spaces of Colonization," *Africa Update*, 14:2, 1–38.

Felek, Özgen and Alexander D. Knysh, editors. 2012. *Dreams and Visions in Islamic Societies*. Albany, NY: State University of New York Press.

Fisher, Robert B. 1998. *West African Religious Traditions: Focus on the Akan of Ghana*. Maryknoll, NY: Orbis Books.

Florschütz, Gottlieb. 1993. *Swedenborg and Kant: Emanuel Swedenborg's Mystical View of Humankind, and the Dual Nature of Humankind in Immanuel Kant*. West Chester, PA: The Swedenborg Foundation.

Fortes, Meyer. 1959. *Oedipus and Job in West African Religion*. Cambridge: Cambridge University Press.

Fortes, Meyer. 1965. *African Systems of Thought*. NY: Oxford University Press.

Fortes, Meyer. 1987. *Religion, Morality and the Person: Essays on Tallensi Religion*. Cambridge: Cambridge University Press.

Freeman, Dena. 2012. *Pentecostalism and Development: Churches, NGOs and Social Change in Africa*. New York: Palgrave Macmillan.

Gerloff, Roswith I. H. 1992. *A Plea for British Black Theologies: The Black Church Movement in Britain in Its Transatlantic Cultural and Theological Interaction with Special Reference to the Pentecostal (Oneness) and Sabbatarian Movements*, 2 volumes. Frankfurt am Main, and New York: Peter Lang.

Gifford, Paul. 2004. *Ghana's New Christianity: Pentecostalism in a Globalizing African Economy*. Bloomington: Indiana University Press.

Gifford, Paul. 2009. *Christianity, Politics and Public Life in Kenya*. London, UK: Hurst & Company.

Gornik, Mark R. 2011. *Word Made Global: Stories of African Christianity in New York City*. Grand Rapids, MI: William B. Eerdmans Publishing Company.

Green, Nile. 2015. "A Brief World History of Muslim Dreams." *Islamic Studies*, 54:3–4, 143–167.

Gyekye, Kwame. 1995. *An Essay on African Philosophical Thought: The Akan Conceptual Scheme,* revised edition. Philadelphia: Temple University Press.

Gyekye, Kwame. 1997. *Tradition and Modernity: Philosophical Reflections on the African Experience*. New York: Oxford University Press.

Hamminga, Bert. 2005. *Knowledge Cultures: Comparative Western and African Epistemology*. Amsterdam: Rodopi.

Haustein, Jörg. 2020. "Religion, politics and an apocryphal admonition: the German East African "Mecca letter" of 1908 in historical-critical analysis." *Bulletin of the School of Oriental and African Studies,* 83:1, 95–125.

Hayashida, Nelson O. 1999. *Dreams in the African Church: The Significance of Dreams and Visions Among Zambian Baptists.* Amsterdam: Rodopi.

Hollenweger, Walter J. 1972. *The Pentecostals.* London, UK: SCM Press, Ltd.

Hollenweger, Walter J. 1997. *Pentecostalism: Origins and Developments Worldwide.* Peabody, MA: Hendrickson Publishers, Inc.

Hymes, David. C. 2012. "Toward an Old Testament Theology of Dreams: a Pentecostal-Charismatic Perspective." *Australian Pentecostal Studies,* 14, 60–88.

Isichei, Elizabeth. 1995. *A History of Christianity in Africa: From Antiquity to the Present.* Lawrenceville, NJ: Africa World Press, Inc.

Jacobsen, Douglas G. 2003. *Thinking in the Spirit: Theologies of the Early Pentecostal Movement.* Bloomington, IN: Indiana University Press.

Jacobsen, Douglas G. 2006. *A Reader in Pentecostal Theology: Voices from the First Generation.* Bloomington, IN: Indiana University Press.

Jędrej, M. C. and Rosalind Shaw, editors. 1992. *Dreaming, Religion and Society in Africa.* Leiden: Brill.

Jenkins, Philip. 2006. *The New Faces of Christianity: Believing the Bible in the Global South.* New York, NY: Oxford University Press.

Jennings, Willie James. *The Christian Imagination: Theology and the Origins of Race.* New Haven, CT: Yale University Press, 2010.

Johns, Cheryl Bridges. 2010. *Pentecostal Formation: a Pedagogy among the Oppressed.* Eugene, OR: Wipf and Stock.

Kalu, Ogbu. 2006. *Power, Poverty and Prayer: The Challenges of Poverty and Pluralism in African Christianity, 1960–1996.* New Jersey: Africa World Press, Inc.

Kalu, Ogbu. 2008. *African Pentecostalism: An Introduction.* Oxford: Oxford University Press.

Keener, Craig S. 2011. *Miracles: The Credibility of The New Testament Accounts,* vol. 2. Grand Rapids, MI: William B. Eerdmans Publishing Company.

Keener, Craig S. 2016. *Spirit Hermeneutics: Reading Scripture in Light of Pentecost.* Grand Rapids, MI: William B. Eerdmans Publishing Co.

Kelsey, Morton T. 1978. *Dreams: a Way to Listen to God.* New York, NY: Paulist Press.

Kelsey, Morton T. 1991. *God, Dreams, and Revelation: a Christian Interpretation of Dreams.* Minneapolis, MN: Augsburg.

Kramer, Milton and Myron Glucksman, editors. 2015. *Dream Research: Contributions to Clinical Practice.* New York: NY: Routledge.

Lajul, Wilfred. 2013. *African Philosophy: Critical Dimensions.* Oxford, UK: Fountain Publishers.

Lakoff, George and Mark Johnson. 1980. *Metaphors We Live By*. Chicago, IL: University of Chicago.

Lamoreaux, John C. 2002. *The Early Muslim Tradition of Dream Interpretation*. Albany, NY: State University of New York Press.

Land, Steven J. 1993. *Pentecostal Spirituality: a Passion for the Kingdom*. New York, NY: Sheffield Academic Press.

Larbi, E. Kingsley. 2001. *Pentecostalism: The Eddies of Ghanaian Christianity*. Accra: CPCS.

Latourette, Kenneth Scott. 1975. *A History of Christianity: Beginnings to 1500*, vol. 1. San Francisco, CA: HarperSanFrancisco.

Lee, Matthew T., Margaret M. Poloma, and Stephen G. Post. 2013. *The Heart of Religion: Spiritual Empowerment, Benevolence, and the Experience of God's Love*. New York, NY: Oxford University Press.

Levison, John R. 2009. *Filled with the Spirit*. Grand Rapids, MI: William B. Eerdmans Publishing Company.

Lohmann, Roger I. 2003. *Dream Travelers: Sleep Experiences and Culture in the Western Pacific*. New York, NY: Palgrave Macmillan.

Luhrmann, T. M. 2012. *When God Talks Back: Understanding the American Evangelical Relationship with God*. New York, NY: Vintage Books.

Macchia, Frank D. 2006. *Baptized in the Spirit: a Global Pentecostal Theology*. Grand Rapids, MI: Zondervan.

Macchia, Frank D. 2012. *Justified in the Spirit: Creation, Redemption, and the Triune God*. Grand Rapids, MI: William B. Eerdmans Publishing Company.

Mageo, Jeannette Marie. 2003. *Dreaming and the Self: New Perspectives on Subjectivity, Identity, and Emotion*. Albany: State University of New York Press.

Marshall, Ruth. 2009. *Political Spiritualities: The Pentecostal Revolution in Nigeria*. Chicago: University of Chicago Press.

Martin, David. 2001. *Pentecostalism: The World Their Parish (Religion and Spirituality in the Modern World)*. New Jersey: Wiley-Blackwell.

Maxwell, David. 2007. *African Gifts of the Spirit: Pentecostalism and the Rise of a Zimbabwean Transnational Religious Movement*. Athens, OH: Ohio University Press.

Mbiti, John S. 2012. *Concepts of God in Africa*, 2nd edition. Nairobi: Acton Publishers.

McFague, Sallie. 1982. *Metaphorical Theology: Models of God in Religious Language*. Philadelphia, PA: Fortress Press.

McGee, Gary B. 2010. *Miracles, Missions, and American Pentecostalism*. Maryknoll, NY: Orbis Books.

Meek, Esther Lightcap. 2011. *Loving to Know: Covenant Epistemology*. Eugene, OR: Cascade Books.

Meyer, Birgit. 2015. *Sensational Movies: Video, Vision, and Christianity in Ghana*. Oakland, CA: University of California Press.

Miller, Donald E. and Tetsunao Yamamori. 2007. *Global Pentecostalism: The New Face of Christian Social Engagement.* Berkeley: University of California Press.

Miller, Patricia Cox. 1994. *Dreams in Late Antiquity: Studies in the Imagination of a Culture.* Princeton, NJ: Princeton University Press.

Nabudere, Dani W. 2011. *Afrikology, Philosophy and Wholeness: An Epistemology.* Pretoria, South Africa: Africa Institute of South Africa.

Neumann, Peter D. 2012. *Pentecostal Experience: An Ecumenical Encounter.* Eugene, OR: Pickwick Publications.

Noel, Bradley Truman. 2010. *Pentecostal and Postmodern Hermeneutics: Comparisons and Contemporary Impact.* Eugene, OR: Wipf and Stock.

Oduyoye, Mercy Amba. 1990. *Hearing and Knowing: Theological Reflections on Christianity in Africa.* Maryknoll, NY: Orbis Books.

Oduyoye, Mercy Amba. 1995. *Daughters of Anowa: African Women and Patriarchy.* Maryknoll, NY: Orbis Books.

Ojo, Matthews A. 2006. *The End-Time Army: Charismatic Movements in Modern Nigeria.* Trenton: Africa World Press, Inc.

Okpewho, Isidore. 1983. *Myth in Africa: a Study of its Aesthetics and Cultural Relevance.* Cambridge: Cambridge University Press.

Omenyo, Cephas N. 2006. *Pentecost outside Pentecostalism: a Study of the Development of Charismatic Renewal in the Mainline Churches in Ghana.* Zoetermeer: Boeckencentrum Publishing.

Onyinah, Opoku. 2012. *Pentecostal Exorcism: Witchcraft and Demonology in Ghana.* UK: Deo Publishing.

Onyinah, Opoku. 2012. *Spiritual Warfare: a Centre for Pentecostal Theology Short Introduction.* Cleveland, TN: CPT Press. 2012.

Onyinah, Opoku and Gibson Annor-Antwi. 2016. *Myth or Mystery: The 'Bio-Autobiography' of Apostle Professor Opoku Onyinah.* UK: Inved.

Osuigwe, Nkem Emerald. 2014. *Christian Churches and Nigeria's Political Economy of Oil and Conflict: Baptist and Pentecostal Perspectives.* UK: Cambridge Scholars Publishing.

Pack, Roger A. 1967. "On Artemidorus and His Arabic Translator." *Transactions and Proceedings of the American Philological Association.* 98, 313–326.

Pack, Roger A. 1976. "Artemidoriana Graeco-Arabic." *Transactions of the American Philological Association.* 106, 307–312.

Palmer, Karen. 2010. *Spellbound: Inside West Africa's Witch Camps.* New York, NY: Free Press.

Pariona, Amber. 2018. "Differences Between Sunni and Shia Muslims." *World Atlas.* 2018. Accessed Oct. 17, 2018. https://www.worldatlas.com/articles/differences-between-sunni-and-shia-muslims.html.

Parker, Stephen E. 2015. *Led by the Spirit: Toward a Practical Theology of Pentecostal Discernment and Decision Making*. Cleveland, TN: CPT Press.

Parrinder, Geoffrey. 1949. *West African Religion: a Study of the Beliefs and Practices of Akan, Ewe, Yoruba, Ibo, and Kindred Peoples*. London, UK: Epworth Press.

Parrinder, Geoffrey. 1951. *West African Psychology*. London, UK: Lutterworth Press.

Plüss, Jean-Daniel. 1988. *Therapeutic and Prophetic Narratives in Worship*. Frankfurt, Germany: Verlag Peter Lang.

Pobee, J. S. 1976. *Religion in a Pluralistic Society*. Leiden: Brill.

Pomerville, Paul A. 2016. *The Third Force in Missions: a Pentecostal Contribution to Contemporary Mission Theology*. Peabody, MA: Hendricksons Publishers.

Pouresmaeil, Ehsan. 2012. "Seeing Allah While Dreaming: a Comparison between Shi'a and Sunni Beliefs." *Journal of Shi'a Islamic Studies,* V:1, 65–80.

Pype, Katrien. 2015. *The Making of the Pentecostal Melodrama: Religion, Media, and Gender in Kinshasa*. NY: Berghahn.

Quayesi-Amakye, Joseph. 2013. *Prophetism in Ghana Today: a Study on Trends in Ghanaian Pentecostal Prophetism*. Scotts Valley, CA: CreateSpace Publishing.

Rattray, R. S. 1916. *Ashanti Proverbs: The Primitive Ethics of a Savage People*. London, UK: Oxford University Press.

Rattray, R. S. 1927. *Religion and Art in Ashanti*. Oxford: Oxford University Press.

Richter, Roxane, Thomas Flowers, and Elias Kifon Bongmba. 2017. *Witchcraft as a Social Diagnosis: Traditional Ghanaian Beliefs and Global Health*. Lanham, MD: Lexington Books.

Ricoeur, Paul. 1970. *Freud and Philosophy: An Essay on Interpretation*. New Haven, CT: Yale University.

Robeck, Cecil M., Jr. 2006. *The Azusa Street Mission and Revival*. Nashville, TN: Thomas Nelson.

Sanders, Cheryl J. 1996. *Saints In Exile: The Holiness-Pentecostal Experience in African American Religion and Culture*. New York, NY: Oxford University Press.

Sanneh, Lamin. 2003. *Whose Religion is Christianity?: The Gospel Beyond the West*. Grand Rapids, MI: William B. Eerdmans Publishing Co.

Sharpe, Eric. 2001. "The Legacy of Bengt Sundkler." *International Bulletin of Missionary Research*, April, 58–63.

Sirriyeh, Elizabeth. 2015. *Dreams and Visions in the World of Islam: a History of Muslim Dreaming and Foreknowing*. London, UK: IB Tauris & Co. Ltd.

Smith, James K. A. 2000. *The Fall of Interpretation: Philosophical Foundations for a Creational Hermeneutic*, 2nd edition. Grand Rapids, MI: Baker Academic.

Smith, James K. A. 2002. *Speech and Theology: Language and the logic of incarnation*. New York, NY: Routledge.

Smith, James K. A. 2009. *Desiring the Kingdom: Worship, Worldview, and Cultural Formation*. Grand Rapids, MI: Baker Academic.

Smith, James K. A. 2010. *Thinking in Tongues: Pentecostal Contributions to Christian Philosophy.* Grand Rapids, MI: William B. Eerdmans Publishing Co.

Smith, James K. A. 2013. *Imagining the Kingdom: How Worship Works.* Grand Rapids, MI: Baker Academic.

Sorgenfrei, Simon. 2018. "Hidden or Forbidden, Elected or Rejected: Sufism as 'Islamic Esoterocism'?" *Islam and Christian-Muslim Relations.* 29:2, 145–165. UK: Informa UK Limited.

Sundkler, B. G. M. 1961. *Bantu Prophets in South Africa,* 2nd edition. London: Oxford University Press.

Synan, Vinson. 1997. *The Holiness-Pentecostal Tradition: Charismatic Movements in the Twentieth Century,* 2nd edition. Grand Rapids, MI: William B. Eerdmans Publishing Company.

Synan, Vinson. 2001. *The Century of the Holy Spirit: 100 Years of Pentecostal and Charismatic Renewal, 1901–2001.* Nashville, TN: Thomas Nelson, Inc.

Synan, Vinson, Amos Yong, and J. Kwabena Asamoah-Gyadu, editors. 2016. *Global Renewal Christianity: Spirit-Empowered Movements, Past, Present, and Future, Volume 3: Africa.* Lake Mary, FL: Charisma House.

Tait, David. 1961. *The Konkomba of Northern Ghana.* Oxford, UK: Oxford University Press.

Tedlock, Barbara. 1992. *Dreaming: Anthropological and Psychological Interpretations.* Santa Fe: New Mexico: School of American Research Press.

Thayer-Bacon, Barbara J. 2003. *Relational "(e)pistemologies."* New York, NY: Peter Lang Publishing.

Thiselton, Anthony C. 2016. *A Shorter Guide to the Holy Spirit: Bible, Doctrine, Experience.* Grand Rapids, MI: William B. Eerdmans Publishing Company.

Trementozzi, David. 2018. *Salvation in the Flesh: Understanding How Embodiment Shapes Christian Faith.* Eugene, OR: Pickwick Publications.

Von Grunebaum, Gustave and Roger Caillois. 1966. *The Dream and Human Societies.* Oxford, England: University of California Press.

Wacker, Grant. 2003. *Heaven Below: Early Pentecostals and American Culture.* Cambridge, MA: Harvard University Press.

Währisch-Oblau, Claudia. 2012. *The Missionary Self-Perception of Pentecostal/Charismatic Church Leaders from the Global South in Europe: Bringing Back the Gospel.* Leiden: Brill.

Wamsley, Erin J. and John S. Antrobus. 2007. "Dream Production: a Neural Network Attractor, Dual Rhythm Regional Cortical Activation, Homeostatic Model." In *The New Science of Dreaming,* Volume 1, Deirdre Barrett and Patrick McNamara, editors. Westport, CT: Praeger Publishers.

Wanly, Yosof. 2016. *Insightful Dreams of the Prophetic Realm: a Brief Analysis.* Publisher unknown.

Wariboko, Nimi. 2012. *The Pentecostal Principle: Ethical Methodology in New Spirit*. Grand Rapids, MI: William B. Eerdmans Publishing Company.

Wariboko, Nimi. 2014. *Nigerian Pentecostalism*. New York, NY: Rochester Press.

Wariboko, Nimi. 2016. "West African Pentecostalism: a Survey of Everyday Theology." In *Global Renewal Christianity,* vol. 3, Africa. Lake Mary, FL: Charisma House.

Wariboko, Nimi. 2018. *The Split God: Pentecostalism and Critical Theory*. NY: SUNY Press.

Wariboko, Nimi. 2020. *The Pentecostal Hypothesis: Christ Talks, They Decide*. Eugene, OR: Cascade Books.

Warrington, Keith. 2008. *Pentecostal Theology: a Theology of Encounter*. London, UK: T&T Clark.

West, David. 2010. *Continental Philosophy: an Introduction*, 2nd edition. Malden, MA: Polity Press.

Williamson, S. G. 1965. *Akan Religion and the Christian Faith*. Accra, Ghana: Ghana University Press.

White, Robert. 1975. *The Interpretation of Dreams: The Oneirocritica of Artemidorus*, translated by Robert White. Park Ridge, NJ: Noyes Press.

Wiredu, Kwasi. 1980. *Philosophy and an African Culture*. Cambridge: Cambridge University Press.

Wiredu, Kwasi. 1996. *Cultural Universals and Particulars*. Indiana: Indiana University Press, 1996.

Wiredu, Kwasi. 2006. *A Companion to African Philosophy*. Malden, MA: Blackwell Publishing.

Wrogemann, Henning. 2016. *Intercultural Theology: Intercultural Hermeneutics,* vol. 1, English edition. Downers Grove, IL: IVP Academic.

Wyllie, Robert W. 1980. *Spiritism in Ghana: a Study of New Religious Movements*. Missoula, MT: Scholars Press.

Yong, Amos. 2002. *Spirit–Word–Community: Theological Hermeneutics in Trinitarian Perspective*. Eugene, OR: Wipf and Stock.

Yong, Amos. 2005. *The Spirit Poured Out on All Flesh: Pentecostalism and the Possibility of Global Theology*. Grand Rapids, MI: Baker Academic.

Yong, Amos. 2010. *In the Days of Caesar: Pentecostalism and Political Theology*. Grand Rapids, MI: William B. Eerdmans Publishing Company.

Yong, Amos. 2012. *Spirit of Love: a Trinitarian Grace*. Waco, TX: Baylor University Press.

Yong, Amos. 2014. *The Dialogical Spirit: Christian Reason and Theological Method in the Third Millennium*. Eugene, OR: Cascade Books.

Yong, Amos. 2014. *The Missiological Spirit*. Eugene, OR: Cascade Books.

Index

Acolatse, Esther   12n26, 74n62, 92–94, 96, 213
African Initiated Churches (AIC)   XIV, 3n7, 67, 68, 71, 73, 74, 77n70, 97, 99, 179, 200
al-Bukhari, Muhammad b. Ismail   49, 213
Alexander, Paul   1n1, 213
Anderson, Allan H.   7, 97–100, 179, 213
Anim, Peter   76
Appiah, Kwame Anthony   20n49, 59–60, 84–86, 88
Aquinas, Thomas   25, 40–42
Asamoah-Gyadu, J. Kwabena   96, 102n73, 181n14, 214, 222
Ashanti   61–63, 75, 85n5, 124n30, 180, 215, 221

Bangura, Abdul Karim   86, 89
Baum, Robert M.   61n7, 82
Brown, Warren S.   194
Bulkeley, Kelly   XI, 6, 13, 16, 17, 25n5, 26n7, 27, 37n44, 37n45, 50n99, 116, 120n12
Busia, K. A.   85–86n5, 125n30, 215

Cartledge, Mark J.   4n8, 6–13, 91n29, 172, 215
Church of Pentecost   60, 75–77, 83, 117, 143, 200, 211, 212, 216
Clarke, Clifton R.   97, 129–130n42, 179–182, 215
CoP. See Church of Pentecost

Daneel, M. L.   68, 73n60
Danfulani, Umar   62n12, 66n32, 80, 88, 92, 95–96, 99, 121, 125, 134, 137, 162–163
Danquah, J. B.   84, 85n4
Dickson, Kwesi   93
Dilley, Roy M.   61, 66–67, 216
Diola   59n1, 60–61, 64–65, 82, 214
Dreams and Visions
   and *abisa*   76–80, 83, 117
   and angelology   134–135
   and *'kra*   62, 63
   and big dreams   14, 15, 37n45, 115–116, 138, 140
   and incubation   28, 31, 50, 80
   and root metaphors   15–17, 101, 113
   and *sunsum*   62–63, 158
   in Islam   31, 41, 47–57, 56–67, 175, 181n14, 214–216, 221–222

   in the Apocrypha   25, 26, 33
   in the New Testament and early Church   35–40
   in the Old Testament   25, 26–33, 34n33, 37, 39, 74n60, 78, 111, 216, 218

Ephirim-Donkor, Anthony   62–63, 82, 86, 87n10, 90–91, 99, 123, 158, 216–217
Epistemology   1–3
   pentecostal epistemology   2, 5, 21, 23, 25, 83, 96, 98, 106, 108, 115, 147, 173, 177, 178, 182, 183, 184, 185, 189, 193, 201, 204

Falola, Toyin   XI, 86, 89, 214, 217

Green, Nile   55, 217

Haustein, Jörg   53, 56
Hayashida, Nelson O.   60, 66n32, 73–75, 83, 94, 143, 202, 218
Hymes, David C.   26, 28–32, 218

Johns, Cheryl Bridges   187–189, 218

Kalu, Ogbu   101, 110–113, 153, 218
Kant, Immanuel   25, 40, 43–46, 105–106, 217
Kelsey, Morton   21–22, 26–27, 29, 31–43, 47, 218

Lamoreaux, John C.   24, 41, 47–48, 51–53, 117, 219
Land, Steven J.   183, 189–190, 219
Luhrmann, Tanya   183, 186–187, 219

Mbiti, John S.   60–61, 73, 219
McFague, Sallie   16–17, 219
McKeown, James   76
methodology   6, 8, 9, 11, 32, 89, 101, 196, 201, 204
Meyer, Birgit   77
Muhammad, the prophet   48, 50, 54, 56

Nabudere, Dani Wadada   86, 89–90

Onyinah, Opoku   60, 75–83, 117, 134, 143, 182, 198, 220

pastoral counseling   74, 75, 78, 94, 202
Plüss, Jean-Daniel   3n7, 182–185, 190, 221

Quayesi-Amakye, Joseph   22, 31n24, 76n68

Rattray, R. S.   61–63, 71, 75, 124n30, 158, 221
recontextualization   76, 78n77, 82, 117, 118, 147
Ricoeur, Paul   17

Sanneh, Lamin   84n3, 92, 96, 221
Shona   68, 73, 216
Smith, James K. A.   2n3, 188n33, 189n35, 192–194, 221
Spirit hermeneutics   3, 100, 118, 137, 138, 147, 175n74, 181, 183, 190, 195, 197, 200
spiritual warfare   19, 96, 101, 108, 111, 112, 114, 131, 132n45, 140, 149, 152, 153, 157, 158, 159, 161, 180, 197, 210, 211

Sundkler, Bengt   66n32, 68, 70, 71n48, 99, 221
Swedenborg, Emanuel   40, 44–46, 217

Tukolor weavers   66–67

Wariboko, Nimi   xi, 4, 22, 46, 80, 90n21, 93n34, 101, 102, 105, 113, 118, 149, 150, 163, 177, 199n77, 200, 223
Wiredu, Kwasi   85n5, 86, 88, 96, 223
witchdemonology   77–81, 177

Yong, Amos   xi, 87n9, 102n73, 137n50, 172, 181n14, 183, 189n35, 195–198, 215, 222–223

Zambian Baptists   3, 27, 59n3, 60, 66n32, 67, 68, 73–75, 94, 200, 218
Zande   88

Printed in the United States
by Baker & Taylor Publisher Services